Egypt in its African Context

Proceedings of the conference
held at The Manchester Museum,
University of Manchester, 2-4 October 2009

Edited by

Karen Exell

BAR International Series 2204
2011

Published in 2016 by
BAR Publishing, Oxford

BAR International Series 2204

Egypt in its African Context

ISBN 978 1 4073 0760 2

© The editors and contributors severally and the Publisher 2011

COVER IMAGE *Front cover illustration: Inlaid gold pectoral from El-Riqqeh, Middle Kingdom. The Manchester Museum 5966. Back cover illustration: Fertility figurine, provenance unknown. The Manchester Museum 10990*
©The Manchester Museum (with thanks to Steve Devine)

The authors' moral rights under the 1988 UK Copyright,
Designs and Patents Act are hereby expressly asserted.

All rights reserved. No part of this work may be copied, reproduced, stored,
sold, distributed, scanned, saved in any form of digital format or transmitted
in any form digitally, without the written permission of the Publisher.

BAR Publishing is the trading name of British Archaeological Reports (Oxford) Ltd.
British Archaeological Reports was first incorporated in 1974 to publish the BAR
Series, International and British. In 1992 Hadrian Books Ltd became part of the BAR
group. This volume was originally published by Archaeopress in conjunction with
British Archaeological Reports (Oxford) Ltd / Hadrian Books Ltd, the Series principal
publisher, in 2011. This present volume is published by BAR Publishing, 2016.

Printed in England

PUBLISHING

BAR titles are available from:

BAR Publishing
122 Banbury Rd, Oxford, OX2 7BP, UK
EMAIL   info@barpublishing.com
PHONE   +44 (0)1865 310431
FAX   +44 (0)1865 316916
www.barpublishing.com

Preface

This volume forms the proceedings of the conference, *Egypt in its African Context*, which took place at The Manchester Museum, University of Manchester, UK, on the 3-4 October 2009. The conference took the form of one day of papers, a selection of which are presented in this volume, and one day of community panel discussions with the key speakers and a screening of the film *Nubian Spirit: The African legacy of the Nile Valley* (BlackNine Films), by the documentary film-maker Louis Buckley. The event was inspired by recent work with Black and other community audiences at the Petrie Museum of Egyptian Archaeology, UCL, lead by Stephen Quirke, and at the Fitzwilliam Museum, Cambridge, lead by Sally-Ann Ashton, both curators of Egyptology collections, addressing issues of prejudice and perceived Eurocentrism in the presentation and interpretation of Ancient Egypt in the museums in the UK. In addition, at the time of the conference, and, indeed, at the time of writing, The Manchester Museum was – and is – in the planning stages of a large-scale redevelopment of its Egyptology and Archaeology galleries, wherein the presentation of Egypt as an African culture will form an aspect of the interpretation.

The conference at Manchester had a number of aims: to address perceptions of Ancient Egypt in the West, in scholarly writing and public understanding; to present a scholarly approach to the subject of Egypt in Africa in order to counterbalance the extreme Afrocentric views within which such a debate is often contextualised; to investigate how community groups and professional Egyptologists can transfer their knowledge and points of view; and to present the work of scholars working on African-centred Egyptology to a wider audience – including the traditional academic Egyptological community. In my opinion, the conference achieved the first three of these aims, and fell short on the last. The conference failed to attract as many academic Egyptologists as desired, this latter failure indicative of what might be described as the academic prejudice which exists within the conservative subject of Egyptology, which frequently resists engagement with what it regards as 'alternative' approaches to its subject. I hope that, with the publication of this volume, with its balance of African-centred and more traditional 'Egyptological' authors, and with further events of this nature, the lack of communication and debate between African-centred and the more traditional Egyptological scholars will begin to be eradicated.

The conference itself had a character that was unusual in my experience of Egyptology conferences: the debate was lengthy and lively, and the audience contained a wide mix of ethnicities. The various speakers covered a broad spectrum of topics, from Predynastic royal imagery to public perceptions of Cleopatra's ethnicity, a spectrum which is reflected in the papers in this volume. Many speakers and delegates did not agree with each others' views. This disagreement on the place of Egypt in Africa, and its role and influence on and by the wider African continent, is reflected within this volume, and makes one aspect of African-centred scholarship very clear: in relation to Ancient Egypt, African-centred interpretations of Ancient Egyptian culture and society are complex, and scholars with this approach have diverse viewpoints and provide nuanced interpretations of the evidence; there is not a single, monolithic 'Afrocentric' view.

The outcomes of the conference include this volume – an attempt to enrich the sparse literature on the subject of Egypt in Africa available to interested people in the UK, an intention to run similar events in other UK museums and universities, and, on a personal level, a broadening of my own understanding of and approach to interpreting Ancient Egypt. The conference and the process of editing the papers in this volume have exposed me to a diverse range of people, backgrounds, views and ideas, and to a literature that the traditional student of Egyptology would not generally come across. It is always important to question what we take for granted; I hope that readers of this volume will contemplate and assess what Ancient Egypt means to them and how they understand its place in the world, and will, whether they find themselves in agreement or not with the authors in this volume, at least open their minds to the debate about Egypt in its Africa context.

The volume is organised into two sections, the first exploring Egypt's influence on Africa, and *vice versa*, the second looking at interpretations of Egypt as an African culture. Each section has an introductory essay, and the volume as a whole is introduced by Bayo Folorunso, the keynote speaker at the conference, and Stephen Quirke, a lead advisor in the project and delegate at the conference. The paper by José Lingna-Nafafé, one of the key speakers at the conference, was a late submission due to unavoidable circumstances, and is for this reason omitted from the discussions in the introductory sections.

Acknowledgements

I would like to thank Sally-Ann Ashton and Stephen Quirke for their advice and support, throughout the project. In addition, thanks are due to Nick Merrimen, Director of the Manchester Museum, whose support allowed the conference to take place, and to Conni Lord, Karen Brackenridge, Scott McManus and Bryan Sitch, for their help throughout the conference. Louis Buckley provided a copy of his film free of charge, and Adele Wagstaff supplied a selection of her artworks from the exhibition, *Faces of Egypt*, for display at the conference, for which I am grateful. Generous funding for the conference was provided by the Heritage Lottery Fund and the African Studies Association of the UK.

For the preparation of this volume, I would like to thank Bill Manley for assisting with the proof-reading, and Steve Devine for his help in formatting many of the images in addition to editing and uploading the video footage of the key speakers to The Manchester Museum's YouTube channel.

Last and by no means least, I would like to thank all those who attended the conference, whose lively and thoughtful contributions made the event the memorable success that it was. In particular, I would like to thank all the speakers, those represented in this volume and those not:

Sally-Ann Ashton, The Fitzwilliam Museum, Cambridge
Solange Bumbaugh, University of Chicago
Gloria Emeagwali, Central Connecticut State University
C. A. Folorunso, University of Ibadan
Charles A. Grantham, Northeastern Illinois University
Shomarka Keita, Research Associate, Howard University and Smithsonian Institution
José Lingna-Nafafé, Birmingham University
Ana I. Navajas Jiménez, Oxford University
Kimani Nehusi, University of East London
Bill Manley, National Museums Scotland
Lyra Monteiro, Brown University
Dellé Odeleye, Anglia Ruskin University
Amon Saba Saakana, Karnak House Publishers and Intef Institute
Abdul Salau, Michigan State University
Robin Walker, Director of Education, Black History Studies Ltd.
Clyde Ahmad Winters, Governors State University, Illinois

The volume also includes papers by Maria Gatto (Yale University) and Alain Anselin (University of Antilles-Guyane) who were unable to attend the conference, for which thanks are due.

Karen Exell
Curator, Egypt and Sudan, The Manchester Museum, University of Manchester
January 2011

While it would be absurd to present the diverse peoples and cultures of that vast land mass as an undifferentiated whole, we will eschew the equal absurdity of depicting ancient Giza as a picturesque suburb of Athens and Rome!
Bret Waller, Director, Indianapolis Museum of Art,
Egypt in Africa (1996), p. 11

Contents

Contributors	1
Introduction: Egypt in its African Context *C. A. Folorunso and Stephen Quirke*	5

Part 1: Egypt in Africa

Introduction: The Strategic Importance of Kemet *Kimani S. K. Nehusi*	11
The Nubian Pastoral Culture as Link between Egypt and Africa: A View from the Archaeological Record *Maria Carmelo Gatto*	21
The Predynastic *Bos primigenius* as a Royal Image of Territory, Boundaries and Power in an African Context *Ana I. Navajas Jiménez*	30
Some Notes about an Early African Pool of Cultures from which Emerged the Egyptian Civilisation *Alain Anselin*	43
Egypt in Afrika and Afrika in Egypt: The Example of Libation *Kimani S. K. Nehusi*	54
Meroitic Worship of Isis at Philae *Solange Bumbaugh*	66

Part 2: Interpreting Ancient Egypt

Introduction: Critical Comments on Essays on Interpreting Ancient Egypt presented at the *Egypt in its African Context* Conference *Charles A. Grantham*	71
Contesting Egypt: Facts, Rhetoric or Sentiment? *C. A. Folorunso*	73
West African Perspectives on Ancient Egypt: African Renaissance *José Lingna-Nafafé*	80
Petrie's Revolutions: The Case of the Qurneh Queen *Bill Manley*	92
Public Understandings of Ancient Egypt in the Formation of Dalit and Afro-American Identities and History Curriculum *Clyde Ahmad Winters*	98
Curating Kemet, Fear of a Black Land? *Sally-Ann Ashton*	105

Contributors

Alain Anselin, University of Antilles-Guyane, Martinique

Alain Anselin teaches Ancient Egyptian language and the description of ancient writing systems (Sciences of Language) at the University of Antilles-Guyane, Martinique. He is the author of many articles in the field of Egyptology, founder of the research group The Ankhou, and chief editor and founder of the *Cahiers Caribéens d'Egyptologie*, and the electronic papyrus *i-Medjat*. He is member of a number of workshop groups, including Early Dynastic Potmarks Workshop (http://www.potmark-egypt.com/), the Writing Workshop in the cadre of the periodical international conference *Egypt at its Origins*, and the workshop La Route de la Traite (International Committee of the Museums of Archaeology and History (ICMAH)), as well as an associated member of the workshop Ngok Lituba (University of Yaounde I). He is a member of the Editorial Board of the review *Présence Africaine*. In addition to Egyptology, Alain has published as an anthropologist. In this area his publications include books on the West Indian migrations (*L'émigration antillaise en France: la troisième île*. Paris, Karthala, 1990) and the slave trade (*Le refus de l'esclavitude: résistances africaines à la traite négrière*. Paris, Duboiris, 2009).

Sally-Ann Ashton, The Fitzwilliam Museum, Cambridge, UK

Sally-Ann Ashton is Senior Assistant Keeper at the Fitzwilliam Museum, Cambridge where she curates the Egyptian and Sudanese collections. She obtained her PhD from Kings College London in 1999. Over the past 10 years she has published extensively on cross-cultural interaction in the Ptolemaic and Roman periods of Egyptian history. Sally-Ann has worked on a number of archaeological projects in Egypt, most recently as Field Director of the North Karnak Survey, the results of which will be published in 2011. For the past five years she has worked with community groups to explore African-centred approaches to presenting Ancient Egyptian culture, and has just completed an African-centred virtual version of the Egyptian and Nubian galleries at the Fitzwilliam Museum. In 2007 she was awarded a Knowledge Transfer Fellowship (Arts and Humanities Research Council, UK) to work full-time for two years in English prisons, exploring the impact of Black History classes on prisoners and staff. She is currently working on a monograph on her research entitled *Experiencing Black History in Prisons*. She continues to teach Black History in prisons, and to support prison education departments with museum resources. Her current research interests are concerned with Nubian identity, and the history of the African comb.

Solange Ashby Bumbaugh, University of Chicago, USA.

Solange Bumbaugh is a doctoral candidate in Egyptology at the University of Chicago. Her interests include Egyptian religion, Roman Egypt and the Meroitic language, religion, and history. The interaction between Meroitic, Egyptian and Greek culture along Egypt's southern border as well as the simultaneous practice of traditional pharaonic religion and early Christianity resulted in a vibrant and unique religious climate which is reflected in the inscriptions carved onto the walls of the Egyptian temples. Solange is currently writing a dissertation on these inscriptions composed in Demotic, Greek and Meroitic and left by Meroitic worshippers in the temples of Lower Nubia.

Caleb Adebayo Folorunso, University of Ibadan, Nigeria

Professor Caleb Adebayo Folorunso is based in, and was until 31 July 2010, the head of, the Department of Archaeology and Anthropology at the University of Ibadan. He studied Archaeology at the University of Ibadan, Nigeria, obtaining the Bachelor of Arts and the Master of Science degrees in 1979 and 1981 respectively, and the doctoral degree at Université Paris I, Sorbonne in 1989. He has been teaching and researching in Archaeology at the University of Ibadan since 1981 in the areas of ethnoarchaeology, historical archaeology and cultural resource management. One of his most recent publications is entitled *Archaeological Sites and Heritage in the Face of Socio-economic Development in Nigeria, since Independence* (2008)[1] and he is generally interested in the subject of heritage conservation.

Maria Carmela Gatto, Yale University, USA

Since 2008 Maria Carmelo Gatto is a Lecturer and Postdoctoral Associate at Yale University. She gained her MA in 1993 from the University of Rome 'La Sapienza', and her PhD in 2001 from the University of Naples 'L'Orientale'. She has also taught at the University of Rome 'La Sapienza', and at the UCLA/RUG Fieldschool in the Fayum, Egypt. Between 2003 and 2005 she was a temporary research curator at The British Museum in the Department of Ancient Egypt and Sudan, in charge of prehistoric and proto-historic pottery collections from the Nile Valley and the deserts. Maria specialises in the prehistory and archaeology of Nubia, Egypt, and Libya. Her research interests include the African Neolithic Model, the origin of complex societies in North Africa, Nubian prehistory and archaeology, the southern frontier of Predynastic and Early Dynastic Egypt, the interaction between Nubians and Egyptians in prehistoric and early historic periods, the Garamantes of Central Sahara and the prehistoric and historic ceramics in the Nile Valley and the Sahara. Maria has considerable experience in field archaeology and pottery analysis. She has worked on excavations in Egypt, Sudan, Libya, Eritrea, Turkey and Italy, and has direct knowledge of most of the prehistoric ceramic collections from Central and Eastern Sahara. Since 2005 she has been the director of an archaeological project in the region between Aswan and Kom Ombo, Egypt.

---

[1] In Naffé, B. O. M., Lanfranchi, R. and Schlanger, N. (eds.) *L'Archéologie préventive en Afrique: enjeux et perspectives*, 135-41. Saint-Maur-des-Fossés, Éditions Sépia.

Charles A. Grantham, Northeastern Illinois University, USA
Charles A. Grantham is currently a docent at the Field Museum of Natural History in Chicago and an Adjunct Professor at Northeastern Illinois University Carruthers' Center for Inner City Studies (CCICS) and at Olive-Harvey City College. Charles is a retired Licensed Certified Prosthetist and a former United States Peace Corps Volunteer. He served in Niger, West Africa and Kenya, East Africa as a consultant in Prosthetics (the design, fabrication, and fitting of artificial limbs) for five years. He has certificates in Prosthetics and Orthotics from Northwestern University, a Bachelor's degree in African Studies (under the tutelage of Dr. Jacob H. Carruthers) and a Master's degree in Inner City Studies from Northeastern Illinois University CCICS. He is a member of the Kemetic Institute in Chicago, Illinois and a member of ASCAC (Association for the Study of Classical African Civilisation). He is the author of *The Battle for Kemet* (Chicago, Kemetic Institute, 2003) and has lectured nationally and internationally on topics pertaining to Africa and Ancient Egypt (Kemet).

Ana I. Navajas Jiménez, University of Oxford, UK
Ana I. Navajas Jiménez gained her PhD from the Autonoma University of Madrid, Spain in 2004. Between 2007 and 2009 she was a Postdoctoral Fellow at Oxford University (Oriental Institute and Wolfson College). Her earlier work and publications focused on the historic periods of Egyptian history, but she soon developed a keen interest in the Egyptian Predynastic period. Her PhD thesis focused on Predynastic White Cross-lined pottery and she has continued to work until the present on this material, producing a number of specialised papers. She is currently finishing the complete corpus of White Cross-lined pottery, work that has allowed her to access new material, unknown until recently, held in different museums especially around Europe. Ana is currently based in Oxford at the Oriental Institute completing this work, as well as working as a tutor on an online course in Egyptology based in Spain, and on a research project connected to the Pyramids texts, based at the Autonoma University of Barcelona, Spain.

Kimani S. K. Nehusi, University of East London, UK
Kimani Nehusi teaches in the Cass School of Education, University of East London. He graduated from Teachers College with a Class I Grade I Trained Teachers Certificate and holds a BA and MA from the University of Guyana, a PhD from University College, London and a Diploma in Egyptology from the University of London. He is a Fellow of the Higher Education Academy (FHEA) of the UK, has been Assistant Examiner in the Caribbean Examinations Council and is regularly consulted by this and many other organisations. Kimani has been an international athlete and National Track and Field Coach of Guyana, has held offices in the Amateur Athletic Association of Guyana and was honoured by the International Amateur Athletic Federation for his services to track and field in Guyana. Kimani has taught and lectured in primary and secondary schools in Guyana and lectured in universities and colleges as well as in many communities in Guyana, the Caribbean, the USA, Afrika and Europe, and held posts at the University of Guyana and the University of London. He founded and was director of the Afrika Studies Centre at the University of East London. His research interests centre on the Caribbean and Afrika and include Resistance and Revolts, Reparations, Language issues, Carnival, Names and Naming, Libation and Education. He has published widely in most of these areas.

Dr José Lingna Nafafé, Birmingham University, UK
Dr José Lingna Nafafé is a Lecturer in the Department of Political Science and International Studies (POLSIS) at the University of Birmingham. He did his BD degree at London University, and his MPhil and PhD at Birmingham University. He previously lectured in the School of Education, Theology Department and in the European Research Institute at Birmingham University. He currently lectures in Postcolonial Theory, Ethnicity and Migration, 20th Century Lusophone History, and Creole, Culture and Society in Luso-Africa-Brazil at the University of Birmingham. José's academic interests centre around five main areas: Europe in Africa and Africa in Europe – Europe and Africa relations, asylum-seekers and refugees in a postcolonial world, postcolonial theories and representation, slavery and labour, and the relations between postcolonial theory and sociology. He has published on power relations between the colonisers and the colonised, social justice, identity and creolisation, slavery in the modern world, and power and language. His book, *Colonial Encounters: Issues of Culture, Hybridity and Creolisation, Portuguese Mercantile Settlers in West Africa* (Witney and New York, Peter Lang, 2007), raises searching questions on the nature of identity, space and representation. José has held the Fernão Mendes Pinto Scholarship, awarded by the Instituto Camões, and worked on representations of Africa: Africa and the outside world, focusing on Abraham Cresques's *Catalan Atlas* (1373) and Richard of Haldingham's *Mappa Mundi* (1290).

Bill Manley, formerly Senior Curator for Egyptian Scripts, National Museums Scotland
Bill Manley is Honorary Research Fellow of the University of Liverpool, and Honorary President of Egyptology Scotland. He gained his PhD at University College, London. He is a best-selling writer about pharaonic Egypt, and has taught at the University of Glasgow since 1996. He was at National Museums Scotland from 2005-2010, and before that was Lecturer in Egyptology at the Universities of Liverpool and London. He has worked with archaeological projects in Egypt and Palestine, published research on subjects including ancient poetry and the history of Egyptology, and also collaborated on the definitive publication of the coffins of the ancient kings of Egypt.

Stephen Quirke, University College, London
Stephen Quirke is Curator at the Petrie Museum of Egyptian Archaeology and Professor of Egyptian Archaeology at the Institute of Archaeology, UCL. His principal research monographs are *The Administration of*

Egypt in the late Middle Kingdom: the Hieratic Documents (New Malden, SIA publishing, 1990), *Titles and Bureaux of Egypt 1850-1700 BC* (London, Golden House Publications, 2004), *Egyptian Literature 1800 BC* (London, Golden House Publications, 2004), *Hidden Hands: Egyptian Workforces in Petrie Excavation Archives, 1880-1924* (London, Duckworth Egyptology, 2010), and, with Mark Collier, *The UCL Lahun Papyri: Letters* (Oxford, BAR Publishing, 2002), *The UCL Lahun Papyri: Religious, Literary, Legal Etc.* (Oxford, BAR Publishing, 2004) and *The UCL Lahun Papyri: Accounts* (Oxford, BAR Publishing, 2006). Recent articles include: Labour at Lahun, in Z. Hawass and J. Richards (eds.), *The Archaeology and Art of Ancient Egypt. Studies in Honor of David O'Connor* (Cairo, The American University in Cairo, 2007), 273-88; Interwoven Destinies: Egyptians and English in the Labour of Archaeology, 1880-2007, in B. Brehony, and A. El-Desouky (eds.), *British-Egyptian Relations from Suez to the Present Day* (London, Saqi Books, 2007), 247-73; with Gianluca Miniaci, Reconceiving the Tomb in the Late Middle Kingdom: the Burial of the Accountant of the Main Enclosure Neferhotep at Dra Abu al Naga, in *BIFAO* 109, 2009, 338-84; with Zahed Tajeddin, Mechanical Reproduction in the Age of the Artwork? Faience and 5000 Moulds from 14th Century BC Egypt, in *Visual Communication* 9, 2010, 341-62.

Clyde Winters, Governors State University, Illinois, USA

Clyde Winters, PhD, is a Lecturer in the College of Education, Governors State University, Illinois. He wrote the guided lesson plans used to teach 6th Grade World History in the Chicago Public Schools, and he was also part of the Committee that wrote the Social Studies Standards for the CPS. He is the author of *Brain Based Learning and Special Education* (Canberra, Anu Press, 2004). Clyde is the author of numerous articles on anthropology, archeogenetics and linguistics. His articles have appeared in the *Journal of Black Studies, Proceedings of the National Academy of Science, Science, Bio Essays, International Journal of Human Genetics, International Journal of Dravidian Linguistics* and *Journal of Modern African Studies*. He has written extensively on Afrocentric historical themes as well as the deciphering of the Meroitic writing used in the Sudan during the Meroitic period, and the Olmec writing system. His most recent book on the Olmec is *Atlantis in Mexico*. He is also the author of *Afrocentrism: Myth or Science*. Both books can be purchased at http://www.lulu.com/.

Introduction: Egypt in its African Context

C. A. Folorunso (University of Ibadan) and Stephen Quirke (University College, London)

1. An Outline of the Volume
C. A. Folorunso

This present volume is a collection of papers that evaluate the Ancient Egyptian civilisation in its African context. The chapters in the first part of the book treat varied subjects on Ancient Egypt including the archaeological evidence for the processes leading up to the emergence of the Ancient Egyptian civilisation, the question of the interpretation of artefacts and symbols used in Ancient Egypt, the origin or antecedents of such artefacts and symbols, rituals of libation, and pilgrimage to and worship in Ancient Egyptian temples. The second part of the book deals with how Ancient Egypt has been viewed and appropriated, including a review of Petrie's views on Ancient Egypt seen within the context of his social, political and philosophical background (Manley), and a report on community engagement and individual research using the Fitzwilliam Museum's Egyptian collections to present Egypt in its African context (Ashton).

Egypt in Africa
To demonstrate that Ancient Egypt was an African civilisation and that it was not just in Africa, it has become imperative to raise other lines of evidence aside from relying on the 'Ancient Model' of history, for which attempts have been made to substitute it with the 'Aryan Model'. Such lines of evidence would include archaeological data that explain the early period of Egyptian civilisation. Maria Carmela Gatto provides archaeological evidence to show that Nubia strongly influenced Egyptian culture in its formative stages during the 5th and 4th millennia BC. The chapter describes the processes of cultural development in the Nile Valley and demonstrates the strong similarity between the Western Desert Neolithic cultural material and that of the Badarian which resulted from massive migration of the desert people to Middle Egypt due to the increasing desert aridity. Gatto concludes that 'Nubia is Egypt's African ancestor' and that 'not only did Nubia have a prominent role in the origin of Ancient Egypt, it was also a key area for the origin of the entire African pastoral tradition' (p. 26).

Another important line of evidence necessary for a proper understanding of Egypt is the establishment of the antecedents and likely sources for Ancient Egyptian iconographic representations and their meanings. Ana I. Navajas Jiménez, through an examination of representations of the *Bos primigenius* (wild ox) during the Predynastic period, provides an insight into the development of iconographic representations in the Nile Valley spanning the Neolithic and the dynastic periods. Navajas Jiménez suggests that the Predynastic populations of the Nile were formed from the flow of people from the Western Desert, highlighting the fact that the production of rock art is an observable feature shared by the communities extending from the Western Desert to the Nile Valley from at least the 6th millennium BC onwards, and that rock art was a common and widespread practice in the Western Desert long before its manifestation in the Nile Valley. Rock art is documented in significant numbers in conjunction with decorated Type C ceramics in areas near to the river valley only from the Naqada I period onward. The iconographic representation of the *Bos primigenius* in the Nile Valley is traced to the Western Desert; in effect, Egypt's earliest iconography was determined by the African context that gave birth to it.

Alain Anselin provides more elements to demonstrate that Egypt was not isolated from its African roots but that it was part and parcel of its neighbouring African communities. The chapter describes what is termed the Saharo-Nubian cultural antecedents of the Egyptian Predynastic culture; both material and immaterial features shared by Egyptian and African cultures and ascribing the commonalities to migrations and contact in the general area from the desert to the Nile Valley. The artefacts considered include headrests that are known in many cultures of Africa, among the Cushitic, Nilotic, Bantu, Zande and Dogon, and a religious staff/emblem shared by the pastoral Saharo-Nubian hinterland of the early Egyptian cultures and Predynastic civilisation, the Egyptian civilisation itself, and contemporary North East African shepherds. In the realm of immaterial culture, language is considered and similarities in words associated with religion, ritual and the mind are discussed. Anselin suggests that 'the Egyptian vocabulary reflects a lengthy ancient pooling of cultural features from Chadic-speakers and Nilo-Saharan speakers, shepherds of the Western Sahara' (p. 49). He also suggests 'that the earliest speakers of the Egyptian languages could be located to the south of Upper Egypt' (p. 50).

Kimani S. K. Nehusi attempts to demonstrate the interconnectedness of Egypt and the rest of Africa through the study of libation practices that are widespread in Africa. Nehusi cites the temple complex at Nabta Playa and an incense burner at Qustul as providing the earliest evidence of what 'may constitute indirect references to the practice of libation in organised political entities that existed before and beyond the state of Kemet' (p. 54). In line with the thesis expressed in the preceding chapters, that there had been population migrations from the south to the Nile Valley, Nabta Playa and Qustul are located to the south of Kemet, the direction from which it 'inherited much of its people and heritage' (p. 55). While Nehusi subscribes to the thesis of south-north population movement and impetus for cultural developments in the Nile Valley, he also suggests, though without citing solid evidence, that the ritual practice of libation spread from Kemet through migrations to other parts of Africa.

Nehusi suggests that in addition to libation ritual, Africans also took with them from Kemet a distinctive world view 'on their migrations to people a continent and other parts of the world' (p. 60). This is recourse to the Hamitic hypothesis that sub-Saharan Africa's cultural developments had their origin in the north, a view that cannot be supported by evidence. The chapter therefore – and in my opinion, contentiously – suggests that the world views of some African peoples, such as Asante and Yoruba, were derived from Ancient Egypt.

Solange Bumbaugh discusses another form of religious link between Egypt and Nubia in the form of Meroitic pilgrimage and worship at the Temple of Isis, located on Philae Island in Upper Egypt. Though the history of the temple and Meroitic pilgrimage and worship there date to the later part of the history of Egypt (332 BC to the 5th century AD), it is a veritable testimony to the connection between Egypt and other regions of Africa. The temple itself seemed to have been conceived and constructed for Nubian worshippers as it is oriented towards Nubia. Nubians were actively involved as priests and worshippers, leaving numerous inscriptions carved on the temple walls that provide an African perspective on the cult of Isis.

Interpretations of Egypt
While the first part of the book presents Ancient Egypt as an African civilisation with its roots in Africa and sharing cultural elements with other regions in the past, the second part of the book treats the question of interpretations of Egypt. My own chapter reviews and evaluates some of the claims and counterclaims made about the cultural influences of Ancient Egypt. The chapter examines the various arguments with the objective of providing an insight into the social and political contexts of the arguments. The claims and counterclaims centre on the nature and identity of the Egyptian civilisation and its relationships with other parts of the world. I tend to ally with the general philosophy established in the first part of the book that Egyptian civilisation had its roots in Africa and was part of the ancient African civilisation, but I reject what I regard as the unwholesome claims of Egyptian influences on cultural developments in sub-Saharan Africa. I consider the claims of Egyptian origins for isolated cultural elements and sometimes insignificant similarities in some cultural elements in sub-Saharan African as unscientific and self-serving. I accept the explanation of commonalities shared by the Egyptians and other African cultures as being derived from a common origin outside the Nile Valley, dating probably to the Neolithic period as supported by archaeological and iconographic data presented in the first part of this volume.

Obviously, Flinders Petrie is an extremely notable person associated with archaeological discoveries in Egypt. Bill Manley has provided an insight into the personality of Petrie and how his social and political background coloured his interpretations of Egypt. Petrie's views on Ancient Egyptian cultural achievements in the actual sense cannot be said to derive from the interpretation of the material evidence; rather they were based on speculations that satisfied his desires and expectations. The Qurneh burial of a woman and a child, for which Manley reviews Petrie's interpretation, is a good example of turning hard evidence on its head to deny that Egypt was an African civilisation. The burial demonstrates clearly Nubian involvement and influence in Egypt in the 16th century BC. Though Petrie had suggested that the skull of the woman was not typically Egyptian, analyses had shown that 'her diet falls between that typical of Egyptian and that of Nubians' (p. 93). Despite the extraordinary and valuable objects associated with the burial, Petrie stated that the burial was of no great value. From Manley's accounts, Petrie would easily pass for a racist who saw nothing good in Ancient Egypt and saw the Ancient Egyptians as incapable of any meaningful cultural achievement. Though Petrie found some supporters for his ideas concerning Egypt's cultural development, and despite being the first person to occupy a professorial chair of Egyptian Archaeology in the UK, Manley shows that his views on this matter were not taken seriously in wider academic circles as his views were thought to be unsubstantiated. On several occasions reviews ridiculed Petrie's writings. Manley notes that an anonymous reviewer of one of his works in 1907 wrote: 'This book, by the best-known of Egyptologists, reminds us of the articles in a certain magazine which were said to be always written by men who were experts on any subjects but those they were asked to write about' (p. 95).

It would be foolhardy to think that the views of a pioneer professor of Egyptian Archaeology such as Petrie would not have impact on the media, Eurocentric academics, museum educators and the general public that seeks knowledge about Egypt. Sally-Ann Ashton inquires into the attitudes of people to interpretations of Egypt in museum exhibitions. From Ashton's accounts one can easily sense some kind of unnecessary racial tension in the interpretation and presentation of Egypt. Ashton's motives and her involvement in the interpretation and presentation of Egypt as an African civilisation have come under suspicion from both sides of the racial divide. While some members of Black communities forget that Martin Bernal, the author of *Black Athena*, is a White Briton, they doubt the sincerity of a White researcher who chooses to present Egypt in its African context. As Ashton notes, the views of scholars of African descent have been ignored by European/Western scholars because the latter doubt the credentials of the former. Of course, Martin Bernal could not be ignored because he comes from a background that could not be questioned, but he has equally been criticised for accepting the 'Ancient Model' of history that ascribed Egypt to Black history. In the same vein, Ashton reports, she was asked by a White student why she was 'letting the side down' by promoting Egypt as part of Black History. I, on the other hand, was also faced with similar situation at the Manchester conference when some Black participants insinuated that I was letting the side down by expressing the view that most claims on the racial identity of the Egyptians would require hard facts in order to be accepted as proven. One may then ask if the history of Egypt is really therapeutic to both side of the racial divide? The next chapter may provide some insight to this question.

It is quite obvious that the achievements of Ancient Egypt as an early centre of civilisation in world history accounts for the interest shown by various groups, to the extent that Ancient Egypt has had influence in identity formation among Black populations in America and India – Clyde Winters describes the Dalits of East India as sharing with Afro-Americans a history of segregation and slavery, and believing that their ancestors originated in the Sudan, from where they migrated to the Indus Valley. Thus their relationship to Egypt and the Sudan links them to Afro-Americans and Africans. As Winters has shown, these two widely separated populations 'locate their origins in Africa and see Egyptian civilisation as part of their ethnic heritage' (p.98) and this idea is part of the liberation history taught in their schools. These Black populations are minorities who feel oppressed and are therefore interested in the role of Blacks in ancient world history in order to assert the accomplishment of the race, for which Ancient Egypt acts as testimony. Winters provides an analysis of the history curriculum taught to African American students, based on the 'Ancient Model' of history derived from the Bible, which states that the 'Black/African people are the children of Ham' and that 'Blacks founded the first civilisations in Asia (Sumer, Babylon, and Elam), Africa (Egypt, Ethiopia and Libya/North Africa) and Europe (Greece and Crete)' (p. 100). Their argument is simply that the original Egyptians were Black Africans. The Dalit history curriculum is also shown to be founded on research linking them to Africa and therefore to Egypt. Here, although we can see general claims to Egypt without specific evidence and based on the purely a racial issue of the Ancient Egyptians as Black Africans, the objective of such claim is very clear: that the Black race made very significant contributions to world civilisation in the past and should not be marginalised.

2. Reflections on power
Stephen Quirke

To Reject or to Use
For the idea of Ancient Egypt in Africa, even a northwest European writer must recognise that the name *Kemet* holds particular powers. As Kimani Nehusi outlines, surviving writings from writing inhabitants of the land apply the name *Kemet*, 'Black Land', to the Nile floodplain, yearly covered by river flood-deposits of fertile black silt – and identify the people there as *remetj en Kemet*, 'people of the Black Land'. Many of those writings contrast the term with *Deshret*, 'Red Land', the rocky and sandy cocoon of the Sahara to west and east of the flood-plain. In this evocation of life force, the word *kem*, 'Black', instantly asserts a positive strength. Kemet becomes a powerful expression to oppose the racism that infects Europe from the genocidal history of colonial enslavements. In spirit Kemet conveys a force and colour sung by writers from the times of the immediate initial resistance through to the Black Power movement and the musician-poets cited by Nehusi. Kemet becomes a contemporary key for exposing what Robert Young has called the White mythologies. For the African-centred study of Kemet, it might be easiest to ignore the Eurocentric field, and start from nothing. Currents of nihilism have been strong in European thinking, not least where conditions seem unchangeable. A direct gesture of rejection can carry immense radical power, as where Aimé Cesaire exposes evils in the colour White in his hymn to Toussaint L'Ouverture, the Haitian leader imprisoned by Napoleon Bonaparte. Among 20th century African political leaders and writers, Kwame Nkrumah and Frantz Fanon shared a different approach, in a sense the opposite of nihilism, perhaps harder to deploy but more damaging to Eurocentric normative power: a dialectical understanding of human history. In the dialectical history by Nkrumah, the negative drive of capitalist economy and its knowledge-base can be negated in revolution, as an abrupt reversal in the direction of history from evil to good. Like Nietzsche-style nihilism, Nkrumah-style dialectics may carry dangers too great for a liberation movement; the opposing power may be too contagious to risk any encounter, the knowledge-base too contaminated. The existence of African political writing within the dialectical approach offers some justification for exploring whether, and how, African and African-centred study could advance most strongly with continuing White-dominated archaeological and historical research. In order to incorporate that knowledge, African-centred Kemet-studies confronts various options: replacing, or overlapping with, or meeting the separated, predominantly White European and Euroamerican, archaeological research communities.

Meetings and Writings
For the third option, meeting, relatively few opportunities have arisen. Against the high expectations of the time, the 1974 UNESCO-sponsored conference on Egypt and Africa for the General History of Africa did not change the Eurocentric climate of research, as recalled by Alain Anselin. Yet over the past decade, his editorial work has supported a more powerful contribution, perhaps the one essential requirement for developing and sustaining any field of study: the creation of a printed forum for research results. The journal *Cahiers Caribéens d'Égyptologie* is anchored in support from universities in Martinique, Cameroon and Catalunya, and so may connect African-centred studies of Kemet across Africa, America and Europe. Although the spoken word and internet resources offer far more forceful immediate impact, the printed word still holds more staying-power in the longer term. The power of print means that face-to-face meetings, as at the Manchester Museum conference, need to be followed up with publication, as well as with further meetings and discussions within and between groups. Print publication is useful because it can have a longer shelf-life, because its distribution can be different to, sometimes wider than, the web-site, and also because the writers materialise together on a level in a way that can make it easier to absorb the full range of their individual writings in combination. From the present papers in written form, readers can grasp challenges and

possibilities in sharper profiles. On four fronts there may now be little difference between African-centred studies and White European archaeology/Egyptology:

1. Origins/prehistory: archaeologists researching the periods before the invention of writing in the Nile Valley present a broad consensus on the Upper Nile and Saharan sources of Kemet (Gatto, Navajas Jiménez);
2. Study of relations between Kemet and Kush: in detailed philological research into relations between different language-communities along the Nile Valley, the focus on border can bring an emphasis on features shared between them as well as features separating them (Bumbaugh);
3. Language: increasing research into the relation between archaeology and linguistics in Africa highlights the African context and home of *r n kmt*, 'language of Kemet', with attention to the material cultural evidence as part of the linguistic horizon (Anselin, Nehusi);
4. Modern reception of Kemet: archaeology and, to some extent, Egyptology have developed more self-critical approaches to understanding their own operation in society, allowing for new studies of institutional impact (Ashton), of earlier archaeologists (Manley), and of groups omitted from the standard histories (Winters).

All these studies offer a platform for varied development and for reassessing the concept of the material unity of Africa as proposed by Mike Rowlands (2003). Admittedly, the various papers stand somewhat in isolation from one another, in a manner that would allow Eurocentric assumptions to survive untested. Yet the print publication allows them material form throughout library networks, both inside and outside archaeological and Egyptological departments. In itself this encourages disciplinary and non-disciplinary readers to encounter a wider range of views. These advances remain limited by one major omission in efforts at change within at least the English debate: I see little chance of progress without the participation of modern inhabitants of Africa in general, and of the Nile Valley, from source to sea. If anyone is to be absent from the table, surely it should be the White Europeans, not the modern Egyptians and Sudanese. At present, the main discussion on the African context of Kemet seems to take place between Africans in America and Europe and White Europeans. Africans in Africa are either not present or a minority presence (Folorunso, this volume). Economic obstacles are certainly one reason: there are cheaper flights, and more funding opportunities, to bring speakers from one northern country to another, than from Africa to Europe. Nevertheless, future development must overcome these logistical problems, because the absence strikes the heart of the debate, its encounter with others. One fundamental tactic of Empire is to 'speak for' other people, who are converted into the object of discussion, without consent. In archaeology, the people are not present, and consent can never be given: instead, the research into material, including written, evidence becomes one means of trying not to speak for past people. Archaeologists discuss, though not enough, whether that attempt has any chance of success, or whether the encounter with the past always involves stepping on others (Shanks and Tilley 1989). Anthropologists have done rather more to analyse their own practices critically, but, even in that university discipline, the structures prove easier to discuss than to change. Edward Said challenged anthropology not to 'represent the colonised', more or less arguing that they could not (Said 1989). Johannes Fabian has done more than any other anthropologist to show how the Eurocentric discipline strips human beings of 'co-evality', the sharing of time and space, through routine practices as embedded as the use of the present tense in anthropological reports (Fabian 1983). Yet even he could only reply to Said that, if well-intentioned anthropologists were not presenting the other to Europe, then who and what would fill the gap (Fabian 1991). The active participation of modern Egyptians and Sudanese, across the range of views in both countries, would remove the risk of repeating the practice of the colonisers who convert others into objects of discussion. Future discussions could return to the spirit of the General History of Africa, with meetings between Egyptians, Sudanese, other Africans in Africa, and Africans in America and Europe. Doubtless the international climate then made it easier than it is now to construct such encounters. Yet the chances of success are well demonstrated by an African-American initiative of the last decade, the conference on race in Egypt, and its publication (Fluehr-Lobban and Rhodes 2003).

African and Arab
The 1974 speakers already lived in the world of Anwar Sadat with his turning of Egypt toward White north America. Yet just behind them, and within their lived experience, Africa and the Arab World had fought together against European and Euroamerican colonial power. African and Arab were not incompatible. Against France, Frantz Fanon fought the armed struggle for African independence on the soil of what for the 21st century are Arab and Berber Algerians. A triumphant Cassius Clay became Mohammed Ali, and Black Power embraced Islam as solution in the Black Muslim movement. In Egypt, too, things had been different in the 1950s and 1960s, when, after rejection by Washington, its preferred economic partner, the government of Gamal Abdel Nasser adopted an Arab Socialism aligned with the African Socialism of Nyerere and Nimeiri, and promoted an African-Asian 'moment' to explore shared cultural histories and futures. The more communist Nkrumah would reject those leaders as selling out to rich White economies, and indeed the subsequent economic paths of the continent tend to support his view that colonialism has recreated itself violently as neo-colonialism. Today the imperial motto 'divide and rule' seems to go uncontested: has empire ever been more successful in securing the power of the privileged not only over, but with the essential assistance of, its victims? A parallel might be drawn between early 21st and late 19th century history. In 2003, London joined the invasion of Iraq launched from Washington, including bombardment of Baghdad as a distant television spectacle; despite or through the embedding of journalists, the US and UK governments and electorates never found the ability to

estimate the human casualties of that invasion. The subsequent occupation has seen the largest presence of African Americans in the Arab World, in the armed forces, disproportionately from poorer sections of society. In 1882, London despatched its armed forces, including prominent Indian, Irish and Scottish contingents, on an invasion of Egypt in order to remove an independently-minded government opposed to British and French management of the Egyptian economy; reports of the invasion do not quantify the human casualty figures for the bombardment of Alexandria, and it seems we have not to ask too hard how many people died there, as in Baghdad. One answer reaches us, though, on the first page of the biographical essays by Hakim Adi and Marika Sherwood in their *Pan-African History*, in the entry on Dusé Mohamed Ali (1866-1945), who remembered his parents as 'an Egyptian army officer and his Sudanese wife' (Adi and Sherwood 2003, 1). The early political career of Dusé Mohamed Ali included the book *In the Land of the Pharaohs*, assembling data to defend Egypt against another example of US-UK alliance – support by Theodore Roosevelt for British 'violence and injustice' as necessary strategies of British occupation of Egypt. Sherwood relates: 'in 1882 his father and brother were killed in the bombardment of Alexandria which led to the British occupation of Egypt. His mother and sisters, whom he never saw again, fled to the Sudan'. So the Pan-African archive includes modern north Africa literally from page 1: in the face of White racism, Fanon wrote 'Black or Arab' (1952, 25: 'un nègre ou un Arabe').

Towards a Presence of African-centred Archaeological Practice in the Nile Valley
In his history of archaeological thought (2006), Bruce Trigger characterised post-independence archaeology in much of the world, including Africa, as neo-colonial. In a global economic context, the encounter with the past might seem a trivial luxury, but economic systems generate and need systems of ideas for support. Despite healthy internal debates of conscience, as a public block both archaeology and history still play their part in regenerating a peculiar Eurocentric sense of the European self as somehow naturally dominant in world history. At the same time, African-centred researchers are not visible in archaeological fieldwork in the Nile Valley. Similarly, research conferences and publications on the history and language of Kemet remain dominated, beyond 90%, by those brought up and trained in European, not African, societies and languages (which include Arabic). The absence is clearly structural, for modern research requires expensive resources that only centres of capital can finance to the full: not so much cutting-edge technological equipment – though advanced computer hardware and software does exclude all but the richest – as the secure provision of the research base in university, library, archive, and museum. The 21st century research machine has two institutional faces, both rooted in a 19th-century history of European middle-class political and scientific revolutions: the Academy, a Paris export, especially under Napoleon Bonaparte, from European Enlightenment beginnings, and the University, in its research-anchored frame pioneered in Berlin by Wilhelm von Humboldt. Despite the concentration of research with capital, other structures exist, and today the African and African American universities hold the greatest potential for overcoming any structural absence on the archaeological field, in direct and online training of the next generation.

Communication and Legitimacy
As well as belonging to its continent, the word Kemet also belongs within a vocabulary of its own speakers and times. These may invite readers explicitly to join a language-community, as in the case of prayers to those who live and pass by monuments, asking them to recite a formula for sustenance of those who lived. If such prayers can be conveyed, many readers will surely feel that the words come here through the wrong channels – from a White north-European English-writing academic, whose Irish and Danish forebears also must belong within that European colonial history (Lindqvist 1997). Fanon wrote, 'The European knows and does not know' (1952, 161: 'L'Européen sait et ne sait pas'), presenting the innumerable instances in which well-intentioned White European writers failed to escape themselves. Imprisoned in the narrowest Egyptological space, there are two windows. From one, we can see a radical European tradition that opposed Empire, and inspired many in Africa (Nkrumah 1970). From the other, we can see that, for all our techniques and data, the only sure knowledge we have of Egyptological Kemet is that it did not exist (cf. Derchain). If so, then the initial hope to encounter Kemet needs not more of the European, but of other worlds: of those living in the Valley today, those speaking languages related to theirs and those who feel linked to it by the history of the continent. Inside Egyptology, the Egyptologist can say that there needs to be a different set of meetings. This claim does not decide anything. Decisions to read, reject, incorporate come from social actions of debate, with new meetings between non-European participants.

References

Adi, H. and Sherwood, M. 2003. *Pan-African History: Political Figures from Africa and the Diaspora since 1787*. London and New York, Routledge.

Cesaire, A. 1939. *Cahier d'un retour au pays natal*. Paris, Volontés.

Derchain, P. 1996. Review of D. O'Connor and D. Silverman (eds.), *Ancient Egyptian Kingship*. Leiden, E. J. Brill, 1995, in *Bibliotheca Orientalis* 53, cols. 690-692.

Fabian, J. 1983. *Time and the Other. How Anthropology Makes its Object*. New York, Columbia University Press.

—1991. Dilemmas of Critical Anthropology, in *Time and the Work of Anthropology: Critical Essays, 1971-1991*, 245-64. Reading, Harwood Academic Publishers.

Fanon, F. 1952. *Peau noire, masques blancs*. Paris, Éditions de Seuil.

Fluehr-Lobban, C. and Rhodes, K. (eds.) 2003. *Race and Identity in the Nile Valley: Ancient and Modern Perspectives*. Trenton, N.J., Red Sea Press.

Lindqvist, S. 1997. *Exterminate all the Brutes. One Man's Odyssey into the Heart of Darkness and the Origins of European Genocide.* New York, The New Press.

Nkrumah, K. 1970. *Class Struggle in Africa.* London, Panaf Books.

Rowlands, M. 2003. The Unity of Africa, in D. O'Connor and A. Reid (eds.), *Ancient Egypt in Africa*, 39-54. Walnut Creek, CA and London, Left Coast Press/University College London.

Said, E. 1989. Representing the Colonised: Anthropology's Interlocutors. *Critical Inquiry* 15, 205-25

Shanks, M. and Tilley, C. 1989. *Reconstructing Archaeology.* London, Routledge.

Trigger, B. 2006. *A History of Archaeological Thought.* 2nd Edition. Cambridge, Cambridge University Press.

Part 1: Egypt in Africa

Introduction: The Strategic Intellectual Importance of Kemet

Kimani S. K. Nehusi
University of East London

Introduction
The racial and cultural origin and identity of the people of Kemet, Ancient Egypt, has been the subject of one of the most significant intellectual disputes in the study of Afrika and therefore of the world. This subject, in one form or the other, has been the object of scholarly enquiry, assertion and speculation, of unscientific and even openly racist pseudo-science and misrepresentation, as well as the object of rescue, redemption and pride. The reasons for these extremes of opinion, emotions and conclusions are not difficult to ascertain. The history of Arabs in Afrika over the last 1500 years and of Europeans on that continent over the last 500 years has been a history largely of conquest, domination and oppression. The identity of the people of Kemet has been a contested factor in the resulting hegemonic narratives and in the resistance these called forth. These competing and often contradictory narratives, whether or not informed by a genuine search for truth, have all contributed to the literature on Kemet. This section of the book contains five chapters which offer further evidence of the Afrikan nature of Kemet. This introduction is meant to aid our understanding of these chapters by providing a summary of the debate. A clear idea of the wider intellectual context in which these efforts are located will also assist in our understanding of these chapters.

It is helpful to begin with one of the most important aspects of this issue. To enquire whether ancient Egypt was an Afrikan society, which is the basic question in this dispute, is the same as asking, as Asa Hilliard points out, whether Afrikans are indeed Afrikans (Hilliard 1996, 112). It is the same as asking whether Arabs are really Arabs, or whether Europeans are really Europeans, or Chinese Chinese, and so on. It may be surprising that no one ever asks whether Chinese are Chinese, or Europeans European. But in effect some scholars have asked, and perhaps still ask, whether Afrikans are Afrikan. The fact that such a question occupies the attention of serious academics is generally a testimony to the persistence of pseudo-scientific colonial ideology, and the power of a related and currently dominant mode of perception and thinking, rather than to the triumph of scientific enquiry and logical thinking. How such a mode of perceiving people and thinking about them has become so dominant and so persistent in the minds of so many constitutes the most significant aspect of the context in which this debate was initiated and has unfolded. So too is the investment in countering this academic racism, which has proved a cornerstone in the popular curriculum of Western and Western-dominated societies, where such views are assiduously propagated throughout society, generally by the press, church, governments, education systems, judiciaries and other institutions.

A fundamental principle at stake in all of this is whether the Afrikan people, like any other group of people, should participate in the writing of their own history from a position of equality, which of necessity must also mean from their own perspectives. In the Western world the voices of other traditionally disempowered groups, such as the working class and women, have been increasingly established in recent generations as integral aspects of the 'mainstream' narrative. This idea of equality is supported by the United Nations, whose *Convention on the Rights of the Child* calls for every child to be educated to know and respect her or his history and cultural identity as well as that of others (see http://wboesww.org for full text; as well as UNICEF 2002; UNICEF and UNCESCO 2007). Further, it appears timely that this world body has declared 2011 the International Year for People of African Descent (United Nations A/Res/64/169).

However, despite claims of multiculturalism and other forms of equality, conscious and organised racism remains an aspect of life in modern Britain and the rest of the Western world. Academia is not immune to this inhuman scourge, which affects relations among people and generally lessens the well-being and the life chances of those who face discrimination.

Origins of and Reasons for the Debate
Scholarship appears unanimous that there were forms of discrimination in the ancient times, but that the major roots of racial discrimination in today's world lie in the European subjugation of large parts of the earth (Asante 1996a, 33; Asante 1996b, 116-7; Carruthers 1999, 3-18; Drake 1987; Harris 1998, 2; Hilliard 1996, 112-5; Snowden 1996, 107-8), though in the study of Afrika it is imperative to add the previous Arab colonisation of large parts of the continent. When Europe enslaved and later colonised Afrika it did not only subjugate the land and its people; it also colonised the social history of the continent, including its images (Clarke 1994, 8, 88; 1998, 35). The reason for this is that colonisers are compelled to demean the colonised and everything about them, including their culture, in order to try to justify their activity (Achebe 2009, 61; Cabral 1980, 138-54; Said 1993). Every system of organised oppression needs a system of supporting, validating, and even on occasion valorising values, attitudes and behaviours which serve to justify and reproduce that system in the minds of oppressor and oppressed alike. Enforced self-ignorance as the basis of imagined superiority among oppressors and ingrained inferiority among the oppressed is a very powerful weapon in the armoury of oppression. It is chiefly for this reason that White racism emerged as

dogma to support that system of institutionalised inhumanity termed, after its various phases, enslavement, colonisation, neo-colonisation, etc. The institutions in Europe and in colonised societies dominated by Europe upheld and reproduced negative stereotypes of Afrikans in history, literature, religion, sciences, physical images, art and all other aspects of representation. Over many centuries both coloniser and colonised were assiduously inculcated with these lies, falsifications and misrepresentations (consult, for example, Drake 1987, 13-32; Diop 1974, 43-84; Harris 1998, 1-19; Rashidi 1994, 105-8; Reynolds-Marniche 1994, 109-25, for additional statements and critiques of these myths, which are not recounted here). Basil Davidson has remarked that 'the facts of Africa's own history have always been, and remain, an entirely convincing denial of the mythologies of modern racism, in the name of whose lies and legends many have suffered persecution … in the entire continent' (Davidson 1991, xxi). He ought to have added that Afrikans in communities abroad have also historically suffered racist persecution, and that such persecution continues to this day, both on the continent and in its communities abroad.

Academic racism and intellectual violence accompanied the physical, social, cultural, psychological and spiritual genocide of the *Maafa* or great Afrikan holocaust that was occasioned by Arab and European subjugation of Afrika and were an integral aspect of this great catastrophe. History was ethnically cleansed of Afrikan achievement. Everything Afrikan was ascribed negative value. The result for Afrikan people has been that peculiar ordering of humanity along a continuum with Arab and European 'superiors' at one end and supposedly Afrikan 'inferiors' at the other. The world has witnessed the most extreme forms of this doctrine in Nazi Germany and Apartheid South Africa. The continuing consequences of the *Maafa* reside in the underdevelopment of Afrika and its people: an active process of disabling a people and exploiting their human and material resources, in the negative self-image of Afrikans so assiduously propagated – and still propagated – by the dominant ideology of the institutions and places dominated by this strain of Arab and European world views, in the negative or severely diminished concept of self inculcated over many generations in the victims, in the consequence of achievement that does not match ability or potential. Afrikan identity was amputated, distorted and erased and Afrikans were disabled in the most fundamental way.

The reasons why Kemet has obtained such importance reside in the fact that it is the first civilisation in the world and that it exerted a tremendous influence upon every subsequent civilisation, most especially upon European civilisation via the Greeks as explained by James (1954), Bernal (1987), Browder (1992), and many others. But such achievements do not match the image of the primitive and the barbarian Afrikan that apologists for the *Maafa* have assiduously created and propagated. So the Ancient Egyptians could not be the same as other Afrikans, or even Afrikan. Kemet could not belong to Afrika for the same reason that the Republic of Haiti could not be permitted to succeed. Haiti was an Afrikan state created by a revolution of enslaved Afrikans who triumphed militarily against two armies of the French under Napoleon, an English army, one of the Spanish and another made up of counter revolutionary Whites and mulattoes. Afrikans in Haiti promulgated what was then the most advanced constitution in the world. Haiti and Kemet are examples of outstanding Afrikan agency, humanity and achievement rendered dangerous to the perpetuators of global domination and oppression because they are dramatic illustrations of the falsity of those inaccurate and demeaning notions of Afrika and Afrikans so necessary for the existing world order. The real history of Kemet in particular and of Afrika in general, amounts to an eloquent and profound refutation of the myths of oppression. Such history renders very hollow indeed such claims as 'bringing civilisation' to a people who not only possessed civilisation, but had initiated it. It was therefore necessary to invent another history of Kemet, of Afrika and therefore of the world.

Disabled Afrikans without any agency in their own land, or elsewhere, is a necessary and so preferred image which justified the conquest of Afrika and underpins most European 'aid' to Afrika which is still trumpeted in the Western media, whether it is 'Live Aid' or 'Band Aid'. Meanwhile the same media remains conveniently silent about the continuous organised looting of the continent's resources, the impoverishment of its people and the complicity of sections of its elite that accompany these pretences of the White man's burden, Christian duty, humanism, free trade and so on.

Oppression inevitably calls forth resistance, for that is a measure of humanity in any condition. Afrikans resisted foreign oppression from the inception, and intellectual resistance was always part of that resistance. In addition, there were always honest scholars of other races and cultures who sought the truth in any colour. The evidence shows intellectual resistance with several highpoints, but with a general trajectory towards greater and greater organisation, sophistication and intellectual rigor. The scholarship that points out the Afrikan identity of the majority of the Ancient Egyptians is a part of the intellectual resistance to racist lies, myths and other means of falsification which try to justify the largest crime in human history.

There is a long list of scholars who have contributed to the scholarship that retrieves Ancient Egypt from falsifications and establishes it as fundamentally an Afrikan civilisation. Understandably, there are disagreements, divergences and debate within this group. However they have agreed that Kemet was an Afrikan civilisation, with origins that were Afrikan, a culture that was Afrikan and a citizenry that was composed of an Afrikan majority for its entire existence. Afrikan scholars as well as scholars of Afrika, including Asante and Abarry (1996), Asante and Mazama (2009), Browder (1992), Carruthers (1984, 1999), Davidson (1991), Diop (1977, 1981), Drake (1987), Finch (1994), James (1954),

Massey (1990), Nehusi (2001, 2011 (forthcoming), Obenga (2004), Van Sertima (1986, 1989, 1994), Chancellor Williams (1976) and many others, have contributed in various ways to our understanding of this civilisation. On the other hand the work of their opponents is characterised by ignorance, inconsistencies, omissions, distortions, unfounded and unsupported assertions and outright inventions (see, for example, Davidson 1991, xxi-xxiv; Drake 1987; Hilliard 1996, 112-3). It is entirely illustrative of the unscholarly nature of the latter school's approach to this question that it is not usual for its members to engage with the scholarship of their opponents, particularly those in the Afrikan-centred movement, or to do so in any scientific or rational manner.

Despite the prevalence of the colonial myths, many Afrikans have never lost sight of their relationship to Kemet and the Nile Valley. For example, the Yoruba have two myths of origin, one which begins at Ile Ife and a more ancient one that places their origin near the 'Big Water' – the Nile River (Lucas 1970). The Igbo know that they migrated from 'Egypt and the Sahara region and only dispersed when the Sahara desert emerged' (Umeh 1997, iii). There are many similar stories held in common by other people in West Afrika and recent research has confirmed migrations from the Nile Valley to that part of the Afrikan world as well as the resulting multitude of links that express themselves in multi-faceted cultural and historical continuities and correspondences between the Nile Valley and the rest of Afrika (Armah 2006, 171-98; Buuba 2006, 137-47; Diop 1987, 212-34; Lam 2004, 90-108; Lam 2005-2006, 115-27; Lam 2006; Obenga 2003-2004, 48-63; Sarr 2005-2006, 128-36).

Afrikan communities abroad, especially in the West, resulted mostly from the great terror of capture, the forced march to the coast, and the economic, social, psychological and psychic horrors of the baracoons, the Middle Passage and the plantation, the historical and cultural rupture from the source, a great terror and trauma that is still mostly untreated and inherited and passed on from generation to generation in persons, families and communities in the Afrikan world. In such a climate of direct and continuing physical and psychological violence, cultural genocide, racism and miscellaneous other inhumanities, the wound of separation is always raw because it is renewed each day with its promises of racism, self-ignorance, disablement, dependency and anger. Questions of origins and identity are therefore of the greatest importance and the greatest urgency. It is scarcely surprising, therefore, that many Afrikans fought against the lies and distortions of the popular curriculum. Such resisters had for centuries proclaimed the Afrikan nature of Ancient Egypt and the connection of Afrikans – in the communities abroad as well as on the continent – to that state. The legal termination of physical enslavement, termed emancipation in most literature, did not mean an end to either mental enslavement and economic bondage nor the consequent disablement of the vast majority of Afrikans. In the western hemisphere, particularly but not only in the USA, Robert Alexander Young in 1829, David Walker in 1830, Martin Delany, the Jamaicans T. Scholes, Robert Love and Marcus Garvey, W. E. Blyden of the Caribbean and West Afrika, the Guyanese Norman E. Cameron (1929, xvi) and others argued Ancient Egypt as an Afrikan country and specifically connected Afrikans in the communities abroad to that state. These 'old scrappers', as they are called by Prof. Anderson Thompson (Carruthers 1984, 36; 1986, xi), are well represented in the scholarship of this period. Movements such as the Harlem Renaissance, Negritude, Negrismo in Cuba, and Black Power, fed a growing recognition and understanding of Pan-Afrikanism. Afrikans born abroad, including Blyden, Marcus Garvey, George Padmore, C. L. R. James, Ras Makonnen and J. H. Clarke, worked along with Kwame Nkrumah, Jomo Kenyatta and other Afrikan anti-colonial and anti-imperialist leaders born on the continent. Many of these leaders were intellectual lights in their own right and their work has contributed towards the intellectual liberation of Afrika (Beatty 2006, 79-99; Carruthers 1984, 36-7; Caruthers 1999, 10-13; Clarke 1986, 45-54; Drake 1987).

The single most important scholar in the recovery of the Afrikan nature of Kemet from the pseudo-scientific and often racist dogma of White supremacy is Cheikh Anta Diop. A multi-disciplinary scholar who 'specialized in history, linguistics, Egyptology, and the use of scientific tests for determining the approximate age of some archaeological finds' (Drake 1987, 137), Diop was familiar with several European languages, Ancient Egyptian, Woloof and several other Afrikan languages and was also a physicist. It seems that there can be hardly anyone else at any time more eminently qualified to investigate this topic. His work has been extensively studied, debated and on occasion modified (assessments include Carruthers 1999; Clarke 1986, 47-53; Drake 1987; Van Sertima 1986). Diop advances facts to show that in origins, physical features, blood type, skin type, culture (including language), kingship, matriarchy, hairstyles etc., the Ancient Egyptians were Afrikans and that as the history of the state unfolded they were joined by other peoples (Diop 1974; 1977; 1981; 1989; 1991; Diop *et al.* 1997). It is scarcely surprising that Diop has been the target of some of the most unscholarly and often racist attacks from modern defenders of the European master race project.

A decisive turning point in the debate over the nature of Kemet was reached at the 1974 UNESCO conference in Cairo, Egypt. Diop and Théophile Obenga demolished the arguments posed by their opponents. A general conclusion of the official report is instructive: 'Although the preparatory working paper ... sent out by UNESCO gave particulars of what was desired, not all participants had prepared communications comparable with the painstakingly researched contributions of Professors Cheikh Anta Diop and Obenga. Consequently there was a real lack of balance in the discussions' (Diop *et al.* 1997, 102).

The movement among Afrikan scholars to reclaim all of Afrikan history has in recent times become known as the

Afrikan Centred Movement, which is distinguished by multi-disciplinary approaches combined with a rigorous methodology for the study of Afrika from perspectives which include those of Afrika. The notion of the intellectually disabled Afrikan is permanently buried by the Afrikan Centred Movement and the search and practice of viable Afrikan alternatives to imposed disablement in every field of human endeavour.

The study of Ancient Egypt has been a fairly accurate reflection of some of the most significant forces that helped to shape the world which is unfolding in the 21st century. One of the distinguishing features of the growing scholarship in search of truth about this land has been an increasing willingness to engage with the work of colleagues of all backgrounds. In recent times the resulting dialogue has been reflected in the work of Van Sertima, Celenko and O'Connor and Reid. The current volume is the latest contribution to this very healthy development. In contrast, the work of the defenders of the oppression of Afrika and its peoples continues to be intellectually racist and is characterised by ignorance, misrepresentation and a studied avoidance of scholarship committed to rigorous scientific methodology in search of truth in any colour. A very notable example of the latter is the continued pretence of most 'mainstream' Eurocentric scholars in the West that Afrikan-centred scholarship does not exist. It is the norm among such scholars, such as they may be, not to mention any Afrikan scholar who examines Afrika through Afrikan eyes. It seems clear that for such scholars, it is all well and good to write the history of Afrika, but only if it is done from a Eurocentric perspective. Intellectual liberation and intellectual racism continue to mark and mar the march of humanity down the opening decades in the century of instant communication and the global village.

There are some relevant questions about the place of Kemet in the Afrikan context that are rarely or never asked. As we proceed with this summation and analysis of some of the arguments advanced by scholars of Ancient Egypt, it will be helpful to have some of these questions in mind. First, how can a civilisation which was born Afrikan in Afrika and grew out of the ground there become 'not African'? If it was not Afrikan then what was it? How come it became 'not African'? In considering answers it will perhaps be helpful to note some facts – no longer disputed – that are part of the historical, cultural and geographical context in which Kemet is situated.

Physical Appearance or Phenotype: Eye-witness Accounts and Self-presentation
In the history of this world there was a period when the racial and cultural identity of the Ancient Egyptians was not a contested issue – in European scholarship or elsewhere. Curiously, and quite decisively for the correct answer to the question before us, this was a time when the Ancient Egyptian civilisation was in full swing, and ancient European eyewitnesses reported who they saw and what they saw, with their own eyes and in their own words. These eyewitnesses include Diodorus Siculus (1935, I, 34-44), Solon, Herodotus, Aristotle, Lucian, Lycinus and many others (Blyden 1994, 130-5; Diop 1974, 1-9; 1981, 36-8). These ancient eyewitnesses from foreign lands attest the Afrikan nature of Kemet, which the people of Kemet proclaimed. There was no contradiction on this issue among these eye-witnesses. Yet, later Europeans, who have not witnessed these things with their own eyes, have contradicted these very eye-witnesses whose work they often use, selectively, to try to justify the European master race project. Part of the reason may well be that such an open admission would have committed them to providing reasons for their express rejection of such conclusions when there is no logic for such rejection. In any event there are some very obvious contradictions in the prevailing attitudes of modern Europe to these ancient European scholars. These ancients are on the one hand celebrated as the founders of civilisation while on the other hand their observations and conclusions about the people of Kemet as the real founders of civilisation are dismissed and the fact that many of them were educated in Kemet conveniently omitted. Some of the best evidence on the identity of the Ancient Egyptians has therefore come to us from the ancients themselves – both Egyptians and Europeans, especially Greeks. These were expositions of self-knowledge on the part of the people of Kemet, and eye-witness reports by both. These were not intended to prove any point about the identity of the people of Kemet, for there was no debate about that fact among the eye-witnesses. Therefore their attribution of identity is often unintended and unbiased. These two groups of sources therefore offer some of the most independent and strongest corroboration of the fact of the Afrikan identity of Kemet.

It should not be surprising that a number of modern scholars have concluded that the majority of the people of Kemet were Afrikans and cite the appearance of the people as preserved in the Sphinx and other physical representations of the majority of the population of the country (Browder 1992; Nobles and Nobles 2006, 168-75; Van Sertima 1991; 1994).

The Peopling of Kemet and its Southern Orientation
This line of argument points out that humanity itself was born Afrikan in Afrika and that the first 'high cultures' as well as Kemet, the first civilisation and the next step up in terms of development, were also evolved in Afrika by these first people of the world. Afrikans therefore founded the archetypes of the arts and sciences which still govern human perception and behaviour and so gave to humanity its humanity.

Humanity's birthplace is quite probably somewhere in the Nile/Great Lakes region of the continent. It was from this ancient heartland that Afrikans migrated to people a continent, later other parts of the earth. Subsequent long residences in differing environments resulted in mutations of Afrikans into different types of humanity commonly called races today. As Afrikans migrated out of the original heartland the Kongo-Ubangi and Nile river valleys became the first great transcontinental cultural highways. Civilisation moved from south to north. There were a number of Afrikan societies that boasted very advanced social organisation and other outstanding achievements: Kush, Nubia, Ta-Seti. Significantly, all of these were located in the vicinity of Kemet, but in the south, in inner Afrika, closer to the heartland where humanity was born. Then there was Kemet, the most outstanding of them all. Kemet has become the most known and admired flower from this Afrikan tree. But it was not its only bloom. These and other aspects of the antecedents of Kemet are not fully known, though scholars are advancing knowledge in this area, as attested by several of the chapters in this section (see Anselin, Gatto, Navajas Jiménez).

The inhabitants of Kemet were therefore Afrikan from the inception, and though there were infusions of others, such as the 'Peoples of the Sea', the Hyksos, Assyrians, Persians, Greeks, Romans, Arabs and Turks, none of these people were the founders of the Ancient Egyptian civilisation which, until relatively recent historical times, was always predominantly Afrikan. One fact that appears to confuse many observers today and appears to give credence to an 'Arab' Ancient Egypt is that the current inhabitants of Egypt are overwhelmingly Arab. The Arab people occupied Egypt *en masse* only in historically recent times, in the 7th century AD to be exact. This was long after the heyday of Kemet, which lasted from at least 3000 BC to AD 625. The Arab occupation of Kemet was part of a general invasion and occupation of North Afrika. Today the north-south divide in countries such as the Sudan and Mauritania amounts to a continuing zone of confrontation between Arabs and Afrikans, though this is often an over simplified statement of the situation. It is necessary to remember that Egypt is and always has been geographically part of Afrika, but has become alienated from its geographical and cultural location in some aspects of the modern discourse. If the people of Kemet were not Afrikan, what were they? When and how did they arrive in that or any other part of Afrika? How come, as we shall see below, did they have an Afrikan culture and an Afrikan world view?

The Phenotype or Physical Features, and Genotype or Genetic Make-up, of the Ancient Egyptians
The physical appearance of the Ancient Egyptians is an obvious arena of contestation, since race is almost entirely calculated on physical appearance. Ancient eye-witness testimonies to the Afrikan identity of the majority of the inhabitants of Kemet have been mentioned above. Yet many defenders of the 'not African' thesis descend into complex arguments employing the pseudo-scientific device of cranial measurements in order to arrive at their pre-determined conclusions. Simultaneously, some of these very scholars are patronising or even openly racist to the living examples of the very same 'not Africans' – on account of their phenotype: how they look, their physical characteristics (see Drake 1987, 361-62 for a discussion of Wallis Budge, who was ambivalent on this question throughout his long career). It is strange and illogical indeed that today the race of the Ancient Egyptians is not openly discussed by scholars who inhabit a race-conscious world in which the vast majority of Ancient Egyptians would have been constantly discriminated against on a daily basis on account of their Afrikan race. It appears that nowadays the Ancient Egyptians are white, Arab or 'not African' only by innuendo.

The famed 25th Dynasty is often termed the Nubian or Black Dynasty, as though they are distinctive with regard to their race or phenotype and their national origin. However, the Ancient Egyptians' own representations of themselves leave no doubt that the first dynasties were racially Afrikan, and that even after the accession of some families with members who displayed allegedly 'not African' features, some of whom were of mixed race, many of these very families supplied pharaohs whose physical features would mark them as very Afrikan in the racist criteria of modern Western society. In this regard the term 'Nubian' may be misleading, since the Nubians were all 'very African' in their physical appearance and the Ancient Egyptians did not represent them as physically different from themselves. 'Nubian' is a national rather than a racial category. But even such a national distinction is misleading when explaining the racial identity of the majority of the population of Ancient Egypt for most of its history. Some scholars agree that after immigration produced significant proportions of 'not Africans' and mixed race people in the Delta region, called Lower Egypt, there was a south-north divide in which, generally, the further south one went the more the 'very African' types in the population predominated. We shall see below that the south is the origin of much of Ancient Egypt, the original population, its gods, spiritual doctrine, its mythology, the keeper of its national shrines and a constant source of renewal and national continuity that would remain, throughout its history, the spiritual and cultural heartland and capital of the country (Diop 1974; Drake 1987). The 25th Dynasty is therefore not distinctive in that regard either. Kashta, Shabaka, Shabataka, Taharka and Pianky were not distinctive pharaohs because of their 'very African' physical features, but neither would have been their non-Afrikan rivals after the accession of the latter. Even after the end of the 25th Dynasty, Kemet, as before, continued to be led by pharaohs, many of whom would be termed 'Black' or 'very African' in today's world.

Today it is common for scholars, whether by affirmation or by omission, to contribute to the assumption that the Ancient Egyptians were the same people as the modern Egyptians – often while deliberately avoiding any direct mention of the issue. An instance of the use of images in the work of Joyce Tyldesley on Hatshepsut (1996) supplies a good example of this trend. On the cover, the very first part of the book that would be seen by the observer, is an imaginary physical representation of how Hatshepsut actually appeared. Here, Hatshepsut is unmistakably white or European in appearance. Within the book, Plate 10 is a photograph of a red granite sphinx of Hatshepsut, a physical image of Hatshepsut supplied by her Ancient Egyptian contemporaries, people who actually saw her and represented what they saw with their own eyes. They supply a remarkably different version of Hatshepsut from the one dreamt up by an artist who was apparently not looking at the subject – or who did not represent what they saw. In today's world, in which judgments on humans beings are still made by many according to physical features, and the fortunes of Afrikan people and others are still determined by economic, social, mental and other structures that were constructed in past eras and justified by racism, such deviations from truth, whether or not intentionally constructed, are neither sensitive, nor innocent, nor harmless.

The mistranslation of 𓂜𓏤𓈉 (Faulkner 1991, 137 with several variations; see also Allen 2000, 461 and Gardiner 1988, 575), *Nḥsy* = *Nahasy*, *Nehsi* as 'Black' in such a way as to suggest a fundamental distinction between the Ancient Egyptians and the other Afrikans has been opposed as inaccurate, unhistorical, unscientific and worse (Carruthers 1984, 21; Diop 1981, 42; Drake 1987, 141; Grantham 2003, 9-22).

Some scholars emphasise the later mixed race and European rulers of Kemet as though they are representative of the entire line of rulers. The Western media has popularised these falsehoods, which are now common in television programmes and magazines. This is the same as deciding that all the presidents of the USA were Afrikan merely because one of them, Barak Obama, the present incumbent, is physically an Afrikan. Others emphasise the Nubian Dynasty (the 25th) as though those pharaohs are vastly different from the majority of the others, which is roughly the same as emphasising the fact that both George Bush senior and George Bush junior were White presidents of the USA, which gives the impression to the unsuspecting that it is not normal for presidents of the USA to be White. The inference is that they must have a different identity from that of the other presidents, who were all White males.

The people of Kemet were certain of their Afrikan identity. Even though for much of their history they appeared to have regarded all others, including other Afrikans, as less cultured or even uncultured, they graphically represented both themselves and other Afrikans as Afrikans.

Language and Southern Orientation
Language is an inventory of and a witness to a people's perceptions, thoughts and experiences (see Anselin, this volume). The language of the people of Kemet therefore tells us some more about their own perception of themselves. Diop and Carruthers have pointed to the importance of the language of Kemet as an indicator of the southern orientation of the people of the country. The people of Kemet referred to southern Egypt as Upper Egypt and northern Egypt as Lower Egypt (Carruthers 1984, 19). Diop (1991, 108) emphasises that the language of Kemet enshrines a southern orientation of the people. Carruthers (1984, 18-22) points out that the words in this language for 'up' are interchangeable for 'south'. Neither Diop nor Carruthers says whether the terminology of Upper and Lower Egypt was instructed by the topography of the land – the south of the country is higher than the north. However, it is clear from the context of their analysis that this topographical fact is an irrelevant coincidence. The south or up was clearly a place of reverence, as we shall see below: 'Now we understand better why the Egyptian turns towards the South, the heart of Africa, land of his origins, land of his ancestors, "land of the gods", just as the Moslem today turns towards Mecca. That is why the right hand designates the West and the left hand the East' (Diop 1991, 108).

Quite apart from the evidence from the *Medew Netjer* cited by Diop and Carruthers, a number of other scholars reached the very conclusion of the southern origin of the majority of the Ancient Egyptians, but for slightly different reasons. W. E. B. DuBois, the great Afrikan-American scholar, is among those who reached this conclusion about the southern origin of the Ancient Egyptians at a fairly early date (DuBois 1915, 21, 46; 1965, 106), a conclusion that has now become commonplace (see, for example, Drake 1987; Monges 1997; Van Sertima 1991, 1994). It is not at all difficult to understand the reason for this southern orientation. The people of Kemet consciously pointed towards the south as their place of origin. This is the reason why that direction held great significance to them. To the Ancient Egyptian, the south, the headwaters of the Nile in the Great Lakes region of Afrika, where humanity was born, was a sacred place. In Kemet water drawn from the River Nile, especially from the region of the First Cataract, was highly prized for the pouring of libation, a pan-Afrikan ritual (see Nehusi, this volume; Nehusi forthcoming), since tradition had it that the water drawn from this area was guaranteed to be pure because it was nearer than anywhere else in Kemet to the symbolic source of the river (Blackman 1912, 71; Smith 1993, 43). Such a conclusion appears to be verified in the name the people of Kemet gave to this region of their country. It is 𓈎𓃀𓈗𓊖 *ḳbḥw, kebehu* (Gardiner 1988, 596), which must mean, literally, 'pure land' or 'pure region'. This term is also consistent with the name the people of Kemet gave to the extreme south of their country, (of which this region was a part): 𓎗 *wpt-t3, wepet-ta* = 'Earth's beginning' (Gardiner 1988, 560). This term means, literally, 'the beginning of all land', 'the place where the water comes out of the land.' It was obviously a sacred place to the citizens of Kemet, who knew that that was the direction of their origin, for in fact they referred to Afrika south of their country by names such as *Ta-Kenset*, literally 'placenta-land', *Ta-Khenti* = 'the land of beginnings' and *Ta-Takhu* = 'the land of the spirits', that is, 'where the souls of ancestors dwell' (Finch 1994, 38-9) or 'God's Land', 'The Land of the Ancestors' (Drake 1987, 162-3, 273). It is helpful here to recall that, to the Ancient Egyptians, ancestors were revered persons and therefore their dwelling place was sacred on account of both that and the related fact of it being the place of their origin. These exact cultural attitudes towards ancestors and the place of their burial are alive all over the Afrikan world today. This Ancient Egyptian belief that the southern region of their country was a sacred and perhaps even a pristine place also finds expression in the term 'Herr ( ) des Kataraktengebiets' (Erman and Grapow 1982 Vol. 5, 29), literally 'Master of the Cataracts', but more precisely 'Owner of the Cataracts', one of the titles given to Khnum, who was a Creator Divinity. To the people of Kemet, this sacred land in Upper or Southern Egypt, near to the First Cataract and contiguous with inner Afrika, is the place of origin of Osiris (Wosir), the culture hero and bringer of civilisation to Egypt and eventually everywhere else. He would later become Judge of the Underworld, and he and Auset (Isis), his sister-wife, would become two of the most significant figures in the long history of the land and eventually of other lands, including Greece, the Roman Empire and Europe in later ages (Drake 1987, 166). The knowledge of inner Afrika 'as the chief source of the spiritual – "The Land of the Gods" or "The Land of the Spirits"' has persisted even after the Arab invasion and domination of Kemet (Williams 1976, 36, 110, 136).

Within Egypt the south was commonly recognised as the residence of the ancestral divinities, shrines and mystical power. 'All Egyptians shared the tradition that the holiest spots in Egypt were in the very Negroid south … The rulers there had high mystical status, and southerners were people who were believed to have close contact with "the ancestors" and were custodians of the earliest sources of mystical power, such as the shrine of Hathor… and above all, the shrine of Hapi, god of the Nile, at the first cataract. During low Niles and floods, pharaohs travelled to the latter site to seek a change in the behaviour of the river' (Drake 1987, 175-6). Specific expression of this reverence of the south as the origin of ancestors is illustrated in the oft recounted story of pharaoh Pepi II and the Baka (pigmy) man who is referred to in the literature of Egyptology as a dwarf. This man was from the 'Land of Punt' or 'Land of the Spirits'. He was highly regarded because of this origin as well as his related knowledge of 'the dances of the ancestors' (Drake 1987, 186; see Lichtheim 1976, 26-7). Such reverence for the south seems to have exerted a powerful influence upon the Asiatic usurpers called the Hyksos, who persistently 'sought the prestige of an alliance with the South' (Drake 1987, 197). The recognition of the south as the initiator and spiritual and cultural heartland of Kemet is almost universal to this day, for the Old Kingdom, which was unmistakably rooted in the Afrikan south, is widely understood to be the formative and classical era of Kemet.

Those who propose a 'not African' origin and identity of the builders of Kemet are thus posed with an insurmountable problem. The facts show that these builders were from the south, from inner Afrika and that the general trajectory of development and progress in human affairs was generally from south to north. If they were 'not African', then who were these builders of Kemet? We return here to Asa Hilliard's question.

There is a very narrow definition of 'Negro' by some Egyptologists in order to get around what, for them, is a problem. There are two insurmountable problems with this tactic. The first is that Afrikans in their genotype, their physical characteristics, do not confirm to the narrow physical parameters of thick lips, broad noses and very dark skin selected and ascribed to *all* Afrikans by racist scholarship. Afrikans possess the widest gene pool among humanity and range in colour from high yellow to the bluest black, from the tightest peppercorn curls to straight hair, from the broadest to very narrow nostrils. The definition of those Egyptologists excludes a vast number of Afrikans from being Afrikan! It is therefore inaccurate and misleading. The other problem with this approach is that it does not confirm to the modern reality of the odious categorisation of humanity by physical characteristics. It is important to be clear that this writer does not support such racism. However, it is disingenuous for some scholars to claim that Afrikans were 'not Afrikan' when in contemporary society the very people would have been actively discriminated against because of these very same features which make them Afrikan.

One argument that is part of the debate on the Afrikan nature of Kemet is the meaning of the word *kmt*, *Kemet* itself. In the *Medew Netjer* this word is deployed by the Ancient Egyptians to refer to their country. It is traditional for Egyptologists to interpret it to mean 'Black Land' (Faulkner 1991, 286; Gardiner 1988, 597). However, Afrikan-centred scholars, beginning with Cheikh Anta Diop (1981, 41-2) and including Carruthers (1999, 239-40) and Newsome (1983, 128) have challenged this interpretation (see also Drake 1987, 141). Perhaps the fullest and most recent argument from this latter school is to be found in the work of Charles Grantham (2003, 1-7), who points out that according to the grammatical rules and the usage of the *Medew Netjer*, the word is a noun in which the adjective is followed by the determinative , that there is no dispute that in the *Medew Netjer* the term (*km*) means 'black', that there is therefore a dispute over the meaning of which is normally translated as 'town', 'village' or 'city' and that it is necessary 'to determine if the ancient Egyptians named their country after the color of the soil or the color of their skin' (Grantham 2003, 3). His conclusion is that 'the most appropriate reading of is either 'Black City', 'Black Town', or 'Black Settlement' (Grantham 2003, 5-6).

The racial and cultural identity of the people of Kemet was not a contested issue at the time this society was extant. In fact, in that era there was no great accent upon differentiating humanity based upon 'race' and eye-witnesses were all certain of its Afrikan identity. However, it is of no co-incidence that these matters first became contested during the period of European colonisation of large parts of the world, most importantly and tragically of Afrika. It is against the background of these intellectual developments, differences, divergences, disputes, agreements and commonalities that the following chapters may best be read, interrogated and understood.

References

Achebe, C. 2009. *The Education of a British-Protected Child*. London, Penguin Classics.

Allen, J. P. 2000. *Middle Egyptian*. Cambridge, Cambridge University Press.

Armah, A. K. 2006. *The Eloquence of the Scribes: A Memoir on the Sources and Resources of African Literature*. Popenguine, Senegal, Per Ankh.

Asante, M. K. 1996a. Early African Cultures: An Afrocentric Perspective. In T. Celenko (ed.), *Egypt in Africa*, 33. Bloomington, Indiana, Indianapolis Museum of Art/Indiana University Press.

—1996b. European Racism Regarding Ancient Egypt. In T. Celenko (ed.), *Egypt in Africa*, 116-7. Bloomington, Indiana, Indianapolis Museum of Art/Indiana University Press.

Asante, M. K. and Abarry, A. S. (eds.) 1996. *African Intellectual Heritage: A Book of Sources*. Philadelphia, Temple University Press.

Asante, M. K. and Mazama, A. (eds.) 2009. *Encyclopedia of African Religion*. Vols. I and II. Los Angeles, SAGE.

Beatty, M. H. 2005-2006. Martin Delany and Egyptology. *Ankh: Revue d'Égyptologie et des Civilisations Africaines* 14-15, 78-99.

Bernal, M. 1987. *Black Athena: The Afroasiatic Roots of Classical Civilization. Volume I. The Fabrication of Ancient Greece, 1785-1985*. London, Free Association Books.

Blackman, A. M. 1912. The Significance of Incense and Libations in Funerary and Temple Ritual. *Zeitschrift für ägyptische Sprache und Altertumskunde* 50, 69-75.

Blyden, E. W. 1994. *Christianity, Islam and the Negro Race*. Baltimore, MD., Black Classic Press.

Browder, A. 1992. *Nile Valley Contribution to Civilization: Exploding the Myths*. Vol. I. Washington, DC., The Institute of Karmic Guidance.

Buuba, B. D. 2005-2006. Les migrations Sereer: jalons de la saga africaine et sénégalaise. *Ankh: Revue d'Égyptologie et des Civilisations Africaines* 14-15, 8-33.

Cabral, A. 1980. *Unity and Struggle*. London, Heinemann.

Celenko, T. (ed.) 1996. *Egypt in Africa*. Bloomington, Indiana, Indianapolis Museum of Art/Indiana University Press.

Carruthers, J. H. 1984. *Essays in Ancient Egyptian Studies*. Los Angeles, University of Sankore Press.

—1999. *Intellectual Warfare*. Chicago, Third World Press.

Clarke, J. H. 1986. Africa in the Ancient World, in M. Karenga and J. H. Carruthers (eds.), *Kemet and the African Worldview: Research, Rescue and Restoration*, 45-54. Los Angeles, University of Sankore Press.

—1994. *My Life in Search of Africa*. Monograph Series 8. Cornell University, Africana Studies and Research Center.

—1998. *Christopher Columbus and the Afrikan Holocaust: Slavery and the Rise of European Capitalism*. New York, A&B Publishers Group.

Davidson, B. 1991. *Africa in History: Themes and Outlines*. New York and London, Simon and Schuster.

Diop, C. A. 1974. *The African Origin of Civilization: Myth or Reality*. New York, Lawrence Hill and Company.

—1977. *Parenté génétique de l'égyptien pharaonique et des langues négro-africaines*. Dakar, Institut Fondamental d'Afrique Noire.

—1981. Origin of the Ancient Egyptians. In G. Mokhtar (ed.), UNESCO *General History of Africa II: Ancient Civilizations of Africa*, 27-57. Berkeley, University of California Press/UNESCO.

—1987. *Precolonial Black Africa. A Comparative Study of the Political and Social Systems of Europe and Black Africa, from Antiquity to the Formation of Modern States*. Trans. H. Salemson. Westport, Conn., Lawrence Hill and Company.

—1989. *The Cultural Unity of Black Africa: The Domains of Matriarchy and of Patriarchy in Classical Antiquity*. London, Karnak House

—1991. *Civilization or Barbarism: An Authentic Anthropology*. Trans. Y.-L. Meena Ngemi. New York, Lawrence Hill and Company.

Diop, C. H., Leclant, J., Obenga, T. and Vercoutter, J. 1997. *The Peopling of Ancient Egypt and the Deciphering of the Meroitic Script*. London, Karnak House.

Drake, St. C. 1987. *Black Folk Here and There: An Essay in History and Anthropology*. Vol. I. Los Angeles, University of California, Center for Afro-American Studies.

DuBois, W. E. B. 1915. *The Negro*. New York, Henry Holt and Co.

—1965. *The World and Africa: An Inquiry into the Part Which Africa Has Played in World History*. New York, International Publishers.

Erman, A. and Grapow, H. 1982 [1926-1953]. *Wörterbuch der ägyptischen Sprache*. Vols. I-V. Berlin, Akademie Verlag.

Faulkner, R. O. 1991. *A Concise Dictionary of Middle Egyptian*. Oxford, Griffith Institute.

Finch, C. 1994. Nile Genesis: Continuity of Culture from the Great Lakes to the Delta. In I. Van Sertima (ed.),

Egypt Child of Africa. Journal of African Civilizations 12, 35-54. New Brunswick, Transaction Publishers.

Gardiner, A. 1988. *Egyptian Grammar: Being an Introduction to the Study of Hieroglyphs*. 3rd Edition, revised. Oxford, Griffith Institute.

Grantham, C. A. 2003. *The Battle for Kemet*. Chicago, Kemetic Institute.

Harris, J. E. 1998. *Africans and their History*. New York, Meridian.

Hilliard, A. G. 1992. The Meaning of KMT (Ancient Egyptian) History for Contemporary African American Experience. *Phylon* 49(1-2), 10-22.

—1996. Are Africans African? Scholarship over Rhetoric and Propaganda, Valid Discourse on Kemetic Origins. In T. Celenko (ed.), *Egypt in Africa*, 112-5. Bloomington, Indiana, Indianapolis Museum of Art/Indiana University Press.

James, G. G. M. 1954. *Stolen Legacy*. New York, Philosophical Library.

Lam, A. M. 2003-2004. L'origine des peuls: les principales thèses confrontées aux traditions africaines et à l'égyptologie. *Ankh: Revue d'Égyptologie et des Civilisations Africaines* 12-13, 63-90.

—2005-2006. Égypte ancienne et Afrique noire: quelques nouveaux faits qui éclairent leurs relations. *Ankh: Revue d'Égyptologie et des Civilisations Africaines* 14-15, 114-27.

—2006. *La Vallée du Nil: berceau de l'unité culturelle de l'Afrique noir*. Paris and Dakar, Kephera and Presses Universitaires de Dakar.

Lichtheim, M. 1975. *Ancient Egyptian Literature. Volume I. The Old and Middle Kingdoms*. Berkeley, Los Angeles, University of California Press.

Lucas, J. O. 1970. *Religion in West Africa and Ancient Egypt*. Apapa, Nigerian National Press.

Massey, G. 1990. *Ancient Egypt, the Light of the World*. New York and Chesapeake, ECA Associates.

Monges, M. Maát-Ka-Re. 1997. *Kush, The Jewel of Nubia: Reconnecting the Root System of African Civilization*. Trenton, NJ., Africa World Press.

Nehusi, K. 2001. From *Medew Netjer* to Ebonics. In C. Crawford (ed.), *Ebonics and Language Education of African Ancestry Students*, 56-122. New York and London, Sankofa World Publishers.

—2011 (forthcoming). *Libation: An Afrikan Ritual of Heritage in the Circle of Life*. Lanham, MD., University Press of America.

Newsome, F. 1983. Black Contributions to the Early History of Western Medicine. In I. Van Sertima (ed.), *Blacks in Science: Ancient and Modern*. New Brunswick and London, Transaction Books.

Nobles, W. W. and Nobles, V. L. 2006. The Whitening of Black King Tut: Implications for Educating All Children. *Ankh: Revue d'Égyptologie et des Civilisations Africaines*, 14-15, 168-75.

Obenga, T. 2003-2004. Comparaisons morphologiques entre l'Égyptien ancien et le Dagara. *Ankh: Revue d'Égyptologie et des Civilisations Africaines* 12-13, 46-83.

—2004. *African Philosophy: The Pharaonic Period: 2780-330 BC*. Popenguine Senegal, Per Ankh

O'Connor, D and Reid, A. (eds.) 2003. *Ancient Egypt in Africa*. Walnut Creek, CA and London, Left Coast Press/University College London.

Rashidi, R. 1994. From the Center to the Fringe: The Persistence of Racial Myths in Physical Anthropological Theory. In I. Van Sertima (ed.), *Egypt, Child of Africa. Journal of African Civilizations* 12, 81-104. New Brunswick, Transaction Publishers.

Reynolds-Marniche, D. 1994. The Myth of the Mediterranean Race. In I. Van Sertima (ed.), *Egypt, Child of Africa. Journal of African Civilizations* 12. New Brunswick, Transaction Publishers.

Said, E. W. 1993. *Culture and Imperialism*. London, Chatto and Windus.

Sarr, M. N. 2005-2006. Cours d'eau et croyances en Égypte pharaonique et en Afrique noire modern. *Ankh: Revue d'Égyptologie et des Civilisations Africaines* 14-15, 128-35.

Siculus, Diodorus. 1935. *The Library of History*. Vol. I. The Loeb Classical Library 279. London and Cambridge, Heinemann and Harvard University Press

Smith, M. 1993. *The Liturgy of Opening the Mouth for Breathing*. Oxford, Griffith Institute.

Snowden Jr., F. M. 1996. The Physical Characteristics of Egyptians and their Southern Neighbours: The Classical Evidence. In T. Celenko (ed.), *Egypt in Africa*, 106-8. Bloomington, Indiana, Indianapolis Museum of Art/Indiana University Press.

Tyldesley, J. 1996. *Hatchepsut: The Female Pharaoh*. London, Viking.

Umeh, J. U. 1997. *After God is Dibia: Igbo Cosmology, Divination and Sacred Science in Nigeria*. Vol. I. London, Karnak House.

UNICEF. 2002. *A World Fit for Children*. http://www.unicef.org/specialsession/docs_new/documents/A-RES-S27-2E.pdf

UNICEF and UNESCO. 2007. *A Human Rights-Based Approach to Education for All*. New York and Paris. http://unesdoc.unesco.org/images/0015/001548/154861e.pdf

Van Sertima, I. (ed.) 1986. *Great African Thinkers, Vol. I: Cheikh Anta Diop*. New Brunswick and Oxford, Transaction Books.

—(ed.) 1991. *Egypt Revisited. Journal of African*

Civilizations 10. New Brunswick and London, Transaction Publishers.

—(ed.) 1994. *Egypt, Child of Africa. Journal of African Civilizations* 12. New Brunswick and London, Transaction Publishers.

Williams, B. 1985. The Lost Pharaohs of Nubia. In I. Van Sertima (ed.), *Nile Valley Civilizations: Proceedings of the Nile Valley Conference, Atlanta, Sept. 26-30. Journal of African Civilizations* 6, 90-104. New Brunswick, Transaction Publishers.

Williams, C. 1976. *The Destruction of Black Civilization: Great Issues of a Race From 4500 B.C. to 2000 A.D.* Chicago, Third World Press.

The Nubian Pastoral Culture as Link between Egypt and Africa: A View from the Archaeological Record

Maria Carmela Gatto
Yale University

Abstract
The cultural relation between Ancient Egypt and Africa is here analysed from an archaeological point of view highlighting the role of Nubia as link between the two. Nubia strongly influenced the Egyptian culture at its formative stage during the 5th and 4th millennia BC. At the same time the nomadic pastoral way of life, which first developed in Nubia, was adopted by most of the northern African cultures. This pastoral background is what links Egypt to Africa.

Keywords: Africa, Egypt, Nubia, pastoral Neolithic, social complexity.

Introduction
On the role of Egypt in the development of African cultures there exists a long-lasting, and mostly contradictory, scholarship. On the one hand, supported by the Ancient Egyptian viewpoint, a cultural independency of Egypt from other African cultures is claimed. On the other hand, most North African countries and ethnic groups declare a strong and direct bond with Egypt. I myself have heard people in a small village at the southern border between Libya and Algeria claiming their descent from the great Egyptian civilisation. The Afrocentric ideas of Cheikh Anta Diop (1974, 1981) and his theories of a 'Black Egypt' are the extreme consequences of such beliefs.

That Egypt, as an African country, was directly involved in the cultural dynamics of its continent has been broadly accepted. The many essays published in a volume edited by O'Connor and Reid in 2003 (*Ancient Egypt in Africa*, Walnut Creek, CA, Left Coast Press/London, UCL), and those in this volume, have enriched the debate and increased knowledge of the issue over the course of the last decade. Nowadays support for the Egypt-Africa connection comes from different fields of research, mainly archaeological, linguistic and genetic, but to what extent and in what way Egypt interacted with the African world still remains to be clarified. What the archaeological work is bringing to light, though, is the irrelevance of the race-based theory, as cultural identities do not necessarily match or relate to race.

In this paper I will focus on the formative period of the Egyptian civilisation, as this is the period when the Ancient Egyptian social identity was forged and when its African foundations are easier to detect.

The Origin of the Predynastic: Western Desert and Central Sudan
With the intensification of archaeological research in the Egyptian Western Desert evidence of prehistoric human occupation has been consistently found in both the oases region and the playas region to the south. Major breaks in the chrono-cultural sequence are related to climatic variations. After a major arid event during the late Pleistocene, which completely dried up the Sahara, forcing the people to cluster along the Nile (and in the Central Sahara massifs), the Holocene period was characterised by better climatic conditions due to a northward shifting of the monsoon summer rain regime (Kuper and Kropelin 2006; Wendorf and Schild 2001). The desert was again settled, although cyclical minor arid spells required the population to move back and forth from the desert to the Nile or to remain in the oases. From the 4th millennium BC another major arid event forced the people to concentrate in the oases area and to settle more permanently to the Nile Valley.

According to Hassan (1988, 144) and many other scholars after him (see Anselin, this volume), the strong similarity encountered between the Western Desert Neolithic material culture and that of the Badarian can be explained by the massive migration of the desert people to Middle Egypt because of the incipient aridity in their territory. The work by Kuper and Kropelin (2006) supports this perspective. According to their results, the settlement pattern between desert and valley varies throughout the Holocene. If the Nile Valley (particularly Nubia) was mostly settled during the Late Pleistocene and from the 5th millennium BC onwards, the desert was settled during the Early and Middle Holocene, when the Nile Valley was basically empty of human occupation. As a matter of fact, no or scanty evidence of human occupation dated to these periods has been found in the Egyptian Nile Valley (problems in site preservation might be a reason for this). However, this is not the case for the middle Nile Valley (corresponding to the geographical region of Nubia). In fact, for Nubia a complete occupational sequence is well attested throughout the Pleistocene and the Holocene. This makes sense if it is assumed that not only desert people were going back to the valley during arid spells, but that they also had a mobile lifestyle with seasonal movements between the two ecosystems. The archaeological record for the Middle Holocene reports only rather small temporary campsites in the desert, and along the valley settlements are rather seasonal. The sites taken into consideration for Kuper and Kropelin's study are only those with good radiometric dates. Thus, all the old data is left aside, creating a gap in the valley occupation that does not coincide with the reality of the archaeological record.

Including the Nubian evidence in the scenario gives a completely different perspective on the issue. The cultural evidence found in the Nabta-Kiseiba region of the southern Western Desert is indeed part of the Nubian cultural tradition, while that from the oases region belongs to a different cultural unit (Gatto 2002a). The Badarian derives the lithic technology primarily from the Oases Neolithic (Holmes 1989).

In his chapter in the *Ancient Egypt in Africa* volume (2003), Wengrow had the correct perception of looking south to find proof of the African foundation of Egypt. According to him 'the similarities between Early Neolithic burials in Middle Egypt and Central Sudan extend beyond the treatment and ornamentation of the corpse to the deposition of functionally similar artefacts within graves' (Wengrow 2003, 127). However, there is a fundamental assumption in Wengrow's article which leads to misinterpretations. Wengrow denies the evidence of Early Holocene autochthonous cattle domestication in the Nabta-Kiseiba region of southern Western Desert (as proposed by Wendorf and Schild 1980, 1998, 2001; and criticised among others by Grigson 2000; MacDonald and MacDonald 2000; A. B. Smith 1986). Rather he locates the beginning of the Neolithic in the late 5th millennium BC, when clear evidence of domestication is contemporarily present both in Egypt and Sudan (Wengrow 2003, 126). Findings of domesticated cattle, dated to *c*. 7000 BC, have been reported in the past years from the Kerma area (Honegger 2007; Honegger *et al*. 2009). Although not so early as that discovered at Nabta, the Kerma datum definitely pushes back in time the beginning of the Neolithic in the Middle Nile Valley, at least between the Second Cataract and the Dongola Reach.

Furthermore, the Sudanese sites Wengrow takes into consideration are only those associated with the Khartoum Neolithic and located between the confluences of the White Nile with the Blue Nile and the Atbara River, that is to say, the Khartoum Region. The Early Neolithic phase in the Khartoum Region indeed dates to the 5th millennium BC and no evidence for an earlier date has been found so far. Between Badari and Khartoum, however, there is an entire section of the Nile and surrounding deserts the archaeological record of which Wengrow unfortunately does not mention at all. This region is known by the name of Nubia.

Definition of Nubia
In a traditional geographical definition Nubia is the section of the Nile Valley between the First and the Sixth Cataract of the river: a 'corridor' linking Egypt to the sub-Saharan regions of Africa (Adams 1977). Current anthropological and archaeological research suggests that this geographical definition is narrowly conceived given the evidence of Nubian cultures, which cover a much larger and more fluid area. A cultural definition of Nubia, thus, must take into account the desert regions to the east and west of the Nile, as well as the areas of exchange and interaction between Nubians and nearby people.

Frontiers, as zones of cultural interface and fluidity in group affiliations, are socially charged places where innovative cultural constructs are created and transformed (Lightfoot and Martinez 1995). In the Nubian case, its northern and southern frontiers became more fluid and socially active by the 5th millennium BC, when Middle and Upper Egypt, on one side, and the Khartoum Region on the other, became strongly influenced by the Nubian culture. This corresponds to the spread of cattle pastoralism along the whole Nile Valley. Cultural boundaries, as unbounded constructs, move through time for different reasons. Generally speaking, during the prehistoric period and part of the historic period Nubia as a cultural territory included the Nile Valley between the First and the Fourth Cataract and the nearby deserts.

Nubia and the African Neolithic Model
The African pathway to food production differs consistently from those developed in other areas of the world. The Neolithisation in the Near East, Mesoamerica and Eastern North America was primarily focused on the domestication of plants: it occurred in well-watered localities with relatively abundant resources, and yield was probably the major concern during intensification. In Africa, Neolithisation was based on cattle domestication: it occurred in unstable, marginal environments, and predictability and scheduled consumption were the driving forces behind the process (Marshall and Hildebrand 2002). So far, the earliest evidence for domestic cattle in Nubia and Africa has been reported from Bir Kiseiba and Nabta Playa, dated to *c*. 8400 and 7750 BC respectively (Gautier 1980, 1987, 2001; Wendorf, Schild and Close 1984; Wendorf and Schild 2001). Unfortunately the sample is small, poorly preserved and from unsealed cultural contexts. All this, together with the difficulties in finding clear evidence of morphological changes, has led to an ongoing criticism of the discovery (Clutton-Brock 1981; Grigson 2000; Muzzolini 1993; A. B. Smith 1984, 1986; Wengrow 2003).

However, the Combined Prehistoric Expedition (CPE) interpretation of the findings as domesticated was based on an ecological assumption: without human intervention, no wild cattle could survive in the unstable environment of the desert (Wendorf, Schild and Close 1984; Wendorf and Schild 1998). Support for the CPE's hypothesis can be gathered from different sources. Cattle remains interpreted as domesticated and dated to 7000 BC were found in a stratified context at Wadi el-Arab, a recently discovered site in the Kerma region (Chaix 2009; Honegger 2007; Honegger *et al*. 2009). Although so far the findings have been only briefly published, it seems to have more secure morphological traits and stratigraphical provenance than the Nabta-Kiseiba findings, thus in spite of the paucity of the sample, it is hard to question the interpretation. The Wadi el-Arab discovery confirms autochthonous cattle domestication in Africa prior to the arrival of the domesticated sheep/goat from the Levant (*c*. 6000 BC; Close 1992). It also, and for the first time, locates such early evidence of domesticated cattle along the Nile Valley and not just in the desert. As a matter of fact, the deserts and the Nile Valley were both part of the territory seasonally in use by the population at that time.

Morphological and genetic research seems to provide further support for the topic. According to Grigson (1991, 2000) Egyptian cattle of the 4th millennium BC were morphologically distinct from Eurasian cattle (*Bos taurus*) and Zebu (*Bos indicus*), meaning that African cattle may have been domesticated from the local wild

Bos primigenius before the aforementioned date. Nevertheless, Grigson strongly questioned the Nabta-Kiseiba findings, because, according to her, they are not conclusive enough to confirm the chronology of the African domestication. Genetic studies indicate that the wild cattle in Eurasia and in Africa diverged 22,000 years ago and suggest an autochthonous domestication for the latter (Blench and MacDonald 2000; Bradly *et al.* 1996; Caramelli 2006). Linguistic research also provides help in supporting the CPE's theory. The detailed work done by Ehret (2006) on linguistic stratigraphies in North-eastern Africa revealed how terms connected with cattle herding are older than those associated with agriculture, chronologically placing their origin at the beginning of the Holocene.

The zoological, genetic and linguistic studies thus not only suggest an African origin for cattle domestication, but also provide a precise time frame and geographical location which, generally speaking, fits well with that proposed by the CPE. A further element which might give support to the matter comes from the archaeological record, namely the pottery.

During the period spanning the mid 7th-beginning 6th millennium BC the population living along the Nile from the Second Cataract to the Kerma Basin, in the Nabta-Kiseiba region and in the Atbai produced distinct pottery traditions with zonally applied decorative patterns (Gatto 2002b, 2006a, in press a). The territorial dispersion of these ceramics included both the valley and the desert, often overlapping one another but having their own specific territorial distribution, which likely corresponded to the cultural territory of one of the hunter-gatherer-forager and cattle-keeper groups living in the area at that time.

From the beginning-first half of the 6th millennium BC (the chronology varies from area to area) a rocker packed dotted zigzag pattern, applied over all the exterior surface and coupled with rim band decorations is characteristic everywhere (the data from the Kerma region are still scanty but seem to follow the same pattern; Gatto 2006c; Honegger *et al.* 2009). Because pottery decoration is one of the most common cultural markers, and it clearly has this meaning throughout all of Nubian history (Gatto 2002a), this change in the pottery decoration may be symptomatic of other changes in the society and economy of the Early Holocene Nubian population. The change may be the decisive moment when cattle herding became the main economic activity, giving origin to the Neolithic in Nubia and in Africa. The homogeneous pottery tradition may be related to the new 'Neolithic' society.

The southern Dongola Reach, as well as the Laqiya region and the Wadi Howar, were left aside from the Nubian territory at this time; they had their own traditions with both northern and southern influences. Conversely, the Fourth Cataract and the Nile-Atbara region, demonstrate a heterogeneous assemblage of ceramics, indicating that these regions were areas of interface between the Nubian tradition and the Khartoum tradition to the south.

The arrival in Africa of domesticated sheep and goats from the Levant around 6000 BC seems to confirm a local and earlier domestication of cattle; in fact, only populations already able to manage domesticated livestock could have adopted the newcomers so easily, spreading them very rapidly all over the Sahara. One of the arguments Grigson used against the CPE's thesis centred on: «whether people with a mobile lifestyle had a level of social organisation complex enough to allow them to achieve such a major co-operative step, bearing in mind that domestication of herbivores is usually thought to have been associated with sedentism» (Grigson 2000). The Nubian Early Holocene pottery-producer groups were hunter-gatherers of the delayed-return type with a developed social organisation and well-structured ideas of ownership and collaboration. Thus these groups were perfectly able to manage the process of cattle domestication.

According to the Scheduled Consumption Model proposed by Marshall and Hildebrand (2002), hunter-gatherers, when settled in the marginal environment of the Eastern Sahara at the beginning of the Holocene, domesticated cattle to ensure their predictable availability as a food source and for ritual purposes. Wild cattle were a predictable resource along the Nile Valley and a special and close relationship between this animal and the local population dates back to at least the Final Palaeolithic period. At Gebel Sahaba in the Toskha area, in a graveyard found by the same CPE and dated to *c.* 12,000-11,500 BC (Wendorf 1968, 954-95), burials with skulls of wild cattle were reported. At Qurta, in the Kom Ombo Plain, and at Wadi Abu Subeira, north of Aswan, rock drawings representing wild cattle were recently discovered and dated to the Final Palaeolithic (Huyge *et al.* 2007; Storemyr *et al.* 2008). The aforementioned evidence suggests that the strong and long-lasting tie between the Nubian hunter-gatherer-fishers and the cattle was more than economic: in the Nile Valley the cattle had a symbolic significance prior to domestication (see Navajas Jiménez, this volume). The latter aspect might have played a major role in securing the cattle presence in the desert, at least at the beginning of the process.

The Final Palaeolithic population also developed an intensive management of plant resources, as documented at Wadi Kubbaniya around 16,000 BC (Wendorf, Schild and Close 1989). There, plants were harvested and processed on grinding stones. Wild cattle were part of the fauna recovered on site. The continuation of such activity during the Early Holocene is well attested in the El Nabta and Al Jerar sites at Nabta-Kiseiba (Wendorf and Schild 1980, 2001). However, plant productivity was very much vulnerable to variation in rainfall and the desert climatic conditions were not stable enough to depend on them for the development of agriculture. During the 7th millennium BC, thanks to a favourable climate, plant productivity acquired a very important role in the economy of the desert dwellers, maybe equally as important as cattle herding. The climatic deterioration of the 6th millennium BC caused the abandonment of plant productivity in the desert, but it is likely that it continued along the Nile. Areas such as the Dongola Reach certainly were highly favourable for this kind of economic practice. Cattle were certainly better suited to the desert environment conditions because they could be moved to exploit different areas according to necessity (Marshall and Hildebrand 2002), and the Nubian deserts were particularly suitable for cattle: both the Nabta-Kiseiba region and the Nubian Eastern Desert (or Atbai) had plains with playas and wells, thus enough grasslands and water for herds.

In Nubia it is difficult to understand the timing of the change from a pre-domesticated pastoral society (pottery-making, delayed-return hunter-gatherer-fisher and cattle-keepers) to a Neolithic society. As a matter of fact, most of the activities connected with the Neolithic package in other areas of the world (including pottery) were already present in Nubia. Conversely, activities connected to a non-food producing economy (such as hunting-gathering and fishing) continued to be present in the Neolithic Nubian society. In fact, apart from the primary position taken by cattle domestication, the rest of the economic spectrum of the Nubian population remained much the same, greatly relying on hunting, gathering and fishing according to the ecological niches the population was exploiting, at least during the early phase of the Neolithic. Along the Nile, of course, fishing was favoured over hunting or herding, for which the desert was a better environment. As stated above, a hint of such a change may be given by indicated by the pottery: variations in decorative techniques and patterns seem to show how the Nubian society adjusted to the new lifestyle.

The Widespread Nature of the Nubian Culture
From the end of the 6th millennium BC climate conditions started to deteriorate consistently and a long seasonal occupation of the desert was no longer possible. This also implied a shift towards a specialisation of the economic activities performed there. Cattle and sheep-goat husbandry, and hunting, were the basic activities of the Nubian people in the desert during the Mid-Holocene, in addition to collecting raw materials.

As a consequence of such activities, the Nile Valley faced an increase in the stable population and a need to use the Valley's subsistence potentiality as much as possible. Fishing and foraging/farming were the main activities that could be performed along the Nile; husbandry and hunting as alternatives were limited. The Nubian section of the Nile Valley, particularly the region from the First to the Third Cataract, is quite narrow, thus not suitable for medium to large scale foraging/farming. The Kerma Basin and the Seleim Basin were the only sections of the Nubian valley broad enough to sustain increased population density and large-scale foraging/farming.

It is worth remembering that domesticated grains reached northern Egypt from the Levant only at the end of the 6th millennium BC and it probably took another millennium or so for them to be adopted by the Nubian population.

As a matter of fact the oldest evidence of domesticated grains in Nubia dates to the second half of the 5th millennium BC, from the cemetery KDK1 in Kadruka. There, remains of barley glumes have been recorded in many tombs (Reinold 2006, 158). The inaccessibility of domesticated grains for such a long time, and thus a quite late farming development in Nubia, forced the local population to keep foraging autochthonous plants, mainly sorghum. Unfortunately, evidence for a domestication of the latter is very much more recent than the period under discussion here (Marshall and Hildebrand 2002).

A shift towards plant consumption (of domesticated grains?) in the Neolithic population of Nubia (at least those living along the Nile) has been recorded in cemetery R12 at Kawa. The isotope analysis of human remains highlights a change in diet by the second half of the 5th millennium BC (Iacumin 2008, 120). Of course, herding was still the main economic activity and the population, or part of it, divided its efforts between foraging/farming along the Nile and herding in the desert. Only during the Kerma period (c. 1700-1550 BC), with the rise of a state society, did the two economic and social segments became more sharply distinct (Jesse *et al.* 2004; Lange 2006). From that time, however, the Nubian economy developed into an agro-pastoral one, where the pastoral component became fundamental to the construction of social identity and religious beliefs. In this sense cattle held a special place, not only because the Nubians had had a strong relationship with wild cattle since the Late Palaeolithic, but because, from a pastoral point of view, the cattle were far more precious than caprines. The bovine ability to reproduce is conditioned by many factors, such as the age of the cow, which has to be at least two years old in order to become pregnant, the fact that she will only give birth once a year and to one calf at a time (Dahl and Hjort 1983, 33), and the availability of pasture and water. Caprines, on the other hand, are fertile when a few months old and can give birth twice a year (therefore also during the arid season) to more than one kid per time (Dahl and Hjort 1983, 90-3).

During the 5th millennium BC Nubian cultural boundaries became more fluid, probably as a result of another major climatic variation. The monsoon regime retreated further south, this time affecting also the Khartoum region of Central Sudan, and forcing the local population to adopt a pastoral nomad (Neolithic) lifestyle. At the same time, winter Mediterranean rainfall reached the Gilf Kebir plateau (Kropelin 2005) allowing pastoral nomads the use of that ecosystem as well. Although to date there are no records of this kind, winter rains might have influenced other areas of North-eastern Africa.

With the aim of enlarging their land availability and expanding cultural and economic relationships with northern regions, such as the oases region and the Delta (including the Fayum), the Nubians moved north towards Middle Egypt. This spreading trajectory is well recorded along the desert routes of the Western Desert parallel to the river, connecting south-north the Second Cataract area, Dunqul and Kurkur Oases, and the Rayayna Desert (D. Darnell 2002, 2005, 2008; J. C. Darnell and D. Darnell 2009, in press); and east-west the valley with the eastern fringes of Kharga Oasis. Evidence of a Nubian-related presence is moreover reported in the Eastern Desert, particularly in Wadi Atulla, a branch of Wadi Hammamat (Friedman and Hobbs 2002), and Wadi el-Lawi, in the Kom Ombo desert (Gatto 2005). Most of the aforementioned evidence, like the contemporary evidence found along the river in Middle Egypt, is defined as Tasian and Badarian (Brunton 1937; Brunton and Caton-Thompson 1928; Friedman and Hobbs 2002). So far evidence of contemporary occupation in Upper Egypt is lacking. This might be connected to the archaeological research or to site preservation issues. As a matter of fact, there is no reason why Upper Egypt was not settled at this time.

The commonalities between the Nubian Neolithic, on one side, and the Tasian, Badarian and Neolithic of Khartoum, on the other, are the result of their strong ties. They share features such as settlement patterns, economic strategy, material culture, particularly pottery, and religious and funerary practices. It must be said, though, that the northern trajectory seems more important for the Nubians, with the result that they share more features with their northern counterparts then with their southern ones. Pottery can be used as an example of this. The Black Topped wares, characteristic of the Nubian tradition up until the Meroitic period (300 BC-AD 300), are basically missing in the Khartoum Neolithic, where instead only a regional variant of the type, defined as Black Rimmed, developed during this period (Gatto 2002). Conversely, Black Topped wares, the oldest example of which dates to around 5000 BC and comes from Nabta Playa (Gatto 2006b), are the most characteristic ceramics of both the Tasian and Badarian societies. The Tasian and Badarian societies were of course also influenced by other surrounding societies, but they were not as influential as the Nubian society in shaping their cultural identity.

One of the major shared features of the pastoral populations of Middle Egypt, Nubia and Khartoum is the focus on funerary rather than domestic spaces, which is typical, for example, of Near East farming populations. For these mobile groups campsites served as temporal loci of social activity where people could gather at a specific time of the year and for specific functions. Their perception of land property and membership was more on a regional scale than on a settlement level. As Wengrow (2003, 133) states: 'Only in mortuary rites was the flux of geographical and social space suspended, and the body of the individual, together with the objects which formed the nexus of his/her relationships with other persons, withdrawn from circulation and laid to rest within a fixed, communal space'. Pastoral groups applied different patterns in ritualising valley and desert landscapes. Formal disposal areas, such as necropolises, are common only along the Nile, with the exception of that found at Gebel Ramlah, in the Nabta-Kiseiba region (Kobusiewicz et al. 2004; Schild et al. 2002). Usually, there is nothing outside the grave visible to the living. The grave is a kind of isolated and bounded world. Offerings are all placed inside the burial. They are clearly directed to the dead and not to the living. For the community the necropolis was already a demarcated space. In the desert, instead, the landscape is marked by stone structures and stone tumuli. They function as a medium for monumentalising and ritualising the desert (the work of J. C. Darnell – 2002, 2007, in press – on the Predynastic rock art provides a very good parallel for this).

Animal offerings, particularly bucrania, are another characteristic of Neolithic necropolises along the Nile (Reinold 2006; Salvatori and Usai 2008). However, this latter feature is missing in the Badarian cemeteries. Here, though in only a few cemeteries, animal graves were recorded, which are quite rare in southern cemeteries (Brunton and Caton-Thompson 1928). The relationship with the animal world seems to have followed two different trajectories in Nubia and in Egypt. If in Nubia and in Khartoum the relationship with the offered animal is individual, in Middle Egypt it is communal. The animal graves are not related to a single human grave but usually to a cluster of graves from the same cemetery. A similar pattern can be found in the Early Naqada cemeteries from the First Cataract area. This evidence, initially defined as B-Group (Reisner 1910) and then attributed to the Early A-Group (H. S. Smith 1966), has no parallel in the A-Group culture (Flores 2003; Gatto 2006d; Roma 2010). Indirectly, and though slightly more recent in date, this gives witness to the presence of a Badarian-related population in Upper Egypt as well.

Social Complexity in Egypt and Nubia
Contrary to what has previously been thought, pastoral societies were able to develop social complexity to attain, in some instances, a state-level society, and the kingdom of Kerma represents the ultimate result of the social stratification achieved by the Nubian pastoral society. In Nubia the process started as early as the Early Holocene delayed-return hunter-gatherer cattle-keepers, and developing during the Early and Middle Holocene. At this period, evidence for social inequality is primarily detected in the funerary sphere. A rapid increase in social stratification occurred during the 5th and 4th millennium BC as result of the new cultural relations between the Nubian world, through Badari, and the Mediterranean world, via the Delta. Being part of this process made it possible for the Badarian culture to reach a high level of complexity, which in few centuries developed into the regional polities of Hierakonpolis, Naqada and Abydos and thereafter to a unified Egypt (c. 3100 BC).

If the Egyptian Predynastic took advantage of the Nubian social development process, Nubia did the same in return. In Lower Nubia at least two polities evolved during the second half of the 4th millennium BC, namely at Sayala/Naga Wadi and at Qustul (H. S. Smith 1993; Williams 1986). These Nubian kings (or, more precisely, chiefs) adopted the same royal iconography as that of the Egyptian kings.

There is no archaeological information for Upper Nubia at this time but it is likely that chiefdoms were present there as well (as many historical Egyptian texts report; Roccati 1982). From the end of the 4th millennium BC a large settlement with huts, storage pits, enclosures for animals and defensive walls was located at Kerma (Honegger 2006). This was the first step towards the urbanisation process from which the Kerma state emerged.

Egypt and the Other: Shaping a New Identity
With the rise of the Naqada culture Upper and Middle Egyptian society took a separate pathway from Nubia, and Nubian elements in Naqada material and beliefs became less and less visible. Representations of bulls in Naqada rock art are a good example, as the animal represented was not domesticated but wild (Hendrickx 2002). Its meaning as royal image of territory, boundaries and power has nothing to do with the meaning of domesticated cattle in a pastoral society, and therefore what a pastoral society would have depicted (Navajas Jiménez, this volume).

Peripheral areas, such as the Aswan region and the Western Desert parallel to the Nile, bear witness to an exception in the aforementioned trend towards cultural independency. There a Nubian component was still detectable during the Naqada period. If we look to the First Cataract from an Egyptian point of view, this area, from the Early Dynastic period (3100-2686 BC), was considered as the geographical, cultural and political border with Nubia. The archaeological discoveries of the past years clearly demonstrate that the First Cataract was not a real border (Gatto 2009; in press b; Gatto et al. 2009; 2010). Cultural material from the Predynastic village and cemetery in Nag el-Qarmila, just north of Kubbaniya, varies consistently from that recorded in other coeval sites further north. The typical Naqada productions are less represented in order to give more space to local productions (such as the shale pottery), including those (a minority) made according to the Nubian tradition.

Such a mixture of cultural elements is less visible in other aspects of the Predynastic and Early Dynastic society in the First Cataract area and elsewhere. In an application of the classical concept of duality, 'Egypt in opposition to the others', which is a metaphor for 'order over chaos', the Nubians were primarily represented in the Egyptian imagery as captured enemies. One such representation is located to the north of Aswan, in Nag el-Hamdulab (Gatto 2009b; Hendrickx et al. 2009; Hendrickx and Gatto 2009). It consists of a series of rock drawings which date back to the end of Dynasty 0 (c. 3100 BC). The rock art tableaux are all part of the same ideological concept. They represent hunting scenes, particularly bulls hunted by dogs and human figures, and boat processions, the latter with archers and enemies in association. A king with the white crown stands on top of two of the boats. The main tableau represents a procession of boats, the first of which is towed by five men, supervised by the king, who is surrounded by two standard-bearers, one fan-bearer and a dog. Those scenes, like many others in Predynastic rock art, symbolise a royal jubilee cycle. They are interpreted as representing a ritualisation of the celebration of these events in terms of their cosmic significance (J. C. Darnell 2009a). Therefore, the king smiting the enemies does not have to be seen as a real event, but as the symbolic representation of order over chaos. The Egyptian royal ideology, thus, needed the 'other' as a justification for its existence. And the Nubians went from being the 'same' to becoming the 'other'.

Conclusion
To sum up, Nubia is Egypt's African ancestor. What linked Ancient Egypt to the rest of the North African cultures is this strong tie with the Nubian pastoral nomadic lifestyle, the same pastoral background commonly shared by most of the ancient Saharan and modern sub-Saharan societies. Thus, not only did Nubia have a prominent role in the origin of Ancient Egypt, it was also a key area for the origin of the entire African pastoral tradition.

References

Adams, W. Y. 1977. *Nubia: Corridor to Africa*. London, Allen Lane.

Blench, R. and MacDonald, K. (eds.) 2000. *The Origin and Development of African Livestock: Archaeology, Genetics, Linguistics, and Ethnography*. London, University College Press.

Bradley, D., MacHugh, D. E., Cunningham, P. and Loftus, R. T. 1996. Mitochondrial Diversity and the Origins of African and European Cattle. *Proceedings of the National Academy of Sciences* 93, 5131-5.

Brunton, G. 1937. *Mostagedda and the Tasian Culture*. London, Bernard Quaritch.

Brunton, G. and Caton-Thompson, G. 1928. *The Badarian Civilization*. London, Bernard Quaritch.

Caramelli, D. 2006. The Origins of Domesticated Cattle. *Human Evolution* 21, 107-22.

Chaix, L. 2009. Les premiers animaux domestiques dans la région de Kerma. In M. Honegger (ed.), *Kerma (Soudan) – origine et développement du premier royaume d'Afrique noire. Archéologie Suisse* 32, 1-5.

Clutton-Brock, J. 1981. *Domesticated Animals from Early Times*. London, British Museum Press.

Dahl, G. and Hjort, A. 1976. *Having Herds: Pastoral Herd Growth and Household Economy*. Stockholm Studies in Social Anthropology 2. Stockholm, University of Stockholm.

Darnell, D. 2002. Gravel of the Deserts and Broken Pots in the Road: Ceramic Evidence from the Routes between the Nile and Kharga Oasis. In R. Friedman (ed.), *Egypt and Nubia. Gifts of the Desert,* 156-77. London, British Museum Press.

—2005. Evidence from the Rayayna Desert and Kurkur Oasis for Long Distance Trade during the Predynastic Period, in B. Midant-Reynes and Y. Tristant (eds.), *Predynastic and Early Dynastic Egypt. Origin of the State. Abstract of Papers*, 31. Toulouse, CNRS.

—2008. The Rayayna Crossroads: Life, Death and the Divine in the Upper Egyptian Desert, in R. Friedman and L. McNamara (eds.), *Abstracts of Papers Presented at The Third International Colloquium on Predynastic and Early Dynastic Egypt*, 40-5. London, British Museum Press.

Darnell, J. C. 2002. The Narrow Doors of the Desert: Ancient Egyptian Roads in the Theban Western Desert, in D. B. and M. Wilson (eds.), *Inscribed Landscapes, Marking and Making Place*, 104-21. Honolulu, Hawaii University Press.

—2007. The Desert. In T. Wilkinson (ed.), *The Egyptian World*, 29-48. London and New York, Routledge.

—2009a. Iconographic Attraction, Iconographic Syntax, and Tableaux of Royal Ritual Power in the Pre- and Proto-Dynastic Rock Art Inscriptions of the Theban Western Desert. *Archéo-Nil* 19, 83-107.

—2009b. The Wadi of the Horus Qa-a: A Tableau of Royal Ritual Power in the Theban Western Desert. Yale Egyptological Institute in Egypt website: http://www.yale.edu/egyptology/ae_alamat_wadi_horus.htm.

—in press. Ancient Egyptian Rock Inscriptions and Graffiti, in I. Shaw and J. Allen (eds.), *Oxford Handbook of Egyptian Archaeology*. Oxford, Oxford University Press.

Darnell, J. C. and Darnell, D. 2009. The Archaeology of Kurkur Oasis, Nuq' Maneih, and the Sinn el-Kiddab. Yale Egyptological Institute in Egypt website: http://www.yale.edu/egyptology/ae_kurkur.htm

—in press. The Archaeology of Kurkur Oasis, Nuq' Maneih, and the Sinn el-Kiddab, in D. Raue, S. J. Seidlmayer and P. Speiser (eds.), *The First Cataract – One Region, Various Perspectives*. Cairo, Sonderschriften des deutschen archäologischen Instituts Abteilung Kairo.

Diop, C. A. 1974. *The African Origin of Civilization: Myth or Reality?* New York, Lawrence Hill and Company.

—1981. Origin of the Ancient Egyptians. In G. Mokhtar (ed.), UNESCO *General History of Africa II: Ancient Civilizations of Africa*, 27-57. Berkeley, University of California Press/UNESCO.

Ehret, C. 2006. Linguistic Stratigraphies and Holocene History in North-eastern Africa, in K. Kroeper, M. Chlodnicki and M. Kobusiewcz (eds.), *Archaeology of Early North-eastern Africa*, 1019-55. Poznan, Poznan Archaeological Museum.

Flores, D. V. 2003. *Funerary Sacrifice of Animals in the Egyptian Predynastic Period*. British Archaeological Reports S1153. Oxford, BAR Publishing.

Friedman, R. and Hobbs J. 2002. A 'Tasian' Tomb in Egypt's Eastern Desert. In R. Friedman (ed.), *Egypt and Nubia. Gifts of the Desert*, 178-91. London, British Museum Press.

Gatto, M. C. 2002a. Ceramic Traditions and Cultural Territories: The 'Nubian Group' in Prehistory. *Sudan & Nubia* 6, 8-19.

—2002b. Early Neolithic Pottery of the Nabta-Kiseiba Area: Stylistic Attributes and Regional Relationships. In K. Nelson (ed.), *Holocene Settlements of the Egyptian Sahara, Vol. 2, The Pottery of Nabta Playa*, 65-78. New York, Kluwer Academic/Plenum Publishers.

—2005. Nubians in Egypt: Survey in the Aswan-Kom Ombo Region. *Sudan & Nubia* 9, 73-6.

—2006a. The Khartoum Variant Pottery in Context: Rethinking the Early and Middle Holocene Nubian Sequence. *Archéologie du Nil Moyen* 10, 57-72.

—2006b. Prehistoric Nubian Ceramic Traditions: Origin, Development and Spreading Trajectories, in I. Caneva and A. Roccati (eds.), *Acta Nubica*, 103-6. Roma, Istituto Poligrafico e Zecca dello Stato.

—2006c. *Preliminary Report on the Most Ancient Pottery from the Kerma Region*. Unpublished Report for the Swiss Archaeological Mission in Sudan, Geneva.

—2006d. The Nubian A-Group: A Reassessment. *Archéo-Nil* 16 – *Les civilisations préhistoriques du Soudan ancien. Hommage à Francis Geus*, 61-76.

—2009a. Egypt and Nubia in the 5th-4th Millennia BC: A View from the First Cataract and Surroundings. *British Museum Studies in Ancient Egypt and Sudan* 13, 125-45.

—2009b. The Aswan Area at the Dawn of Egyptian History. *Egyptian Archaeology* 35, 10-13.

—in press a. The Holocene Prehistory of the Nubian Eastern Desert, in H. Barnard and B. Duistermaat (eds.), *History of the People of the Eastern Desert from Prehistory to Present*. Los Angeles, Cotsen Institute of Archaeology UCLA.

—in press b. Beyond the Shale: Pottery and Cultures in the Prehistory of the Egyptian Western Desert, in P. Davoli, R. S. Bagnall and C. Hope (eds.), *New Perspectives on the Western Desert of Egypt*. Lecce, Universita' del Salento.

Gatto, M. C., De Dapper, M., Gerisch, R., Hart, E., Hendrickx, S., Herbich, T., Joris, H., Nordström, H-Å., Pitre, M., Roma, S., Swiech, D. and Usai, D. 2009. Predynastic Settlement and Cemeteries at Nag el-Qarmila, Kubbaniya. *Archéo-Nil* 19, 184-204.

Gatto, M. C., Castangia, G., Caruso, S., Curci, A., Pitre, M. and Roma, S. 2010. Le village prédynastique de Nag el-Qarmila, Aswan: problèmes de préservation et essais d'interprétation. *Cahiers Caribéen d'Egyptologie* 13-14, 7-25.

Gautier, A. 1980. Contribution to the Archaeozoology of

Egypt, in F. Wendorf and R. Schild (eds.), *Prehistory of the Eastern Sahara*, 317-44. Dallas, Southern Methodist University.

—1987. Prehistoric Men and Cattle in North Africa: A Dearth of Data and a Surfeit of Models. In A. E. Close (ed.), *Prehistory of Arid North Africa*, 163-87. Dallas, Southern Methodist University.

—2001. The Early to Late Neolithic Archaeofaunas from Nabta and Bir Kiseiba, in F. Wendorf and R. Schild (eds.), *Holocene Settlements of the Egyptian Sahara, Vol. 1, The Archaeology of Nabta Playa*, 609-35. New York, Kluwer Academic/Plenum Publishers.

Grigson, C. 1991. An African Origin for the African Cattle: Some Archaeological Evidence. *African Archaeological Review* 19, 119-44.

—2000. Bos Africanus (Brehm)? Notes on the Archaeozoology of the Native Cattle of Africa, in R. Blench and K. MacDonald (eds.), *The Origin and Development of African Livestock: Archaeology, Genetics, Linguistics and Ethnography*, 38-60. London, University College Press.

Hassan, F. A. 1988. The Predynastic of Egypt. *Journal of World Prehistory* 2, 135-86.

Hendrickx, S. 2002. Bovines in Egyptian Predynastic and Early Dynastic Iconography. In F. A. Hassan (ed.), *Droughts, Food and Culture. European Research Workshop on Ecological Change and Food Security in Africa's Later Prehistory*, 275-318. New York, Kluwer Academic/Plenum Publishers.

Hendrickx, S. and Gatto, M. C. 2009. A Rediscovered Late Predynastic-Early Dynastic Royal Scene from Gharb Aswan (Upper Egypt). *Sahara* 20, 147-50.

Hendrickx, S., Swelim, N., Raffaele, F., Eyckerman, M. and Friedman, R. 2009. A Lost Late Predynastic-Early Dynastic Royal Scene from Gharb Aswan. *Archéo-Nil* 19, 167-76.

Holmes, D. 1989. *The Predynastic Lithic Industries of Upper Egypt. A Comparative Study of the Lithic Traditions of Badari, Naqada and Hierakonpolis*. British Archaeological Reports 469. Oxford, BAR Publishing.

Honegger, M. 2006. La culture du Pré-Kerma de Haute Nubie. *Archéo-Nil* 16, 77-84.

—2007. Aux origines de Kerma, in C. Bonnet, M. Honegger and collaborateurs (eds.), *Les fouilles archéologiques de Kerma (Soudan)*. Genava, n.s., 55, 201-12.

Honegger, M., Bonnet, C., Dubosson, J., Jakob, B., Fallet, C. and Ruffieux, P. 2009. Archaeological Excavations at Kerma (Sudan). *Documents de la mission archéologique suisse au Soudan*. Neuchâtel, Université de Neuchâtel.

Huyge, D., Aubert, M., Barnard, H., Claes, W., Darnell, J. C., De Dapper, M., Figari, E., Ikram, S., Lebrun-Nélis, A. and Therasse, I. 2007. 'Lascaux along the Nile': Late Pleistocene Rock Art in Egypt. *Antiquity* 81(313) (http://antiquity.ac.uk/projgall/huyge/index.html).

Iacumin, P. 2008. Stable Isotopes as Dietary Indicators of Neolithic Nubian Population, in S. Salvatori and D. Usai (eds.), *A Neolithic Cemetery in the Northern Dongola Reach: Excavation at Site R12*, 113-22. Sudan Archaeological Research Society Publication Number 16. British Archaeological Reports International Series 1814. Oxford, BAR Publishing.

Jesse, F., Kröpelin, S., Lange, M., Pöllath, N., Berke, N. and Berke, H. 2004. On the Periphery of Kerma: The Handessi Horizon in Wadi Hariq, Northwestern Sudan. *Journal of African Archaeology* 2(2), 123-64.

Kobusiewicz, M., Kabaciński, J., Schild, R., Irish, J. D. and Wendorf, F. 2004. Discovery of the First Neolithic Cemetery in Egypt's Western Desert. *Antiquity* 78(301), 566-78.

Kröpelin, S. 2005. The Geomorphological and Palaeoclimatic Framework of Prehistoric Occupation in the Wadi Bakht Area, in J. Linstädter and U. Tegtmeier (eds.), *Wadi Bakht: Landschaftsarchäologie einer Siedlungskammer im Gilf Kebir. Africa Praehistorica* 18, 51-65. Cologne, Heinrich Barth Institute.

Kuper, R. and Kröpelin S. 2006. Climate-Controlled Holocene Occupation in the Sahara. *Science* 313, 803-7.

Lange, M. 2006. The Archaeology of Wadi Hariq (NW-Sudan). Results from 1999 and 2001 Excavations, in K. Kroeper, M. Chlodnicki and M. Kobusiewicz (eds.), *Archaeology of Early North-eastern Africa. In Memoriam of Lech Krzyzaniak. Studies in African Archaeology* 9, 273-96. Poznan, Poznan Archaeological Museum.

Lightfoot, K. G. and Martinez, A. 1995. Frontiers and Boundaries in Archaeological Perspective. *Annual Review of Anthropology* 24, 471-92.

MacDonald, K. and MacDonald, R. H. 2000. The Origins and Development of Domesticated Animals in Arid West Africa, in R. Blench and K. MacDonald (eds.), *The Origin and Development of African Livestock: Archaeology, Genetics, Linguistics, and Ethnography*, 127-62. London, University College Press.

Marshall, F. and Hildebrand, E. 2002. Cattle before Crops: The Beginning of Food Production in Africa. *Journal of World Prehistory* 16(2), 99-143.

Muzzolini, A. 1993. The Emergence of a Food Producing Economy in the Sahara, in T. Shaw, P. Sinclair, B. Andan and A. Okpoko (eds.), *The Archaeology of Africa: Food, Metals and Towns*, 227-39. London, Routledge.

O'Connor, D. and Reid, A. (eds.) 2003. *Ancient Egypt in Africa*. Walnut Creek, CA. and London, Left Coast Press/University College London.

Roma, S. 2010. Sepolture animale nella preistoria della Valle del Nilo egiziana e sudanese: contesti, evidence archeologiche e interpretazioni. Unpublished PhD thesis. Napoli, Universita' di Napoli 'L'Orientale'.

Reinold, J. 2006. Les cimetières préhistoriques au Soudan – coutumes funéraires et systèmes sociaux, in I. Caneva and A. Roccati (eds.), *Acta Nubica*, 139-62. Roma, Istituto Poligrafico e Zecca dello Stato.

Reisner, G. A. 1910. *The Archaeological Survey of Nubia. Report for 1907-1908. Vols. I and II*. Cairo, National Printing Department.

Roccati, A. 1982. *La littérature historique sous l'ancient empire égyptien*. Paris, Éditions du Cerf.

Salvatori, S. and Usai, D. (eds.) 2008. *A Neolithic Cemetery in the Northern Dongola Reach: Excavation at Site R12*. Sudan Archaeological Research Society Publication Number 16. British Archaeological Reports International Series 1814. Oxford, BAR Publishing.

Schild, R., Kobusiewicz, M., Wendorf, F., Irish, J. D., Kabaciński, J. and Królik, H. 2002. Gebel Ramlah Playa (Egypt). In Jenerstrasse 8 (eds.), *Tides of the Desert: Contribution to the Archaeology and Environmental History of Africa in Honor of Rudolph Kuper. Africa Praehistorica* 14, 117-24. Cologne, Heinrich Barth Institute.

Smith, A. B. 1984. Origins of the Neolithic in the Sahara, in J. D. Clark and S. A. Brandt (eds.), *From Hunters to Farmers: The Causes and Consequences of Food Production in Africa*, 84-92. Berkeley, University of California Press.

—1986. Cattle Domestication in North Africa. *African Archaeological Review* 4, 197-203.

Smith, H. S. 1966. The Nubian B-Group. *Kush* 14, 69-124.

—1993. The Princes of Sayala in Lower Nubia in the Predynastic and Protodynastic Periods, in C. Berger, G. Clerc and N. Grimal (eds.), *Hommages à Jean Leclant*, Vol. 2, 361-76. Cairo, Institute Française d'Archéologie Oriental.

Storemyr, P., Kelany, A., Negm, M. A. and Tohami, A. 2008. More 'Lascaux along the Nile'? Possible Late Palaeolithic Rock Art in Wadi Abu Subeira, Upper Egypt. *Sahara* 19, 155-8.

Wendorf, F. (ed.) 1968. *The Prehistory of Nubia*. Dallas, Forth Bergwin Research Center and Southern Methodist University Press.

Wendorf, F. and Schild, R. (eds.) 1980. *Prehistory of Eastern Sahara*. Dallas, Southern Methodist University.

—1998. A Late Neolithic Regional Ceremonial Center and Ranked (?) Groups in The Egyptian Sahara, in F. Alhaique, C. Arias, B. E. Barich, C. W. Beck, N. J. Conard, J. De Grossi Mazzorin, M. Heyworth, L. Krzyzaniak, A. Martini, M. Masseti, N. Negroni Catacchio, M. Patou-Mathis, J. P. Raynal, M. K. Striedter, A. Tagliacozzo, T. Tillet, S. Vannucci, F. Wendorf and C. Peretto (eds.), *Proceedings VIIIth Congress UISPP – Workshops Vol. I*, 575-82. Forlì, Abaco.

—(eds.) 2001. *Holocene Settlements of the Egyptian Sahara, Vol. 1, The Archaeology of Nabta Playa*. New York, Kluwer Academic/Plenum Publishers.

Wendorf, F., Schild, R. and Close, A. (eds.) 1984. *Cattle Keepers of the Eastern Sahara: The Neolithic of Bir Kiseiba*. Dallas, Southern Methodist University.

—(eds.) 1989. *Prehistory of Wadi Kubbaniya. Vols. 2 and 3*. Dallas, Southern Methodist University.

Wengrow, D. 2003. Landscapes of Knowledge, Idioms of Power. The African Foundations of Ancient Egypt Reconsidered, in D. O'Connor and A. Reid (eds.), *Ancient Egypt in Africa*, 121-35. Walnut Creek, CA and London, Left Coast Press/University College London.

Williams, B. B. 1986. *Excavations between Abu Simbel and the Sudanese Frontier. The A-Group Royal Cemetery at Qustul: Cemetery L. Oriental Institute Nubian Expedition, Vol. III*. Chicago, Chicago University Press.

The Predynastic *Bos primigenius* as a Royal Image of Territory, Boundaries and Power in an African Context

Ana I. Navajas Jiménez
University of Oxford

Abstract

The king's ability to take different theriomorphic shapes to defeat his enemies recurs in all periods of Ancient Egypt's history as a visual proof of the divine origin of the monarchy, related, in the case of the *Bos primigenius*, with the African continent. One of the best known images is that of the pharaoh in the shape of a bull trampling his enemies on the Narmer Palette. It is my belief that there is enough as yet unused archaeological material from the Predynastic period (5500-3100 BC) which may help to explain why this animal, and not another, was chosen to represent one of the facets of the chief/king. In the present work the figure of the bull will be studied from the very beginning, with the production of rock art, to the Naqada period (Naqada I: 4000-3500 BC) when it was visualised on C-ware pottery. The close connection between the bull, the perception of the territory and the reaffirmation of the chief's figure as the leader of the community against the enemies became the main contexts for the use of the *Bos primigenius* as the metaphor of the chief.

Keywords: *Bos primgenius*, hunting, leadership, Narmer Palette, Predynastic Egypt, rock art, territory, Type C ceramics, warfare.

Introduction

The Narmer Palette (Cairo, Egyptian Museum CG 32169; JE 14716) is perhaps one of the best-known documents in all the archaeological evidence of Protodynastic Egypt (3100-2686 BC). Ever since it was discovered in the Hierakonpolis deposit by the archaeologist James Quibell, a large amount of literature has been written explaining, from different points of view, each of its iconographic and/or historical aspects (Millet 1990; Schulman 1991-1992; Trigger 1979; Wengrow 2001; Wilkinson 2000). The aim here is not to provide a new interpretation of this historical document, an attempt which would in any case have a shadow cast over it by the specific analyses carried out previously, but instead to focus on the image of the *Bos primigenius* which appears on the back of the palette, where the king, taking on the form of a wild bull, tramples on an enemy whilst simultaneously charging at what appears to be a kind of fortification. The bull is one of the many zoomorphic elements which the pharaohs of Egypt adopted when they had to come face to face with an enemy. The Cairo stela CG 34010 provides evidence of this, showing how Thutmosis III (18th Dynasty, r. 1479-1425 BC) was able to change according to the enemy he was facing: he took on the form of a bull when he fought Keftiu (Crete) and Isy (possibly Cyprus; see Lichtheim 1976, 38, n. 5), a crocodile against Mitanni, a lion against the Tjehenu (Libyans) and a falcon when facing enemies from the ends of the earth (Urk. IV 610, 8-619, 2; Lichtheim 1976, 35-9).

One of the first authors to try to explain why the bull was chosen was the historian Henri Frankfort (1948). He saw the matter from a theoretical perspective, modern for the time, and explained some aspects of the Egyptian monarchy within an entirely African context. According to Frankfort, it was the importance that livestock had acquired in Egyptian society that led to the identification of the image of the bull with Hathor, and this was clarified for the first time in the Narmer Palette (Frankfort 1948, 172). David Wengrow, following the same line of thought, studied the palette in a much broader sense, viewing it within the context of the fifth-millennium BC livestock-raising societies of Sudan and the Nile Valley. He pointed out, in specific relation to the bull, that, '[i]n the bottom register of the obverse the ruler's actions in subduing them are again represented, this time through the visual metaphor of a bull battering down the walls of an enclosure and trampling a foe. Decorated palettes of the same general period show the ruler in other animal forms: as a bird of prey, scorpion, cobra, or lion. All are creatures that, like the bull, are capable of sudden and decisive action. This no doubt served to identify him with qualities of self-assertiveness, and the ability to render his opponents passive and helpless' (Wengrow 2001, 94-5). We can thus see that up to the present day the icon of the wild bull has in general terms been explained as the result of the importance which livestock had acquired in the Neolithic (*c.* 8800-4700 BC) and Predynastic (5500-3100 BC) societies of the Nile Valley and, in a more specific sense, that it has been assumed to be the image adopted by the king because, like other animals of different species, it displayed the ability to act immediately and effectively, both of which were desirable qualities in a leader. However, it is important to highlight the fact that what was represented in the Narmer Palette was not a domesticated bull, but *Bos primigenius*, that is, the wild ox species, and it is precisely for this reason that we must analyse this decision to choose the 'wild' ox, as opposed to the 'domesticated' one. It is my belief that there is enough as yet unused archaeological material from the Predynastic period which may help to explain why this animal, and not another, was chosen to represent one of the facets of the chief/king. While it is true that various animals were used as a metaphor for the leader, as a number of authors mention, it is no less true that each of these may have been chosen for a different reason. In this paper my intention is to examine the specific case of the *bos*, and the focus will be on an evaluation of the available evidence regarding the figure of *Bos primigenius*, prior to the Narmer Palette. The contexts used will therefore be both general (rooted in Saharan and Nilotic culture) and specific (*bos* as an image of the chief/king).

The African Context

The study of the Predynastic populations of Naqada I within an African context is an exercise which does no more than look at a reality that must be seen as a first step to the understanding of its cultural and social manifestations. The idea that the Predynastic populations of the Nile began to form as a result of the flow of people from the Western Desert and the contacts made with the inhabitants of that region, continues to gain currency. The depopulation caused by the rise in temperatures and the migratory movement towards the more favourable habitats of the Nile (particularly after 5300 BC) was perhaps the fundamental process that led to contacts between these regions (Riemer and Kindermann 2008, 623-4). According to Maria Gatto, besides, the early A-Group, the Late Neolithic culture of the Western Desert and the Badarian culture should be considered as 'the northernmost regional variants of the Nubian Group' (Gatto 2006, 232), and this is without mentioning the role played by the oases of the Western Desert as connectors between the different sociocultural contributions of the various populations (Barich and Lucarini 2008; Riemer 2008; Riemer *et al.* 2008; Reimer and Kindermann 2008).

From this perspective, it is a great deal easier to explore possible commonalities (Rowland 2003) throughout this extensive territory, and then to analyse the various manifestations of the material culture of the Nile and particularly possible shared ideas and beliefs. One of these observable features or commonalities shared by all these communities from at least the sixth millennium BC onwards is the production of rock art. The creation of rock art was a common and widespread practice in the Western Desert, including the oases, and its chronology, though difficult to determine with precision, coincides on a broad scale with the populations that inhabited the various territories associated with it. In this sense, the process of climate change undergone by this entire region from 5300 BC onwards, which affected the different areas at different times, is considered a viable way of dating the manifestations of rock art in each place (Riemer 2009). In the Nile Valley manifestations of rock art appear later, with the majority of them concentrated at this time in the Eastern Desert (Huyge 2003) and only from the Naqada I period onwards in significant numbers in areas near to the river valley (Darnell 2009). There are, however, examples of rock art which may be dated to the Paleolithic (Huyge 2009) and Epipaleolithic (Huyge 2005) periods. The other great iconographic manifestation which appears in parallel in the Nile Valley is decorated Type C ceramics. It is interesting to note that it is precisely when the Naqada I culture sprang up in the Nile Valley that both manifestations (rock art and decorated ceramics) began to develop; the Badarian populations settled there previously did not seem to be very interested in this type of symbolic cultural phenomena. This implies that, at least in theory, the first Naqada I populations may have had access to instances of rock art before their arrival in Nile Valley, or that at least they were accustomed to them, while the Badarians, for whatever unknown reason, were not. In reality it would prove very difficult to explain the dramatic appearance of figurative motifs in the Naqada I period, both in terms of ceramics and in rock art, without any previous tradition, and it is known that such a tradition already existed in the Western Desert.

Decorated Type C Ceramics and Rock Art
The iconographic representations which developed on Type C ceramics have been explained primarily through their comparison with later artistic productions. The most notable conclusion of this methodology has been to include them within the most primitive or least evolved category of 'Egyptian art', given that the techniques employed later are not present here (Davis 1976). A more in-depth study, however, shows us that it is much more illuminating to study the iconographic elements of these ceramics in conjunction with the rock art which similarly developed previously and appeared simultaneously in the Naqada culture. There is no doubt that both the decorated Type C and D ceramics and the rock art which began to be produced in the deserts near the Nile Valley form part of the same cultural complex (Darnell 2009). It seems that, at their root, the subjects and the symbolic language used express the same system of beliefs shared by the various communities that created these compositions. The iconographic differences that may be found between one context and other may in fact be explained more by the different medium in which each of the images was located, depending on whether the context was the ceramic bowl (where space is managed in an immediate, finite way calculated by the creator) or the rock wall (where space is understood in a broader context, the surface area is normally large, and there may be a number of creators). This is why each context may be studied in conjunction but also separately, as the planning is unique to each medium.

It is hard to calculate the number of Type C ceramic pieces that survive today (perhaps around 600), and their content is highly variable, perhaps owing to the different reasons for which they were created. Although the majority of these productions were deposited in tombs as part of funerary rites, it cannot be discounted that they fulfilled another purpose too. They have been found in habitats at El-Mahâsna, for example, in a context which, according to Anderson, is clearly ritual in nature (Anderson 2006, 258-60). As they were an object of prestige, it is my belief that they were also used in trade exchanges, possibly with a view to establishing relations between different settlements (Navajas 2006). On the other hand, the celebration of important events in the community may also have formed a valid pretext for the creation of some of the pieces.

The group of pieces where the main iconographic motif is the depiction of the wild animals that lived in the desert and the hunting of some of them is particularly reminiscent of rock art. It would not therefore be unreasonable to consider that one of the principal reasons why production techniques of highly specific iconographic subjects (such as the wild animals of the desert) should be so developed on Type C ceramics might be because a traditional, ancestral iconographic language (that of rock art) was being reproduced in a new medium (the pot). This new medium obviously conditioned the way the images were produced (especially as regards the management of space), and at the same time favoured the creation of a new syntax and the appearance of new subjects, such as geometric and floral motifs and the various combinations of these (Figure 1), though it should not be forgotten that geometric decoration was used in other Neolithic ceramic traditions.

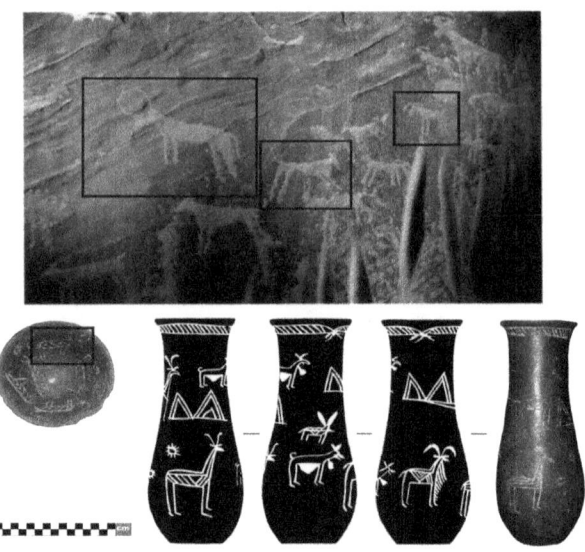

Figure 2. Top: rock art at Gilf Kebir, Wadi Hamra (Le Quellec *et al.* 2005, 150, no 361). Lower left: bowl, London, Petrie Museum UC15335 ©Petrie Museum of Egyptian Archaeology, UCL; Lower right: Oxford, Ashmolean Museum E.2778 (author's photograph); drawing E2778 in Payne 1993, no. 424, fig. 30 (special thanks to the Department of Antiquities, Ashmolean Museum, for access to this material).

Figure 1. Top: rock art at Gilf Kebir, Wadi Hamra (Le Quellec *et al.* 2005, 150, no 359); Lower left: vase, London, Petrie Museum UC15333 ©Petrie Museum of Egyptian Archaeology, UCL; Lower right: drawing, UC 15333 in Petrie 1921, plate XXV C96E.

The animal species which were painted on Type C ceramics coincide with those that were represented in rock art contexts in the Western Desert, such as *Oryx dama*, *Oryx beisa*, *Ammotragus lervia*, *Gazella dorcas*, *Giraffa camelopardalis* (Figure 2), and hunting dogs (Navajas 2007; Riemer 2009, 36-9). This could be explained as much by the need to give expression to traditions maintained since the sixth millennium BC (along with the symbolic value that these brought with them) as by original decisions, apart from the fact that these animals formed part of the savannah landscape which surrounded the Nile Valley in the period of Naqada I. This could provide an explanation, for example, for the combination of giraffe and mouflon on the same bowl (London, Petrie Museum UC15338), despite the knowledge that the image was a product of the imagination rather than a representation of reality (Figure 3). This might also indicate why the hunting of the mouflon with dogs was one of the most favoured hunting subjects in Type C ceramics (see Oxford, Ashmolean Museum E.2778; Figure 2), just as it had been in rock art, and how a new animal which lived in the Eastern Desert, the ibex, was included (Osborn and Osbornová 1998, 181) in the Naqada I repertoire, as part of the new reality of which the populations began to form a part (Figure 4).

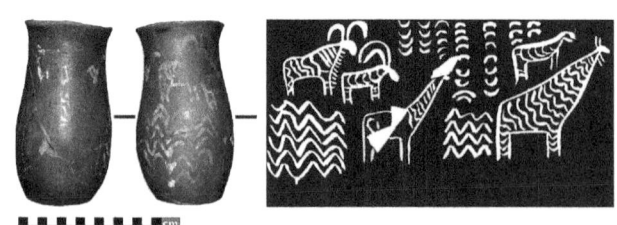

Figure 3. Top: rock art (Winkler 1939, plate LIV). Lower left: vase, London, Petrie Museum UC15338 ©Petrie Museum of Egyptian Archaeology, UCL; Lower right: drawing UC15338 in Petrie 1921, plate XXV C99.

Figure 4. Top from left to right: vase, Oxford, Ashmolean Museum 1895.482 (author's photograph); double vase, Pennsylvania, University of Pennsylvania Museum of Archaeology and Anthropology E1418 © Penn Museum; drawing of E1418 in Kantor 1953, fig. 4-D. Bottom from left to right: bowl, Oxford, Ashmolean Museum 1895.487 (author's photograph); drawing of bowl, Princeton University Art Museum 30-491 (Kantor 1953, figure 4-A); vase, London, Petrie Museum UC15332 ©Petrie Museum of Egyptian Archaeology, UCL; drawing, UC15332 in Petrie 1921, plate XXV C98.

It might be said that the 'imaginary' production of Type C ceramics was the result of a fusion of the traditional and the new, the consequence of the recent settlement of the territory by these populations. The fauna of the Nile was the fresh contribution, the result of the new habitat. Other animals, however, were new to the ceramic representations, like the aforementioned ibex, but also the hyena (Navajas 2005) and, for example, the wild ass (Figure 1). The production techniques used in the ceramic figures also shared a great deal with those employed in the traditional rock art: the bodies and legs of the animals are reproduced in a relatively stereotyped fashion, without any kind of realism, as was the case in rock art. It is true that the design of the forms of the bodies of the animals in Type C ceramics had more to do with the traditions of the workshop where they were produced and possibly with the set of pieces that were manufactured at the same time than with any other motif related to the species of animal that was represented, but, above all, animals were, as in rock art, identified by the design of their horns, and this is at times the only element which allows us to identify them (see Anselin, this volume). The interaction between animals is non-existent (London, Petrie Museum UC15332) and even the hunting scenes lack the dynamism that they ought to display (Figure 4).[1]

[1] The cases of the Oxford bowl (Ashmolean Museum 1895.487), the Oxford vase (Ashmolean Museum 1895.482) and the Princeton plate (University Art Museum 30-491) are noteworthy in this respect. These were explained by Finkenstaedt (1981) as grazing scenes. The confusion is down to the fact that in most hunting scenes the bodies of both the dogs and their prey display an identical design, and it is only the composition of the scene that allows its attribution to the category of hunting rather than grazing scene, as Kantor (1953) pointed out. There

To sum up, all of these are also significant characteristics of the rock art production found in, for example, the Ouenat/Gilf Kebir, as referred to recently by Reimer (2009, 36-9).

The figure of *Bos primigenius* was also represented in this rock art context. The oldest images of it come from the Paleolithic period and were carved at el-Hosh, 30km south of Edfu, and at Qurta, 40km south of Edfu (Huyge 2009). In the Western Desert, rock art was created in some areas around Gilf Kebir, but these were never apparently connected to the hunting scenes found around them (Figure 2), and the animal was represented on its own (Le Quellec *et al.* 2005, 150, 304-5). In comparison with other animals, in fact, the bull was not the object of any special dedication, with the exception of Paleolithic rock art, but it was certainly an animal that had a special importance among all those painted on the Type C ceramics of Naqada I.

Bos primigenius on Decorated Type C Ceramics

There are two facts which are fundamental to our understanding of much of the iconography which developed on Type C ceramics. The first of these is that it arose at a time of significant leadership structures, which generated a principle that regulated the very creation of the pieces, given that they were, above all, prestige products distributed among a highly specific audience and in highly specific places. The second is that the new

is little doubt today that all these scenes, along with others represented on these vases, must be considered as true hunting scenes (Hendrickx 2006; Navajas 2007).

environment of the Nile was integrated within the symbolic world, and so the traditions of the desert were merged with the new life that had sprung up in the Nile Valley.

Figure 5. Bowl, London, British Museum 49025 © The British Museum; drawing of 49025 in Scharff 1928, Plate XXVII 5.

The Nile was depicted in Type C ceramics through the image of certain animals that lived there. Just as was the case with those creatures that epitomised the mental image of the desert, so were only a few privileged enough to form part of that of the river. In order of importance, the hippopotamus, the crocodile and, in smaller numbers, fish and tortoises were all chosen for a particular reason, but it was above all the hippopotamus and the crocodile that were fundamental, so much so that they might be described as the representatives of the Nile region. The animal identified with a territory may be considered a fundamental element, at least as regards Type C ceramics, and this idea can be seen very clearly in a bowl unearthed at El-Mahâsna (London, British Museum 49025). This exceptional piece may be viewed as the first cosmography ever represented in the Nile Valley (Figure 5). The bowl, as previously mentioned, allowed the development of a new syntax between the various elements, given that both the inside and the outside could be decorated, a circumstance which obviously was impossible on a wall surface. On this bowl, the inside was used to represent the Nile, and the outside to depict what we consider to be the desert, or, if preferred, the non-Nilotic territory which was within the borders of the inhabited area. This means that the physical limits of the new space were precisely established, and that animals were the *pure metaphors* used to represent these borders. The desert, on the outside, was depicted from the Nile Valley through the image of two remarkable animals, the elephant and the wild bull, just as those that represented the Nile on the inside were equally remarkable, the hippopotamus and the crocodile (Friedman 2004, 151-3; Navajas 2009, 73-5). These animals were, in essence, the very territory itself.

The iconographic cycles that were developed around the figure of *Bos primigenius* have a great deal to do with those that were painted around the hippopotamus (Navajas 2009). The bull was represented as a powerful animal, the most notable characteristic of which was its fighting spirit, shown as it was charging with its head down (Berkeley Museum of Anthropology 6-2927, and Hammamiya 1649).[2] It is, however, above all the hunting of the animal which forms the main subject for depiction, using nets (Oxford, Ashmolean Museum E.2784),[3] nets and dogs (London, Petrie Museum UC15334), being pursued by dogs (Cairo, Egyptian Museum CG 2076, London, Petrie Museum UC15331),[4] and caught in a circular trap (Oxford, Pitt Rivers 1901.2981). As well as these images, another bowl in which a hunter appears (Princeton 30-493; Figure 6) must also be mentioned; here, the individual is holding the rope-harness of two dogs that are pursuing their prey, which is unquestionably a *bos*, while two other bulls also appear in the scene (one of them with a dog very close to it). There is yet another bowl worthy of mention in this context, too (Cairo, Egyptian Museum CG2076), where there is on the outside an individual holding a rope which leads to the back of the large quadruped. Sadly, the head of this animal has been lost (the bowl is in fragments) and it is not possible to identify the species. Comparative iconographic analyses, however, lead us to believe that this may be a depiction of the hunting of *Bos primigenius* with a lasso, a cycle which appears in Naqada I rock art of the same period (Darnell 2009, 95, fig. 17).

In general, the hunting of wild animals in the desert was a subject of special interest in Naqada I ceramics, though in some cases the hunting is only suggested by the presence

---

[2] London, Petrie Museum UC15335 may also form part of this category. It is not my belief that the central element depicted on the Berkeley and Hammamiya bowls can be explained as a trap, and that bulls are therefore being hunted, as is the view of Graff (2009, no. 60).

[3] Oxford, Ashmolean Museum E.2784. The animal depicted on this bowl shares the iconographic characteristics of the bull represented on the inside of the Cairo bowl (Cairo, Egyptian Museum CG 2076). I do not believe this animal to be a dog (Graff 2009, no. 20), given that it seems clear that horns projecting forward have been depicted and the snout of the animal is pointing downwards, as on Cairo, Egyptian Museum CG2076.

[4] My recent interpretation of this bowl (London, Petrie Museum UC15331; Navajas 2009) is somewhat different. It was my original belief that the bowl depicted four bulls in pairs, linked by their hindquarters, but further iconographic study (most of the pot is very damaged and/or lost) has shown that in fact there are two large animals (two bulls) and two slightly smaller ones, which could be dogs pursuing the large animals in a typical hunting scene.

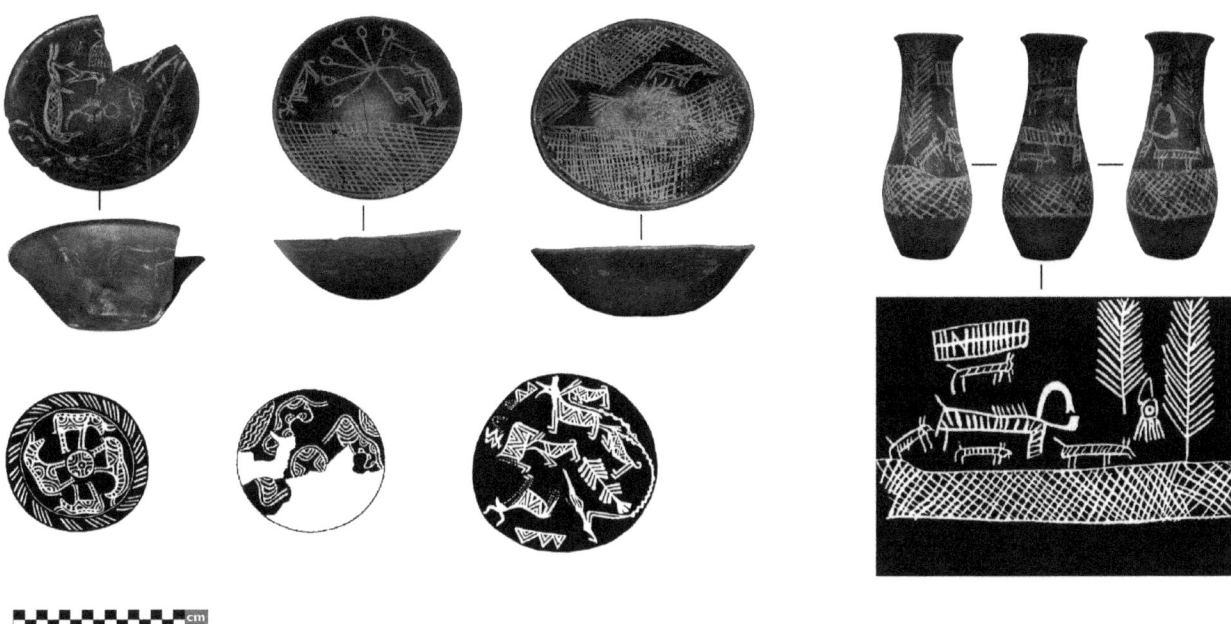

Figure 6. Top from left to right: bowl, Cairo, Egyptian Museum CG2076 © The Cairo Museum; bowl, Oxford, Pitt Rivers Museum 1901.29.81 ©Pitt Rivers Museum; bowl, Oxford, Ashmolean Museum E.2784 (author's photograph); vase, London, Petrie Museum UC15334 ©Petrie Museum of Egyptian Archaeology, UCL; drawing of UC15334 in Petrie 1921, Plate XXV C96L. Bottom from left to right; bowl, Berkeley Phoebe A. Hearst Museum of Anthropology 6-2927 (Lythgoe and Dunham 1965, fig. 3); bowl, Hammamiya Tomb 1649 (Brunton and Caton-Thompson 1928, plate XXXVIII, 49k), scale unknown; bowl, Princeton University Art Museum 30-491(Kantor 1953, fig. 4-B).

of dogs and other essential elements such as nets and traps (Hendrickx 2006; Navajas 2007). The presence of humans, however, only appears in two categories of representations of hunting, namely the hunting of the hippopotamus (hunting with harpoon) and that of the wild bull, the two animals which, as the reader will recall, constitute the pure metaphor of the two territories. In both cases, the emphasis placed on just one person, the hunter, strongly indicates that it is the chief of the community who is being represented. As mentioned earlier, these ceramics arose at a time of strong leadership and were produced and distributed within highly specific circles, and therefore the message too was very specific. The representation of activities like the hunting of the hippopotamus and the bull would consequently provide a reaffirmation of the figure of this leader, because if, as I believe, it was the leader who was hunting both the hippopotamus (the Nile) and the bull (the desert), there is no doubt that he was the individual who was capable of guaranteeing the stability of the community (through control of the entire territory). There is no need to state that each animal is the most dangerous in its environment, and that if a man was able to kill them, his status within the community would be extremely high.

The Abydos U-415 Vase

The construction of the authority, both real and symbolic, of the leader through the activity of hunting and therefore control of territory is crucial to the understanding of the following step in the transformation, doubtless best shown in the U-415 vase from Abydos (Cairo, Egyptian Museum (?); Hartung 2002). It is on this absolutely exceptional vase that the chief assumed for the first time the total appearance of an animal (another *pure metaphor*), none other than *Bos primigenius* (Figure 7).

The vase consists of two registers. On the upper one, the chief is depicted in a presentation of enemies or victory scene (the enemies have ropes tied around their necks and arms), but the fundamental aspect is that the chief is represented larger than any other character, and displays the attributes which from then on would become archetypical of the chief/king: the bull's tail and the mace. He also carries a phallic-shaped case and wears a multiple headdress (perhaps made of feathers), elements that are characteristic of the Naqada I period. On the lower register, the chief is represented in three different stages of the same act: killing (with harpoons) two pregnant female hippopotamuses, and one male, and in this case the leader is also wearing the bull's tail. The massacring of the two pregnant females is an essential detail, since this sacrifice, the killing of the lineage, depicts a projection in time: the chief is thus avoiding harm that might have been caused by future generations. With males, females and unborn babies, the existence of both present and future generations is annihilated. But even more than this, the degree of control and effectiveness could not be greater, because it is *Bos primigenius*, itself the metaphor of the leader, that helps to defeat one of the hippopotamuses. In the same register two planes of reality have thus been depicted, one real (the chief hunting with a harpoon), and the other symbolic (the chief transformed into a bull).

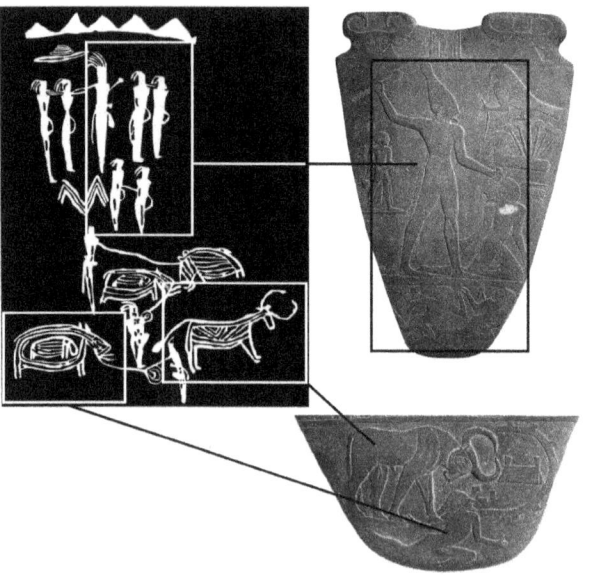

Figure 7. Vase, Abydos U-415. Drawing by the author after Dreyer *et al.* 2003, 81, Abb. 5; Narmer Palette, Cairo, Egyptian Museum CG32169 © Cairo, Egyptian Museum (Saleh and Sourouzian 1987, 8a, 8b).

There is no doubt about the fact that it is a bull's tail that the chief wears in the upper part of the register, since it is clear that it is the leader who has hunted and defeated the bull previously, according to the iconographic evidence of other bowls (Princeton 30-493; Figure 6), which is fundamental, and it is also obvious that the bull appears in the lower register. The conqueror assumes, therefore, the essence of the defeated animal in a double depiction. The chief in his human persona, but with the attributes of the bull, subjugates enemies that are both human and animal, while the chief in his animal aspect, in the form of a bull, defeats an enemy that is another animal as fearsome as himself, the hippopotamus. In this sense, the forces are balanced, since, faced with a cosmic enemy (the hippopotamus),[5] the chief has to be the perfect opponent (against each enemy, an appearance), that is, the bull itself, its equal or counterpart in the desert (if the cosmovision depicted on the aforementioned El-Mahâsna vase is taken into account).

It is traditionally assumed that most Predynastic and Protodynastic images must be explained more in terms of their symbolic value (paradigms and virtual models that form part of the cosmic sphere) than any real value. It is my belief, however, that the fact that an image eventually becomes archetypical does not imply that it may not initially have fulfilled a real need, that is to say, that there might have been a specific event that led to the creation of this image and later events that called for it to be reused. It is quite probable that if images are used to transmit violent events, such as massacres and the display of enemies, then this is because they reflected what might have happened in reality. War or violence must have been an integral part of Naqada I society just as it was in later periods (Gayubas 2006, 51-74; Gilbert 2004). This vase, along with three other Type C vases (London, Petrie Museum UC15339; Cairo, Egyptian Museum CG 99072; Brussels, MRAH E.3002), could be the first iconographic documentation found in an archaeological context which shows the conflicts that Abydos might have had with another settlement outside its community.[6] Which community might it has been that had such a conflict with Abydos? There are two possibilities: either it was a neighboring settlement on the Nile, or another from outside the Valley. In general terms, any individual that did not form part of the community would have been considered an enemy, or at least this is what ethnographic comparisons suggest. War, indeed 'se presenta, pues, como un mecanismo que no busca otro objetivo que remarcar la identidad del grupo y sostener su indivisión: es una condición y un refuerzo para la definición del grupo de parentesco como tal' (Gayubas 2006, 57).[7]

It might, nevertheless, be logical to consider that the individuals in chains that appear on the Abydos U-415 vase might have been from a community outside the Nile Valley. If the chief of the Abydos vase took on an attribute of the bull – its tail – when he displayed an attitude of victory over human enemies, then this is possibly because the enemies that led to the creation of this original image lived in a territory linked with the one where the bull also lived or was hunted. That is to say that the chief wore a trophy of an animal (the bull) that he had defeated, which in turn led to his assuming the power and strength of this animal and, as a result, when he had to fight against a population that lived in the territory of the bull (a territory that was not in the Nile Valley, but outside it, that is, the desert), he also took on these attributes.[8] The conclusion that might be drawn from this

---

[5] There is no doubt whatsoever that one of a number of characteristics that the hippopotamus took on in this period was that of an animal that had to be killed. The cycle of hippopotamus hunting with harpoons on Type C ceramics is proof of this, though the clearest example is that of the bowl in question here.

[6] Only two vases have been found in a clear archaeological context, that of the Cairo, Egyptian Museum CG99072 (Abydos U-239), and the piece analysed here, Abydos U-415. Both share all the iconographic characteristics typical of the productions of Abydos. Although in this respect Graff is more cautious (Graff 2004, 76-7), it is my belief that at this time only Abydos was capable of generating so precise an iconography, in addition to its attribution to this location for purely stylistic reasons.

[7] War is 'therefore to be viewed as a mechanism with no other objective than to underline the identity of the group and maintain its indivisibility; it is both a precondition and a reinforcement for the very definition of the kinship group'.

[8] In the period contemporary with this Abydos vase, the Tasian population tended to live in certain areas of the desert in the vicinity of Upper Egypt (Darnell, D. 2002; Friedman 2002). It is known that this community hunted, and perhaps the hippopotamus was one of the

is that the chief was capable of dominating both the territory (hunting) and the people who lived in it (war), and this image, codified from the very beginning, later became an archetype when a similar event (a display of victory and specifically the massacre of the enemy) had to be remembered, independently of where the enemy in question came from. The image therefore possessed the force and power to perpetuate itself while the historical and/or ritual background might vary on each occasion.

As regards archaeological evidence linking the bull with the elite of the period, there is clear proof in the necropolis Hk6 at Hierakonpolis, an extraordinary site which still has a great deal to reveal about the true role it played in the Predynastic and Protodynastic periods. This site also shows the true importance that the other animal, the elephant, must have had in the period in question (Naqada I-II). Two tombs, one of a bull, tomb 19 (Warman 2000; Warman 2003; Van Neer et al. 2004), and another of an elephant, tomb 33 (Friedman 2009; Majer 2009; Marinova and Van Neer 2009), were discovered in the same area of necropolis Hk6. In addition, the tomb of another elephant, tomb 24 (Friedman 2003a; Friedman 2003b; Friedman 2004; Friedman 2006; Van Neer et al. 2004, 103-5), was found in another part of the necropolis clearly linked to the tomb of quite an important member of the community (tomb 23; Adams 2002a; Friedman 2005; Friedman 2008; Van Neer et al. 2004, 88-90), given that this latter was surrounded by a palisade and various structures that suggest that some kind of worship took place over a considerable period of time. Surprisingly, the tomb of the elephant was found within a similar structure. The care which was taken over the burial rituals of sacrificed animals was indeed not so far from that granted to members at the top of the Hierakonpolis hierarchy (Adams 2002b; Friedman 2004: 142-5; Majer 2009, 8-9; Oldfield and Jones 2003). The connection between animals on one hand (as part of a cosmography) and between them and the chief on the other (a manifestation of the chief himself), is therefore no coincidence, and perhaps both of these interpretations must be made as regards the funerary rituals of Hk6. From a cosmographic viewpoint, the bull and the elephant would both form part of that whole group of animals that was buried in Hk6 and which might well provide a message to the whole known world which had to be controlled or which was under the control, at least in theory, of the chief. The bull, as we have already seen, could be representing a particular area of the desert which was considered to be under control, perhaps the same area as where it was hunted. As regards the elephant, the equivalent to the bull in the cosmography of the British Museum vase and also alluding to a territory outside the Nilotic world, it would

seem by analogy to be associated with an area outside the borders of the Valley. One possible origin of elephants in this period, more likely than the deserts that surrounded Upper Egypt, was Nubia, and so the possibility should not be discounted that the elephant, as part of this cosmovision, was referring to some Nubian territory which, as is suggested by Renée Friedman, 'may have represented control over those regions, a control which Hierakonpolis was well situated to enforce' (2004, 163).[9] Finally, both animals' status as manifestations of the leader himself and, as such, as symbols of power and prestige, was expressed in the special care that was taken in their burials, and in this sense the elephant was at this time the animal which carried the greatest symbolic weight at Hierakonpolis.

The Abydos Vase/Narmer Palette

Both bull and elephant therefore were animals which expressed the power and prestige of the leader. The bull is more closely linked to Abydos itself (U-415 vase and cycles of bull hunting), while the elephant, as we have seen, was developed above all in the Hierakonpolis area (tomb 24).

The image which continued to express the qualities of the leader and which prevailed in later historical periods, however, was that of the bull, whereas the elephant began to form part of an iconography that is harder to interpret (perhaps because its focus is more cultural), up to the point when the link was lost (Whitehouse 2002). One explanation for the survival of the symbol of the bull is doubtless intimately related to the warlike image that the chief/king continued to favor in the depiction of his figure, especially as regards the defeating of enemies (at least as far as the monarchs of Abydos were concerned, seeing as the famous Narmer Palette refers to a king of Abydos). The bull went on appearing in hunting scenes involving the chief (Tomb 100 at Hierakonpolis; Quibell and Green 1902, plate LXXV) and as a manifestation of the king himself, this time as the observer of a hunting scene, in the Hunters' Palette (London, British Museum 20790, 20792; Paris, Musée du Louvre E 11254; Cervelló 1995; Tefnin 1979). The ideological background behind this concept not only survived, but necessarily had to renew itself, given that the image was revitalised when it was re-codified in the Narmer Palette and in the so-called Bull Palette (Paris, Musée du Louvre 11255).

Although the Narmer Palette (Figure 7) displays new features which define the new leader in iconographic terms (Wilkinson 2000, 28), the king continued to make use of the two indispensable elements that explained and

---

animals hunted, or so it seems from the representations that appear in rock art (Darnell 2002, J. C. 146, fig. 17; Darnell 2009, 88, fig. 7). This would mean that perhaps they had to go to the Nile to hunt the hippopotamus, and so there must have been some interaction with the Nilotic societies. They might have had at some point a conflict of interests with Abydos, and this could have been the incident which is commemorated on these vases - the celebration of a victory against this community.

---

[9] We are unable to throw light on the question of whether this territory might be a reference to Elephantine or not (for details of the debate on whether the elephant forms part of the name of Elephantine or Abydos, see Jiménez 2004, 847-58). It seems, however, particularly relevant to mention at this juncture the Berlin Type C vase (Ägyptisches Museum und Papyrussammlung 22388), which depicts three elephants on the rim of the bowl (modelled in clay), and, on the outside, painted under the feet of the elephant, a series of rectangular zigzags imitating mountains. This would seem to be the first occasion that the elephant and the mountains ('The elephant standing on hills') appear together in the same iconographic semantic field.

characterised his role when interacting with an enemy: namely, the mace and the bull's tail, the fundamental essence of the chief's authority and power since the dawn of his leadership. The iconography of the enemy, on the other hand, became more varied in the Naqada II period, taking on new poses, whether showing an upright prisoner with his hands tied, as in Naqada I, or else prostrated, as in the image of the palette (Dreyer 1999, 205, fig. 10b). Since this latter image was probably created to commemorate an important victory of the king over an enemy from the north (i.e. foreigners), the king adopted once more the metaphor of the territorial animal (the bull) which crushes and annihilates another territory and its entire population (as in the Abydos vase with the hippopotamuses), here represented by the destruction of the city walls.

Conclusion

There is no doubt that the ideas and beliefs surrounding cattle created by the inhabitants of the Nile Valley were of great importance in both Neolithic society and the Naqada I period of the 5th and 4th millennia BC. It is not, however, my belief that these concepts were the fundamental element in the construction of the pure metaphor of the chief in the form of *Bos primigenius*. The points of connection between the populations of the Nile Valley and those of the western Sahara may be established by, amongst other evidence, the iconographic and symbolic manifestations of rock art, an art form which in its very essence expressed the world of the wild, of hunting, which is precisely one of those aspects that is common to Type C ceramics. The bestiary transmitted in Type C ceramics was extremely selective, as were the alternatives to the bull used as a representative animal in particular scenes. All the iconographic and archaeological evidence shows that the choice of the bull was a genuinely Nilotic one related to the rise of powerful leadership (at Abydos and Hierakonpolis), and it seems that the most essential requirement for these first leaders was the control of territory, expressed through both hunting and the subjugation of so-called 'enemies'. The bull became representative of a territory (cosmography), one which was controlled by hunting that animal, and consequently the essence of that animal was assumed by the chief himself (the hunter takes the animal's tail). In the following stage, the chief took on the complete image of the bull (that is, the complete metaphor) when he had to carry out punitive campaigns or make war on either the populations that lived in the desert (Naqada I) or on communities from the north (Naqada III). In this sense, it is my view that the creation of the symbolic element may have been very closely linked to the need to construct and consolidate the emerging figure of the chief as a result of real-life events that occurred; that is to say, the hippopotamus and the bull were hunted in real life, and war was waged on any outsider that was believed to be (or indeed really was) a threat to the community. The personification of the chief in the form of a bull also highlights the fact that he was the sole member of the community who possessed the special powers to assume the essence of a powerful and dangerous animal, and, for this reason, it is possible that certain chiefs might already have achieved sacred powers by the time of Naqada I. Judging by the iconographic evidence, it seems therefore that it was above all the capacity to kill and control that was the characteristic that best defined the chief in this early period of development, and this is perfectly manifested in the metaphor of *Bos primigenius*.

References

Adams, B. 2002a. Seeking the Roots of Ancient Egypt. A Unique Cemetery Reveals Monuments and Rituals from Before the Pharaohs. *Archéo-Nil* 12, 11-28.

—2002b. Decorated Sherds from Renewed Excavations at Locality 6, Hierakonpolis. *Cahiers Caribéens d'Égyptologie* 3-4, 5-27.

Anderson, D. 2006. *Power and Competition in the Upper Egyptian Predynastic: A View from the Predynastic Settlement at el-Mahâsna, Egypt*. UMI Dissertations.

Asselberghs, H. 1961. *Chaos en Beheersing. Documenten uit Aeneolithisch Egypte*. Leiden, E. J. Brill.

Ayrton, E. R. and Loat, W. L. S. 1911. *Predynastic Cemetery at El Mahasna*. London, Egypt Exploration Fund.

Barich, B. and Lucarini, G. 2008. The Nile Valley Seen from the Oases. The Contribution of Farafra, in B. Midant-Reynes and Y. Tristant (eds.), *Egypt at its Origins 2: Proceedings of the International Conference "Origin of the State: Predynastic and Early Dynastic Egypt," Toulouse (France), 5th–8th September 2005.* Orientalia Lovaniensia Analecta 172, 569-84. Leuven, Peeters.

Brunton, G. and Caton-Thompson, G. 1928. *The Badarian Civilisation and Predynastic Remains near Badari*. London, British School of Archaeology in Egypt.

Capart, J. 1904. *Les débuts de l'art en Égypte*. Bruxelles, Vromant & Co.

Cervelló, J. 1995. ¿Un precedente del serej faraónico en la paleta predinástica de la caza? *Aula Orientalis* 13, 169-75.

Darnell, D. 2002. Gravel of the Desert and Broken Pots in the Road: Ceramic Evidence from the Routes between the Nile and Kharga Oasis. In R. Friedman (ed.), *Egypt and Nubia. Gifts of the Desert*, 156-177. London, British Museum Press.

Darnell, J. C. 2002. Opening the Narrow Doors of the Desert: Discoveries of the Theban Desert Road Survey. In R. Friedman (ed.), *Egypt and Nubia. Gifts of the Desert*, 132-55. London, British Museum Press.

—2009. Iconographic Attraction, Iconographic Syntax, and Tableaux of Ritual Power in the Pre- and Proto-Dynastic Rock Inscriptions of the Theban Western Desert. *Archéo-Nil* 19, 83-108.

Davis, W. M. 1976. The Origins of Register Composition in Predynastic Egyptian Art. *Journal of the American*

Oriental Society 96, 404-18.

De Morgan, J. 1896. *Recherches sur les origins de l'Égypte. L'âge de la pierre et les métaux*. Paris, Leroux.

Dreyer, G. 1999. Motive und Datierung der dekorierten prädynastischen Messergriffe. In Ch. Ziegler (ed.), *L'art de l'Ancient Empire égyptien. Actes du colloque, Musée du Louvre 1998*, 195-226. Paris, Musée du Louvre.

Dreyer, G., Hartung, U., Hikade, T., Köhler, E. C., Müller, V. and Pumpenmeier, F. 1998. Umm el Qaab. Nachuntersuchungen im frühzeitlichen Königsfriedhof 9./10. *Mitteilungen des Deutsches Archäologisches Institut Kairo* 54, 79-167.

Dreyer, G., Hartmann, R., Hartung, U., Hikade, Th., Köpp, H., Lacher, C., Müller, V., Nerlich, A. and Zink, A. 2003. Umm el-Quaab. Nachuntersuchungen im frühzeitlichen Köningsfriedhof 13./14./15. Vorbericht. *Mitteilungen des Deutsches Archäologisches Institut Kairo* 59, 67-138.

Dreyer, G. and Polz, D. 2007. *Begegnung mit der Vergangenheit-100 Jahre in Ägypten. Deutsches Archäologisches Institut Kairo 1907-2007*. Mainz, von Zabern.

Finkenstaedt, E. 1981. The Location of Styles in Painting: White Cross-lined Ware at Naqada. *Journal of the American Research Center in Egypt* 18, 7-10.

Fischer, H. G. 1968. Ancient Egyptian Representations of Turtles. *Papers of the Metropolitan Museum of Art* 13, 5-35.

Frankfort, H. 1948. *Kingship and the Gods. A Study of Ancient Near Eastern Religion as the Integration of Society and Nature*. Chicago, University of Chicago Press.

Friedman, R. 2002. A Tasian Tomb in Egypt's Eastern Desert. In R. Friedman (ed.), *Egypt and Nubia. Gifts of the Desert*, 178-91. London, British Museum Press.

—2003a. Hierakonpolis 2003: exhumer un éléphant. *Bulletin de la Société Française d'Égyptologie* 157, 9-22.

—2003b. Excavating an Elephant. *Nekhen News* 15, 9-10.

—2004. Elephants at Hierakonpolis, in S. Hendrickx, R. Friedman, K. M. Cialowicz and M. Chlodnicki (eds.), *Egypt at its Origins. Studies in Memory of Barbara Adams*. Orientalia Lovaniensia Analecta 138, 131-68. Leuven, Peeters.

—2005. Excavating Egypt's Early Kings. *Nekhen News* 17, 4-5.

—2006. Bigger than an Elephant. More Surprises at Hk6. *Nekhen News* 18, 7-8.

—2008. Remembering the Ancestors: Hk6 in 2008. *Nekhen News* 20, 10-11.

—2009. Hk6 Checklist. *Nekhen News* 21, 7.

Garfinkel, Y. 2001. Dancing or Fighting? A Recently Discovered Predynastic Scene from Abydos, Egypt. *Cambridge Archaeological Journal* 11(2), 241-54.

—2003. *Dancing at the Dawn of Agriculture*. Austin, Texas University Press.

Gatto, M. C. 2006. The Early A-Group in Upper Lower Nubia, Upper Egypt and the Surrounding Deserts, in K. Kroeper, M. Chlodnicki and M. Kobusiewicz (eds.), *Archaeology of Early Northeastern Africa*. Studies in African Archaeology 9, 223-34. Poznan, Poznan Archaeological Museum.

Gayubas, A. 2006. Guerra, parentesco y cambio social en las sociedades sin estado en el valle del Nilo prehistórico. In M. Campagno (ed.), *Estudios sobre parentesco y Estado en el Antiguo Egipto*, 51-74. Buenos Aires, Ediciones Del Signo.

Gilbert, G. Ph. 2004. *Weapons, Warriors and Warfare in Early Egypt*. British Archaeological Reports 1208. Oxford, BAR Publishing.

Graff, W. 2009. *Les peintures sur vases de Naqada I-Naqada II. Nouvelle approche sémiologique de l'iconographie prédynastique*. Egyptian Prehistory Monographs 6. Leuven, Leuven University Press.

Grimm, A., Schoske, S. and Dreyer, G. 2000. *Am Beginn der Zeit: Ägypten in der Vor- und Frühzeit*. Munich, Staatliches Museum Ägyptischer Kunst.

Hartung, U. 2002. Abydos, Umm el-Quaab: le cimetière prédynastique U. *Archéo-Nil* 12, 87-93.

Hendrickx, S. 1994. *Antiquités préhistoriques et protodynastiques d'Égypte*. Brussels, Musées royaux d'Art et d'Histoire.

—1998. Peaux d'animaux comme symboles prédynastiques, à propos de quelques représentations sur les vases White Cross-lined. *Chronique d'Égypte* 73, 203-30.

—2002. Bovines in Egyptian Predynastic and Early Dynastic Iconography. In F. A. Hassan (ed.), *Droughts, Food and Culture. European Research Workshop on Ecological Change and Food Security in Africa's Later Prehistory*, 275-318. New York, Kluwer Academic/Plenum Publishers.

—2006. The Dog, the Lycaon Pictus and Order over Chaos in Predynastic Egypt, in K. Kroeper, M. Chlodnicki and M. Kobusiewicz (eds.), *Archaeology of Early Northeastern Africa*. Studies in African Archaeology 9, 723-49. Poznan, Poznan Archaeological Museum.

Huard, P. and Leclant, J. 1973. Figurations de pièges des chasseurs anciens du Nil et du Sahara. *Revue d'Égytologie* 25, 136-77.

Huyge, D. 2003. Grandeur in Confined Spaces: Current Rock Art Research in Egypt, in P. G. Bahn and A. Fossati (eds.), *Rock Art Studies. News of the World 2. Developments I Rock Art Research 1995-1999*, 59-73. Oxford, Oxbow Books.

—2005. The Fish Hunters of El-Hosh: Rock Art Research and Archaeological Investigations in Upper Egypt (1998-2004). *Bulletin des Séances de l'Académie*

Royale des Sciences d'Outre-Mer 51, 231-49.

—2009. Late Palaeolithic and Epipalaeolithic Rock Art in Egypt: Qurta and El-Hosh. *Archéo-Nil* 9, 109-20.

Jiménez, A. 2004. Elephants Standing on Hills or the Oldest Name of Elephantine, in S. Hendrickx, R. Friedman, K. M. Cialowicz and M. Chlodnicki, (eds.), *Egypt at its Origins. Studies in Memory of Barbara Adams*. Orientalia Lovaniensia Analecta 138, 847-58. Leuven, Peeters.

Kantor, H. J. 1953. Prehistoric Egyptian Pottery in the Art Museum. *Record of The Art Museum (Princeton University)* 12, 67-83.

Le Quellec, J.-L., de Flers, P. and de Flers, Ph. 2005. *Peintes et gravures d'avant les pharaons. Du Sahara au Nil*. Paris, Fayard.

Lichtheim, M. 1976. *Ancient Egyptian Literature, Vol. II. The New Kingdom*. Berkeley, Los Angeles and London, University of California Press.

Lythgoe, A. M. and Dunham, D. 1965. *The Predynastic Cemetery N 7000. Naga-ed-Dêr. Part IV*. Berkeley, University of California Press.

Majer, J. 2009. Elephant Hunting at Hierakonpolis. *Nekhen News* 21, 8-9.

Marinova, E. and Van Neer, W. 2009. An Elephant's Last Meal. *Nekhen News* 21, 10-11.

Millet, N. B. 1990. The Narmer Macehead and Related Objects. *Journal of the American Research Center in Egypt* 27, 53-9.

Navajas, A. I. 2005. The Petrie Museum's Beaker UC 15332, or the First Representation of a *Hyaena Hyaena* in Egypt. *Göttinger Miszellen* 206, 69-86.

—2006. Jefatura y parentesco en Nagada I. Una aproximación a la dispersión de las cerámicas decoradas del Tipo C. In M. Campagno (ed.), *Estudios sobre parentesco y Estado en el Antiguo Egipto*, 75-94. Buenos Aires, Ediciones del Signo.

—2007. La caza con perros en el desierto en la época de Nagada I: Iconografía y Simbolismo, in S. González Reyero, M. Pérez Ruiz, and Cl. I. Bango García (coor.), *Una nueva mirada sobre el patrimonio histórico. Líneas de investigación arqueológica en la Universidad Autónoma de Madrid*. Colección de Estudios 120, 255-71. Madrid, UAM.

—2009. Bos Primigenius/Loxodonta Africa. Iconographie et symbolisme au travers de la céramique White Cross-lined. *Chronique d'Égypte* 84, 50-87.

Olfield, R. and Jones, J. 2003. What was the Elephant Wearing? *Nekhen News* 15, 12.

Osborn, D. J. and Osbornová, J. 1998. *The Mammals of Ancient Egypt*. Warminster, Aris and Phillips.

Payne, J. C. 1993. *Catalogue of the Predynastic Egyptian Collection in the Ashmolean Museum*. Oxford, Ashmolean Museum.

Petrie, W. M. F. 1901. *Diospolis Parva. The Cemeteries of Abadiyeh and Hu. 1898-9*. London, Egypt Exploration Fund.

—1902. Prehistoric Egyptian Pottery. *A Monthly Record of Anthropological Science* 2, 113.

—1920. *Prehistoric Egypt*. London, British School of Archaeology in Egypt.

—1921. *Corpus of Prehistoric Pottery and Palettes*. London, British School of Archaeology in Egypt.

Petrie, W. M. F. and Quibell, J. E. 1896. *Naqada and Ballas 1895*. London, British School of Archaeology in Egypt.

Quibell, J. E. and Green, F. W. 1902. *Hierakonpolis. Part II*. London, Egyptian Research Account.

Randall-MacIver, D. and Mace, A. C. 1902. *El Amrah and Abydos 1899-1901*. London and Boston, Egypt Exploration Fund.

Ranke, H. 1950. *The Egyptian Collections of the University Museum*. University Museum Bulletin 15. Philadelphia.

Riemer, H. 2008. Interactions between the Desert and the Nile Valley. Introduction, in B. Midant-Reynes and Y. Tristant (eds.), *Egypt at its Origins 2: Proceedings of the International Conference "Origin of the State: Predynastic and Early Dynastic Egypt," Toulouse (France), 5th–8th September 2005*. Orientalia Lovaniensia Analecta 172, 565-8. Leuven, Peeters.

—2009. Prehistoric Rock Art Research in the Western Desert of Egypt. *Archéo-Nil* 19, 31-46.

Riemer, H., Pöllath, N., Nussbaum, S., Teubner, I. and Berke, H. 2008. El Kharafish. A Sheikh Muftah Desert Camp Site between the Oasis and the Nile, in B. Midant-Reynes and Y. Tristant (eds.), *Egypt at its Origins 2: Proceedings of the International Conference "Origin of the State: Predynastic and Early Dynastic Egypt," Toulouse (France), 5th–8th September 2005*. Orientalia Lovaniensia Analecta 172, 585-608. Leuven, Peeters.

Riemer, H. and Kindermann, K. 2008. Contacts between the Oasis and the Nile: A Résumé of the Abu Muhariq Plateau Survey 1995-2002, in B. Midant-Reynes and Y. Tristant (eds.), *Egypt at its Origins 2: Proceedings of the International Conference "Origin of the State: Predynastic and Early Dynastic Egypt," Toulouse (France), 5th–8th September 2005*. Orientalia Lovaniensia Analecta 172, 609-33. Leuven, Peeters.

Rowland, M. 2003. The Unity of Africa. In D. O'Connor and A. Reid (eds.), *Ancient Egypt in Africa*, 38-54. Walnut Creek, CA and London, Left Coast Press/University College London.

Scharff, A. 1928. Some Prehistoric Vases in the British Museum and Remarks on Egyptian Prehistory. *Journal of Egyptian Archaeology* 14, 261-76.

—1931. *Die Altertümer der Vor- und Frühzeit Ägyptens*. Staatliche Museen zu Berlin Mitteilungen aus der

Ägyptischen Sammlung. Band IV. Berlin, Staatliche Museen zu Berlin.

Schulman, A. R. 1991-1992. Narmer and the Unification: A Revisionist View. *Bulletin of the Egyptological Seminar* 11, 79-105.

Sethe, K. 1927-30. Urkunden IV. *Urkunden der 18. Dynastie*. Leipzig, J. C. Hinrichs.

Tefnin, R. 1979. Image et histoire. Réflexions sur l'usage documentaire de l'image égyptienne. *Chronique d'Égypte* 54, 218-44.

Trigger, B. G. 1979. The Narmer Palette in Cross-Cultural Perspective, in M. Görg and E. Pusch (eds.), *Festschrift E. Edel*, 409-19. Bamberg, M. Görg.

Van Neer, W., Linseele, V. and Friedman, R. 2004. Animal Burials and Food Offerings at the Elite Cemetery Hk6 of Hierakonpolis, in S. Hendrickx, R. Friedman, K. M. Cialowicz and M. Chlodnicki (eds.), *Egypt at its Origins. Studies in Memory of Barbara Adams*. Orientalia Lovaniensia Analecta 138, 67-130. Leuven, Peeters.

Vandier, J. 1952. *Manuel d'Archéologie Égyptienne. Les époques de formation. La prehistoire. Tome I*. Paris, A. et J. Picard.

Von Bissing, F. W. 1913. *Catologue Général des antiquités égyptiennes du Musée du Caire. Tongefässe erster Teil: bis zum Beginn des Alten Reiches*. Vienna, Adolf Holzhausen.

Warman, S. 2000. How Now, Large Cow? *Nekhen News* 12, 8-9.

—2003. Predynastic Egyptian Bovid Burial in the Elite Cemetery at Hierakonpolis, in S. J. O'Day, W. Van Neer and A. Ervynck (eds.), *Behaviour Behind Bones. The Zooarchaeology of Ritual, Religion, Status and Identity*, 34-40. Oxford, Oxbow Books.

Wengrow, D. 2001. Rethinking "Cattle Cults" in Early Egypt: Towards a Prehistoric Perspective on the Narmer Palette. *Cambridge Archaeological Journal* 11, 91-104.

Whitehouse, H. 2002. A Decorated Knife Handle from the Main Deposit at Hierakonpolis. *Mitteilungen des Deutsches Archaeologisches Institut Kairo* 58, 425-46.

Wilkinson, T. A. H. 2000. What a King is This?: Narmer and the Concept of the Ruler. *Journal of Egyptian Archaeology* 86, 23-32.

Winkler, H. A. 1939. *Rock-Drawings of Southern Upper Egypt*. Vol. 2. London, The Egypt Exploration Society.

Wolterman, C. 2001-2002. C-Ware Cairo Dish CG2076 and D-Ware Flamingos: Prehistoric Theriomorphic Allusions to Solar Myth. *Jaarbericht "Ex Oriente Lux"* 37, 5-30.

Appendix A: Pots Discussed in the Text

Institution and Number	Provenance	References (in date order)
Berkeley, Phoebe A. Hearst Museum of Anthropology 6-2927	Naga ed-Dêr, Tomb N7014	Lythgoe and Dunham 1965, 7-9, Figure 3; Hendrickx 2002, Appendix A, 2; Graff 2009, no. 27; Navajas 2009, 83, Figure 3.
Berlin, Ägyptisches Museum und Papyrussammlung 22388	El-Khôzam	Scharff 1928, Plate XXVII, 2; Scharff 1931, 120, no. 261; Grimm *et al.* 2000, 20-21, no. 11; Navajas 2009, 87, Figure 16.
Brussels, Musées Royaux d'Art et d'Histoire E 3002	Unknown	Vandier 1952, 287, Figure 194; Asselberghs 1961, 302; Hendrickx 1994, 22-3; Hendrickx 1998; Garfinkel 2003, Figure II, 5 a-b; Graff 2009, no. 145.
Cairo, Egyptian Museum CG2076	Gebelein	De Morgan 1896, Plate II, 5; Capart 1904, 109, Figure 76; Von Bissing, 1913, 22-3, Plate VII; Petrie 1920, Plate XXIII, 2; Vandier 1952, 279, Figure 184; Asselberghs 1961, 11, Plate VII; Fischer 1968, Figure 15a; Hendrickx 1998; Wolterman 2001-2002; Graff 2009, no. 74 ; Navajas 2009, 85, Figure 10.
Cairo, Egyptian Museum CG99072	Abydos	Dreyer *et al.* 1998, 111-12, Figure 12, 1; Graff 2009, no. 155; Garfinkel 2001.
London, British Museum 49025	El-Mahâsna, Tomb H97	Ayrton and Loat 1911, 28, Plate XIV; Scharff 1928, 5, Plate XXVII, 5; Vandier 1952, 175, 274, Figure 5; Friedman 2004; Graff 2009, no. 103; Navajas 2009, 86, Figure 14.
London, Petrie Museum UC15331	Unknown	Petrie 1921, Plate XX, C6L; Vandier 1952, 272, Figure 174; Hendrickx 2002, Appendix A, 3; Graff 2009, no. 1 ; Navajas 2009, 83, Figure 5.
London, Petrie Museum UC15332	Unknown	Petrie 1902, 113, Plate H (4); Capart 1904, 105, Figure 75; Petrie 1920, Plate XVII, 67; Petrie 1921, Plate XXV, C98N; Vandier 1952, 272-3; Navajas 2005, Figure 1A-C; Graff 2009, no. 140.
London, Petrie Museum UC15333	Unknown	Petrie 1902, 113, Plate H (2); Petrie 1920, Plate XVII, 68; Petrie 1921, Plate XXV, C96E; Vandier 1952, 273; Graff 2009, no. 151.
London, Petrie Museum UC15334	Unknown	Petrie 1920, Plate XVII, 69; Petrie 1921, Plate XXV, C96L; Hendrickx 2002, 307, Appendix A (2); Graff 2009, no. 143; Navajas 2009, 84, Figure 6.
London, Petrie Museum UC15335	Unknown	Petrie and Quibell 1896, Plate XXIX, C97; Petrie 1921, Plate XXV, C95; Hendrickx 2002, Appendix A, 5; Graff 2009, no. 78; Navajas 2009, 83, Figure 4.
London, Petrie Museum UC15338	Unknown	Petrie 1902, 113, Plate H (1); Capart 1904, 105-6, Figure 75 ; Petrie 1920, Plate XVIII, 73; Petrie 1921, Plate XXV, C99; Graff 2009, no. 136.
London, Petrie Museum UC15339	Unknown	Capart 1905, 106, Figure 73; Petrie 1921, Plate XXV, C100M; Vandier 1952, 271; Garfinkel 2001; Figure 173; Graff 2009, no. 148.
Oxford, Ashmolean Museum E2778	Hu or Abadiya	Petrie 1901, Plate XIV, 93b; Petrie 1921, Plate XXV, C98D; Payne 1993, 63, no. 424, Figure 30; Graff 2009, no. 149; Hendrickx 2006, 726, Table 1;

EGYPT IN ITS AFRICAN CONTEXT

		Navajas 2007, no. 10.
Oxford, Ashmolean Museum E2784	Hu, Tomb B88	Petrie 1901, Plate XIV, 96; Petrie 1921, Plate XX, C6D; Payne 1993, 59, no. 390, Figure 27; Graff 2009, no. 20.
Oxford, Ashmolean Museum 1895.482	Naqada, Tomb 1644	Petrie and Quibell 1896, Plate XXIX, C93; Petrie 1921, Plate XXV, C92; Payne 1993, 62, no. 422, Figure 30; Graff 2009, no. 146; Hendrickx 2006, 726, Table 1; Navajas 2007, no. 2
Oxford, Ashmolean Museum 1895.487	Naqada, Tomb 1644	Petrie and Quibell 1896, Plate XXIX, C91; Petrie 1921, Plate XXV, C93M; Payne 1993, 62, no. 423, Figure 30; Graff 2009, no. 29; Hendrickx 2006, 726, Table 1; Navajas 2007, no. 1.
Oxford, Pitt Rivers Museum 1901.29.81	El-Amrah, Tomb B 161	Randall-McIver and Mace 1902, Plate XV, C96b; Petrie 1921, Plate XXV, C94; Vandier 1952, 271, Figure 173; Huard and Leclant 1973, 141-3, Figure 1.5; Graff 2009, no. 121; Navajas 2009, 84, Figure 9.
Pennsylvania, University of Pennsylvania Museum of Archaeology and Anthropology E 1418	Naqada, Tomb B 102	Petrie and Quibell 1896, Plate XXIX, C91; Petrie 1921, Plate XXV, C91; Ranke 1950, Figure 9; Kantor 1953, Figure 4-D ; Hendrickx 2006, 726, Table 1; Navajas 2007, no. 4; Graff 2009, no. 173.
Princeton, University Art Museum 30-491	Unknown	Kantor 1953, Figures 1-E, 3-A, 4-A; Hendrickx 2006, 726, Table 1; Navajas 2007; Graff 2009, no. 22.
Princeton, University Art Museum 30-493	Gebelein (?)	Kantor 1953, Figures 1-F, 3-B, 4-B; Hendrickx 2006, 726, Table 1; Navajas 2007, no. 5; Graff 2009, no. 52.
Unknown, Abydos U-415	Abydos, Tomb U-415	Hartung 2002, 87-93, Figure 4; Dreyer et al. 2003, Figure 5, Plate 15a; Dreyer and Polz 2007, 189, Figure 261a, b; Graff 2009, no. 161; Navajas 2009, Figure 12.
Unknown, Hammamiya	Hammamiya, Tomb 1649	Brunton and Caton-Thompson 1928, 49-50, Plate XXXVIII, 49k; Graff 2009, no. 30; Navajas 2009, Figure 2.

Some Notes about an Early African Pool of Cultures from which Emerged the Egyptian Civilisation

Alain Anselin
Université des Antilles-Guyane

Abstract

Using primarily linguistic evidence, and taking into account recent archaeology at sites such as Hierakonpolis/Nekhen, as well as the symbolic meaning of objects such as sceptres and headrests in Ancient Egyptian and contemporary African cultures, this paper traces the geographical location and movements of early peoples in and around the Nile Valley. It is possible from this overview of the data to conclude that the limited conceptual vocabulary shared by the ancestors of contemporary Chadic-speakers (therefore also contemporary Cushitic-speakers), contemporary Nilotic-speakers and Ancient Egyptian-speakers suggests that the earliest speakers of the Egyptian language could be located to the south of Upper Egypt or, earlier, in the Sahara. The marked grammatical and lexicographic affinities of Ancient Egyptian with Chadic are well-known, and consistent Nilotic cultural, religious and political patterns are detectable in the formation of the first Egyptian kingships. The question these data raise is the articulation between the languages and the cultural patterns of this pool of ancient African societies from which emerged Predynastic Egypt.

Keywords: Ancient Egypt, Hierakonpolis, linguistic, Predynastic, rock art, Saharo-Nubian.

In those days, we thought that Egypt was only a gift of the Nile...

In 1974, with the intention of publishing the very first *Histoire Genérale de l'Afrique* ('General History of Africa'), UNESCO gathered scholars from Africa (Egypt, Sudan, Senegal and Congo), America and Europe in Cairo to participate in the first colloquium linking Ancient Egypt with its continent, Africa. In spite of the high academic quality of the participants, and the critical examination of the iconographic, anthropological and haematological data, the colloquium did not reveal all the anticipated conclusions about the population of Ancient Egypt. What was the culprit? Genetic studies, which didn't come to fruition until after the 1980s. In addition, in those days it was thought that Egypt was simply a gift of the Nile. For what reason? Until the 1980s, there was a lack of archaeological excavation in Egypt's Western Desert. Today, the historical genetics of the Nile Valley, which is at one and the same time the 'crossroad and refugium', and the 'Saharan affinities' of the Predynastic Egyptians, have begun to be clearly identified (Keita and Boyce 2005).

Since the 1980s, and the renewal of the excavations at Kom el-Ahmar (ancient Nekhen/Hierakonpolis) by a team directed by Michael Hoffman, archaeologists, notably the team led by Fred Wendorf, have given greater attention to the African hinterland of Ancient Egypt, particularly the Saharo-Nubian area, and have excavated a network of sites of ancient African cultures which could provide cultural patterns, ideological features and the framework for the political organisation of the first kingships of Upper Egypt (Friedman 2002a). In this respect, Egypt and Nubia were also 'gifts of the desert' (Friedman 2002b).

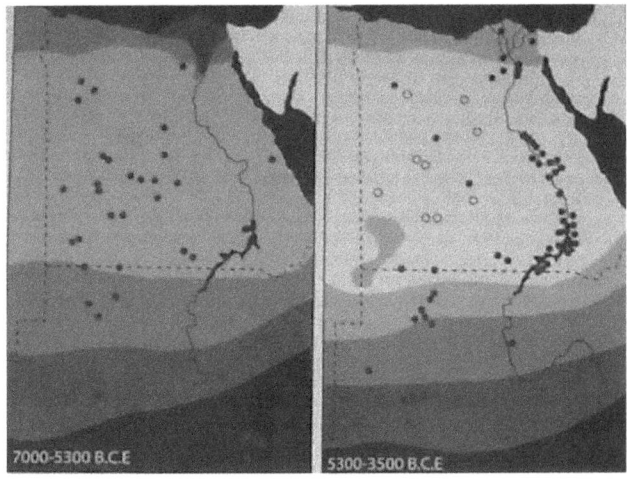

Figure 1. Maps of the Western Desert (after Sadig 2009, 33, fig. 1, a and b).

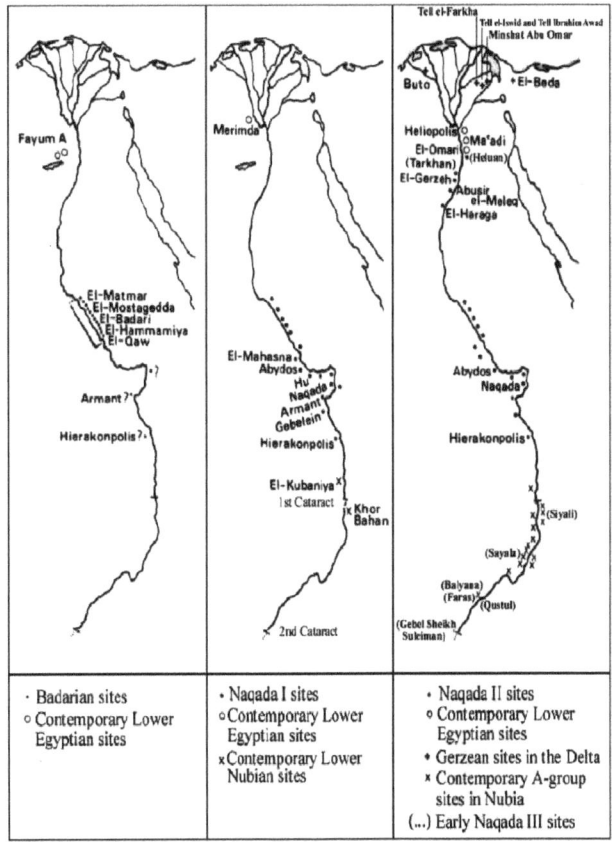

Figure 2. Maps of the main Predynastic sites in Egypt (after Trigger 1983, fig. 1.2).

After 7000 BC, Holocene human settlement expanded all over the Eastern Sahara and Sudan 'fostering the development of cattle pastoralism'; then, 'retreating monsoonal rains caused the desertification of the Egyptian Sahara at 5300BC' (Sadig 2009, 93). During two millennia, the Saharan populations were forced to migrate to ecological refuges such as the desert oases and the 'linear oasis' of the Nile Valley, and to the south, from the desert's western edge in the Chad region and its eastern frontier at the Somalian horn (see Figures 1 and 2). 'The full desert conditions all over Egypt *ca.* 3500 [BC] coincided with the first stages of pharaonic civilization in the Nile Valley' (Sadig 2009, 93). Therefore, the Ancient Egyptians were also the children of the desert.

Then came King Elephant
Today it is accepted that the formation of Egyptian civilisation originated in the expansion of the Naqadan cultures of Upper Egypt, which subsumed the original cultures of the Delta (Maadi-Buto). In this paper I will not be discussing the continuous interaction with the cultures of the Upper Egypt until its 'naqadisation', or the complex relations between Predynastic Egypt and the cultures of the Near East. The southern Naqadan polities traded with the northern polities of the Delta from the time of King Elephant – the burial of an elephant at Nekhen/Hierakonpolis dating to *c.* 3600 BC – and imported Maadi jars as well as Nubian artefacts (Friedman 2003a). I will instead be discussing the links, as historically constituted, of Egypt with its African hinterland from the first kingdoms, revealed through the excavations of Michael Hoffman, Barbara Adams and Renée Friedman over the last thirty years at Nekhen/Hierakonpolis. In placing the kingdom of Nekhen in the context of its African hinterland, we can see that the place where King Elephant was buried emerged at this period from the Badarian cultural background (*c.* 4400-4000 BC) of the Nile Valley and the Western Saharan pool of cultures (see Figures 3 and 4).

Figure 3. Maadi subterranean dwelling (Lower Egypt, Naqada I) (after Hartung 2004, 348)

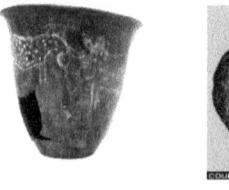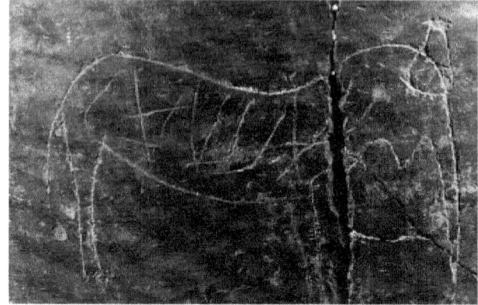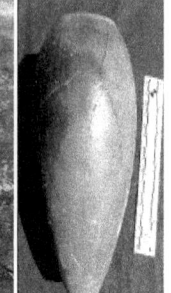

Figure 4. Pottery from the Elephant's tomb, Nekhen Hk24 (Naqada I): imported Maadi jar, C-ware bowl and Black-topped beaker (after Friedman 2003b, 16); Nubian jar from Hk43 (Naqada IIA) (after Gatto 2003, 15b).

Recent archaeological data provided since the 1980s outlines a new map of the formation of Ancient Egypt. Tasian (*c.* 4500 BC) and Badarian Nile Valley sites were not the centres of a Predynastic culture, but peripheral provinces of a network of earlier African cultures around which Badarian, Saharan, Nubian and Nilotic peoples regularly circulated (Darnell 2008).

Saharo-Nubian Cultural Antecedents of the Egyptian Predynastic Culture
The discoveries of archaeologists and rock art specialists over the last two decades uncover a picture of the cultural antecedents or shared characteristics of the Egyptian Predynastic culture supplied by its Saharan hinterland (Anselin 2006a). Here I consider three key features: firstly, in the Gilf Kebir, the rock art can be said to foreshadow the Egyptian myth of the aquatic world of the Afterlife which I call the 'Eau-Delà' (Anselin 2007b); secondly, closer to the Nile Valley, the ceremonial centre and stelae of Nabta Playa document a conception of the Afterlife linked to the key stars of the Egyptian culture: Orion (*S3ḥ*), Sirius (*Spdt*), and the Circumpolar stars (*iḥm-sk*; *Wb* 1, 125.14); and thirdly, we can follow the 'Giraffe road' – not the animals, but their pictures engraved and painted on the rocks of the Western Desert and incised or painted on the Naqadan jars of the Nile Valley cultures.

Zboray presented to the participants at the colloquium *Egypt at its Origins 2* (Toulouse, 5th-8th September 2005) a remarkable scientific inventory of all the sites of the area (Zboray 2005), a valuable tool for all disciplines that serves to invigorate Egyptology. Notably, in the Gilf Kebir, the Wadi Sora group contains many sites that we can interpret as sanctuaries. Kuper and Riemer (2009) propose a chronology as far back as Gilf B1 and B2 that runs from 6600 to 4400 BC, and Gilf C pottery, attested from 4400 to 3500~3000 BC. According to the rock art data and the chronology proposed later by Kuper and

Riemer, Le Quellec was the first to propose a new approach to the relationship between the cultures of the Nile Valley and those of the Sahara, focusing in particular on the Cave of the Swimmers and the Cave of the Beasts (Le Quellec 2005). Pertinently, in Egyptian mythology, the god of the necropolis, Anubis, was the 'Lord of the Cave', *nb ḳrrt*, and the cave, *ḳrrt*, was the place of the dead (Le Quellec 2008, 31). In this similar funerary context, '[t]he famous swimmers, unique to the Sahara, with their filiform and deformed bodies, heading in a series of lines towards the devouring beasts, are very reminiscent of the *nnyw* (drowned people, inert ones) of Egyptian mythology and thus evoke the (aquatic) world of the dead' (Le Quellec and Huyge 2008, 90). Like the Cave of the Swimmers, 'the Cave of the Beasts could illustrate a mythology of the next world similar to some of the mythical tales recorded in the Nile Valley (voracious hybrid beasts, evil spirits caught in the net)' (Le Quellec 2005, 90; Figure 5). From this perspective, many chapters of the *Book of the Dead* (for example, Chapters 127 and 163) and the composite zoomorphic Soul Devourer, *3mmw*, look like a distant echo of the rock art of the far Western Desert of Egypt (Anselin 2007b; Figure 6).

Figure 5. The Cave of the Beast, Gilf Kebir, Wadi Sora (after Le Quellec 2008, 40, fig. 14; 41, fig. 15; see also, Faulkner 1994, 14).

Figure 6. Sheet 3 of the Book of the Dead of Hu-Nefer, showing the 'weighing of the heart' (19th Dynasty; British Museum 9901.3; © The Trustees of the British Museum).

Nearer the Nile Valley, in the South Western Desert, Wendorf and Schild summarise thirty years of excavations as follows: 'the megaliths of the Nabta Playa ceremonial center are an expression of an elaborate Late Neolithic ceremonialism in Africa, the earliest ceremonial center in Africa, marking the dawn of complex societies' (Wendorf and Schild 2004, 11). A first line of a double alignment points 'toward the point where the brightest stars in the belt of Orion rose between around 6150 and 5800 years ago'; a second line 'toward the position of Sirius around 6800 years ago' and a third 'to the rising position of the same star' (Wendorf and Schild 2004, 11). The constellation of Orion, *S3ḥ* in the Egyptian language, the word also meaning 'toe', is associated with Osiris; the rising of Sirius, *Spdt* in Egyptian, is the first chronological reference in the elaboration of the earliest Egyptian calendar. *S3ḥ* and *Spdt* are two key elements of the Egyptian cosmogony. The constellation of Orion and the star of Sirius 'are closely linked to Osiris and Isis' in the Egyptian texts and are attested 18 (Orion) and 22 (Sirius) times in the Pyramid Texts of the Old Kingdom (Gadré and Roques 2008, 7). From this perspective, 'the ceremonial center of Nabta Playa supplies evidence that some of the roots of Ancient Egypt[ian] beliefs, magic and religion lie buried in the sands of the South Western Desert' (Wendorf and Schild 2004, 11) and could be one of the ceremonial high circles belonging to a large network of African cultures of the area (Figure 7).

Figure 7. Nabta Playa, the ceremonial centre (after Wendorf and Schild 2004, 13).

Figure 8. Nabta Playa, the stelae (after Wendorf and Schild 2004, 15).

Wendorf and Schild add: 'The most convincing tie between the myths and religion of Ancient Egypt and the Cattle Herders of the South Western Desert are the group of Nabta Basin stelae, erected [before 4000 BC, which] face the circumpolar region of the heavens, a place where the stars never die and where there is no death at all – as in the Pyramid Texts, where in the Field of Offerings, the deceased, symbolised by the upright megalith, will live as an "effective spirit"' (Wendorf and Schild 2004, 15; see Figure 8).

The African cultures provide good comparisons for this funerary practice. For instance, in the Kordofan region of the Sudan, a Nilotic-speaking people, the Nyimang, still erect a Bull Stone to the dead leader. If the deceased is a *kwai-gosu*, a bull-man, a stone called a bull, *gosu*, crowns the burial mound (Kronenberg 1959).

Throughout the long period of its history, the culture of Ancient Egypt was a network of dynamic phenomena. Some features which were shared with the last cultures of the Eastern Saharan Neolithic were lost when the Old Kingdom arose. For example, omnipresent in the bestiaries of the Saharan rock art, the motif of the giraffe became a star of the Predynastic iconography of Naqada I and II (*c.* 4000-3100 BC), engraved on rock or incised or painted on pottery (Figures 9 and 10). However, actual giraffes were never buried like others animals of the sacred bestiary (elephants, baboons, cattle) in the contemporary elite cemeteries of Nekhen/Hierakonpolis, and they disappear from Egyptian iconography at the end of Naqada III (*c.* 3000 BC).

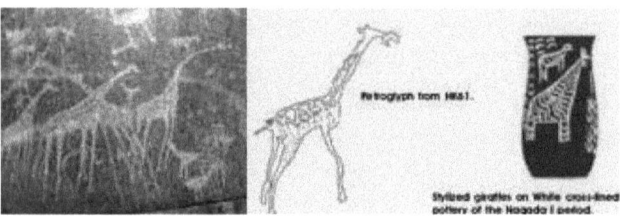

Figure 9. The giraffes of the Gilf Kebir and of the Nile Valley rock art (after Zboray 2005); Rock art and pottery (Hk61, Naqada I) (after Huyge 1998, 9).

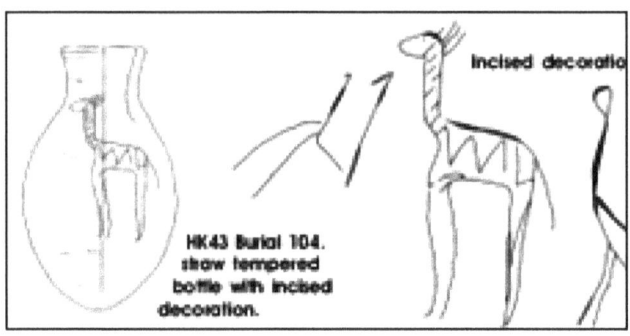

Figure 10. Pottery (Nekhen Hk43, Naqada IIB) (after Friedman 1998, 5).

Some Material and Immaterial Features Shared by Egyptian and African Cultures

In addition to the well-known headrests, the dissymmetric horns of oxen and the *w3s*-sceptre, the Ancient Egyptians shared many features with the cultures of the Nilotic and Cushitic pastoralists, probably as a result of their Saharo-Nubian roots. In particular, the Ancient Egyptian language shares a basic conceptual vocabulary with the languages of these pastoralists.

Material Culture: Some Artefacts

Headrests are known in many African cultures: Cushitic (for example, Beja, Oromo, Somalia), Nilotic (for example, Nyangatom, Turkan), Bantu (for example, Luba, Cokwe, Kuba), Zande and Dogon (Lam 2003). In the Nyangatom culture, the headrest has a religious significance: it is the material double of his owner, just as the favourite ox is the living double (Tornay 2001, 67). This may shed light on the place and the meaning of the artefact in African cultures. In Ancient Egyptian culture, the headrest became a hieroglyph (Figure 11).

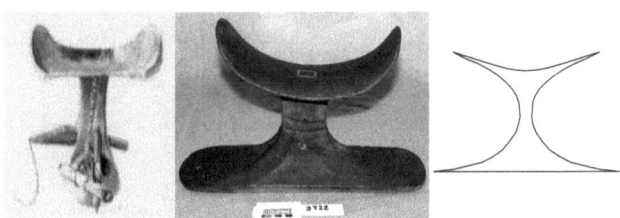

Figure 11. Nyangatom headrest (after Tornay 2001, fig. 14; Lam 2003, Pl. XLIII, fig. 3-4); Ancient Egyptian headrest, 18th Dynasty, Gurob (Manchester Museum 3722, © The Manchester Museum); headrest hieroglyph, Gardiner Q3.

The pastoralists who use headrests often practice dissymmetric shaping of the horns of their cattle, using a variety of plaiting models. Among them, the horn shapes of the *komar* of the Turkana and the *kamar* of the Pokot are a notable modern echo of the dissymmetric horns known from the cemetery of Faras (Nubia, C-Group, *c.* 2494-1550 BC), the rock art figures of Gebel Uweynat (6600-3000 BC), and the bas-reliefs of the Egyptian Old Kingdom (2686-2181 BC; Figure 12).

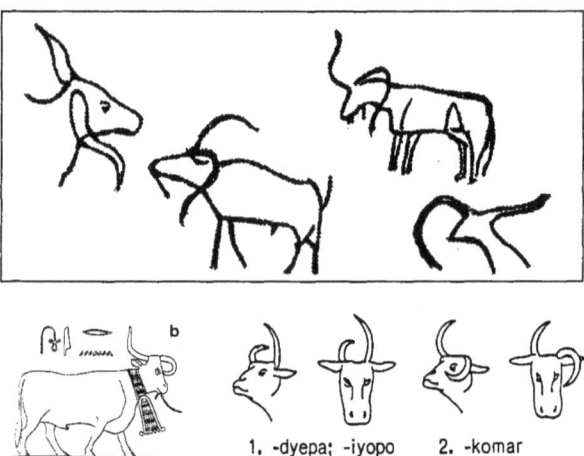

Figure 12. Horn plaiting: dissymmetric horns in Saharan rock art; bas reliefs, Old Kingdom, Egypt; *komar* Turkana, *kamar* Pokot (after Frankfort 1951, 227; Le Quellec 1993, 176, fig. 41, nos. 12, 14; 178, fig. 42, nos. 7, 10; Ohta 1989, 81, figs. 1, 2; Montet 1954, 45).

The pastoral Saharo-Nubian hinterland of the early Egyptian cultures and Predynastic civilisation, the Ancient Egyptian civilisation itself, and contemporary North East African shepherds share some 'powerfacts' or religious artefacts, for which I use the term 'theofacts'. During the ceremony marking the transfer of the post of Director of the South Omo Research Center, the outgoing postholder, Professor Ivo Strecker, gave its emblem, the *woko*, to the incoming Director, Dr Hisada, before the members of the Center, the Elders of the Omo peoples and the academics of the University of Addis Abbaba. Strecker 'explained that this staff with a hook at one end and a fork at the other end was already known in Ancient

Egypt and today is still used in South Omo by the Arbore, the Hamar and others' (Strecker quoted by Thubauville 2009, 1). Its Egyptian ideogram, a straight-handled sceptre with the head of the Seth-animal (Lefebvre 1955, 414) is attested early: ᵖʸʳ, *w3s*. The semantic and phonetic values of the hieroglyph of the *w3s*-sceptre vary. Phonetically, provided with the determinative of the sparrow (*nds*) indicating small things, it is used to write *w3si*, 'to be ruined', but also the word for milk, 'Phon. *i3tt* in , milk, cream' (Gardiner 1988, 509), and the name of the milk goddess: ᵖʸʳ, *I3tt* (*Wb* I, 26.16). Provided with a feather, the sceptre is the symbol of the nome of Hermonthis and its capital, Thebes, in Upper Egypt (*W3st*; Gardiner 1988, 503). Known to the Arbore as *shonkor*, to the Hamar as *woko*, it 'is also extended to the realm of ritual where the fork of the staff is used to ward off what is unwanted (disease, drought, war) and the hook is used to draw close what is wanted (health, abundance, peace)' (Strecker 2000, 1). The *w3s*-sceptre is not only the emblem of the Cushitic-speakers and the Omotic-speakers peoples of the Omo Valley, and of ancient Thebes; as the Egyptian Egyptologist Nagwa Arafa writes, the *w3s*-sceptre was also an attribute of Anubis: 'the *w3s*-sceptre of Anubis is the back of the *k3* (Coffin Texts, Spell 743)' (Arafa 2005). It is the ideogram of this staff that is used to write the name of the Egyptian god, Igay. Arafa has provided a long list of the occurrences of his name, the earliest of which are: (Saqqara, 3rd-4th Dynasty, *c.* 2686-2498 BC); (graffito of Niuserra: *Ig3y nb wḫ3t rsy.t*, 'Igay, Lord of the Southern Oasis', 5th Dynasty, *c.* 2445-2421 BC); (Coffin Texts, Spell 776). 'The God Igay was honored in the oases of the Western Desert' (Arafa 2005, 18, translated by the author). Seth, noted Arafa, is the god of deserts and also the lord of the oases. They are confused in the same cult in the 19th nome of Upper Egypt (Arafa 2005). '[A] rather peculiarly shaped was-sceptre', dating from around the 2nd-4th Dynasty (*c.* 2890-2498 BC), is engraved on a stela of Meri, at a rock art site of the Dakhla Oasis region (Hendrickx *et al.* 2009, 204). This brief overview highlights the connections between the ancient cultures of Western Egypt and the Nile Valley, religious artefacts of contemporary cultures of the Omo Valley and the language of contemporary Chadic-speakers and pastoralists of the Sahel, which provide a set of consistent cognates to the Egyptian word: *w3sj*, 'to be ruined, decay' < ***rus** (the prosthetic *w-* is ruled by the Law of Belova and the correspondence *3* = /r/ is well established by Takács 1999) = Western Chadic: ***rus**, 'destroy'; Hausa: **rúúsā**, 'thrash'; Kulere: **ryaas**, 'break into pieces'; Bole: **ruuš**, 'destroy'; Ngizim: **ràasú**, 'act on an object violently' (Takács 1999, 396); Fulfulde: **ruus-**, 'collapse' (Seydou 1998, 578); Wolof: **ruus**, 'crumble' (Diouf 2003, 294).

Immaterial Culture: Stars in the Mind
The two constellations that caught our attention earlier were the subject of a splendid work by Gadré (2007) who discusses their astronomic meaning and the place they occupied in Egyptian thought. One, Orion, is visible in the southern sky; the other, Ursus Major, in the northern sky (Gadré 2007, 253; 256). As a matter of fact, the constellation of Orion, *S3ḥ*, was conceived as a complex figure that Osiris governs: 'The Sons of Horus, in fact, raised asterisms among the Egyptians, that is to say that they were distributed in astronomical correspondences, in the southern sky as in the northern sky. The southern sky, in fact, offered a fine example of asterism in which a group of three stars, our Orion's Belt, appears surrounded by four others, [and] it was easy to recognise Osiris protected by the Four Sons of Horus' (Mathieu 2008, 12, translated by the author). In this manner, the Egyptians assimilated Orion to Osiris. Chapter 17 of the Book of the Dead reveals that the Four Sons of Horus were a key part of the constellation of Ursus Major: '*jr ḏ3ḏ.t ḥ3 Wsjr, (T)mstj Ḥpy Dw3-mw.t.f Ḳbḥ-sn.w.f pw nty.w m-s3 p3 ḫpš m p.t mḥty.t* – "It is the assembly who are around Osiris, Imseti, Hapy, Duamutef and Qebehsenuef, who are at the back of the Khepesh in the Northern sky"' (Mathieu 2008, 12, translated by the author). But, Mathieu adds, Osiris remains invisible in the stellar configuration. Empty, his place is surrounded by the stars called the four Sons of Horus (Figure 13).

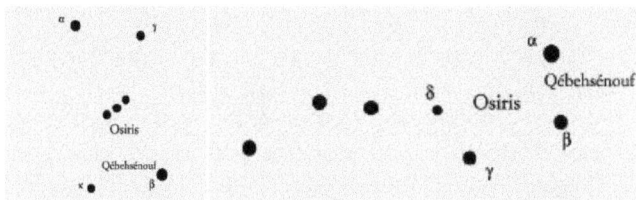

Figure 13. Map of the Egyptian skies: Left: Southern sky, Orion. Osiris, visible, is surrounded by the Four Sons of Horus; Right: Northern Sky, Ursus Major. Osiris, invisible, is surrounded by the Four Sons of Horus (after Mathieu 2008, 14).

The presence of the Sons of Horus in the two skies, the southern one, Orion, and the northern one, Ursus Major, is mentioned in the Pyramid Texts, Spell 576, and in Spell 1143 of the Coffin Texts: '*Hr smsw ḥr(y)-jb sb3.w ḥr(y).w ḫft ḥr(y).w* – "Horus the Elder, who is in the midst of the stars above as well as (the stars) below"' (Mathieu 2008, 12-13, translated by the author). So, if we consider the names of the two key elements of the Egyptian cosmogony that embody Osiris, Orion and Ursus Major, we can weave again a web of African cognates, distributed between the Chadic and Cushitic languages and the Nilotic ones: ᵖʸʳ, ᵍʳ, *s3ḥ*, 'toe' (*Wb* IV, 20) and the constellation of Orion, 'das Sternbild das Orion, bes. Auch als Hauptsternbild des Südhimmels (im Legs. zum, *msn.tjw* des Nordhimmels)' (*Wb* IV 22, 1-3). The Egyptian word is provided with the suffix indicating body-parts: -*ḥ*; that is, it is lexicalised. This suffix is used in contemporary Chadic languages: 'Kera and Kwang share a common prefix k- to mark the names of body-parts' (Jungraythmayr 1977, 18, translated by the author). For example, Kera: **kor**, 'blood'; Kwang: **kowar**; Tumak: **bor** (without the suffix). But, Takács (1995, 99), quoting Skinner (1977, 32) specifies, 'Chadic *-k was also a suffix in the words used for body parts'. He provides some consistent examples for the Angas-sura: *pʷo, 'mouth' > *pʷə > *pʷe; Gerka: **pak** (suffix **-k**), 'mouth'; Angas: **po** (Takács 2004, 110, 295; Anselin 2009a). In Egyptian anatomical vocabulary, this suffix loses its semantic and categorical relevance and appears as a frozen classifier. As Takács notes, 'these postfixes became non-productive very early, possibly in the Old Kingdom or even on [the] «Proto-Egyptian» level (that is before 3000 BC)' (Takács 1995, 101). Certainly, the word for toe belongs to the earliest linguistic horizon, whose remnant is the lexicalisation of the suffix. This is this Chadic-type name that is given by the Egyptians to Orion, the constellation of Nabta Playa. In addition, if we consider that the phonetic value of the hieroglyph of the *percnopterus* vulture, Gardiner G1, well established by Hodge (1968), Lacau (1972), Garba (1996) and Takács (1999), is /ʒ/ = /l/, the cognates of the Egyptian word *s3ḥ* < [*s-l + ḥ*] are: East Cushitic: Somali: **suul**, 'thumb'; Somali-Jabarti: **suul**, pl. **suulal,** 'big toe'; Bayso: **suul**, 'fingernail, claw'; Sidamo: **suul-ičo**, 'fingernail'; South Cushitic: ***cool**, 'finger'; Dahalo: **tsoole**, 'nail, claw'; and Central Chadic: Muturwa: **sĕlĕk**, 'fingernail' (with –k postfix) (Anselin 2009a, 19-20; Takács 1999, 195; 2000, 80-1).

From this perspective, the assimilation of the constellation of Orion to Osiris enters the liturgical vocabulary and enriches it. We know that the Egyptians liked playing with paronyms and closely linking their meanings in this way (for instance, in Egyptian myth, mankind (*rmṯ*) is the tears (*rmy*) of *Rˁ*, the sun god). Although formed from two different roots, *s3ḥ*, toe, and *3n*, light, written with the hieroglyph of a bird, the *Ibis comata* (Gardiner G29), and the solar determinative, the two paronyms designating the Osirian star, *S3ḥ*, , and the Osirian hymns *s3ḥw*, , transfiguration hymns (Hannig 1995, 661), seem not to have been used by chance. *S3ḥ*, 'transfiguration', is a causative of , *3ḥ.w,* '(sun-) light' (*Wb* I, 13), and *3ḥ* designates the transfigured spirit, with the same value as the /ʒ/ of *s3ḥ* for *3ḥ* (Old Kingdom), 'to be splendid, glorious, beneficial' (*Wb* I, 13-14). For /ʒ/ = /l/, and *3ḥ* < *ln, see South Berber: Ghat: **ulaɣ**, 'to be good'; Ayr: **a-laɣ**; North Omotic: *loq, 'good'; South Omotic: *laq; Ari: **laq-mi**, 'to become good'; Bako: **laɣ-mi** (Takács 1999, 62).

In the same way that the words for the human toe and that of Orion, *S3ḥ*, are written with the hieroglyph of an animal body-part, Gardiner F39, occasionally the determinative for 'back', *psd*, whose phonetic reading is *im3ḥ*, the word for the Big Dipper (Ursus Major; the 'Great Bear') is written with the hieroglyph of another animal body-part, the foreleg of an ox, Gardiner F23. , *msḫn*, a writing of or , *msḫtjw*, the constellation of the Great Bear (*Wb* III 148, 1-4), is also the word for, and the writing of, the adze, , the ritual tool of the Opening of the Mouth, linking the offering of the living *ḥpš* to the *k3* of the deceased. The cognates of the Egyptian word *ḥpš*, 'thigh, lower part of leg of humans and animals, forearm' – Demotic: *špš*, 'foreleg'; Coptic: ϣⲱⲡϣ (ϣⲱⲡϣ)(SB), ϣⲱⲡⲉϣ (ϣⲱⲃϣ) (B) and ϩⲱⲡϣ (A) – are distributed in the Nilotic languages: Masaai: **en.gubis**, variant: **en.kupes** (Crazzolara 1978) and nom. sg. **en-kúpês**, acc. pl. **in-kupesîr**, 'front of leg between hip and knee; thigh (in humans and cows); pubic area' (Payne and Ole-Kotikash 2008). In Maa, the name of the thigh is not given to a star. Orion is the **enk-áîbártani**, 'female one who has not been circumcised', not a masculine cultural metaphor or hero; and the Big Dipper, Ursus Major, is not a thigh, but the Seven, '**l-oisápa**. n. pl. [North] Big Dipper constellation; (lit: the seven)' (Payne and Ole-Kotikash 2008). In Nandi: **kupes**, 'thigh', plural **kupes.ua** (Hollis 1909); Pokot: **kᵒpɛɛs**, plural **kipɛsɛi** (Crazzolara 1978); Turkana: **ekipiis**, plural **ngikipiis**, 'forearm', as well as lower part of leg of humans and animals, and the tibia (Ohta 1989, 6-8). The Turkana call the dissymmetry of the horns, **komar** (Ohta 1989, 81), the Pokot, **kamar**. All these Nilotic speakers, the Nandi, the Maa and the Pokot are the primary pastoralists of the Nilo-Saharan peoples. Therefore, the fact that the Pokot culture uses the word **kopees** for the thigh of their **kamar**, 'asymmetrical horned oxen', cannot be a coincidence.

From this perspective, looking at similar cultural features of the North East African pastoralists, we see that the first Ancient Egyptians as well as the Cushitic-speaking and the Nilotic peoples share the art of ruler metaphors which liken the chief or the king to a bull (see Navajas Jiménez, this volume). The bull representing the Horus Narmer charging an enemy city on the lower register of the verso of his famous palette (Cairo Egyptian Museum CG 32169; JE 14716) is well-known, and has contemporary echoes in the Nilotic-speaking culture of the Nyimang of the Nuba Hills, where the leader is a Bull-Man (Kronenberg 1959), or in the Cushitic-speaking culture of the Daaseneč of the Omo, where the political leaders of a generation are called **ara**, literally, 'bulls' (Elfmann 2005, 157).

Immaterial Culture: The Lord of the Divine Words
Around 3700 BC, the elites of Nekhen/Hierakonpolis buried sacred animals such as elephants, young hippopotamuses, wild bull, dogs, cats, cattle, goats and baboons in their cemetery, Hk6 (Friedman 2008). In those days, there was no writing. Later, the immaterial features of the literate culture, the words, were considered sacred. Thoth, the author of these 'Divine Words', with the epithet *nb mdw nṯr* ( ), 'Lord of the Divine Words', was qualified as the Divine Hieroglyphist. The epithet, 'Lord of Divine Words' has traditionally been explained as 'Lord (or founder) of hieroglyphs' (Boylan 1922, 93). But, later, in the texts of the Middle Kingdom (2055-1650 BC), 'the Divine Words … are carefully distinguished from the written signs, and seem to be what is conveyed or expressed by the written signs, rather the signs themselves' (Boylan 1922, 93) for which the Egyptian language uses different words: *sš3* (with a divinity named *Sš3.t*), and *drf*. If we follow the familiar idea of Ancient

Egyptian literature as the written form of recitations of, for instance, funerary offerings, we can suggest that these written standard formulae are the new (and final) form of an ancient religious and ritual 'oral culture'. In this case, 'Lord of the *mdw nṯr*' means 'Lord of Spoken Words', rather than 'Lord of Written Words' or 'Lord of Script', ⌒🏠, *nb sš*. 'The *mdw nṯr* were primarily not signs but words' (Boylan 1922, 94). The Egyptian word, *mdw* (Demotic: **md(.t)**) has a broad and contemporary peripheral range of cognates: Chadic: Kwami: **màad-**, 'to say'; Cushitic: Afar: **mad'a**, 'speech'; Nilo-Saharan: Teda: **meta**, 'to speak', **medi**, 'speech'; and Niger-Congo: Fulfulde: **medd-, met-**, 'to speak' (Anselin 2006b, 147).

Thoth, Lord of Speech and Script, was frequently associated with the baboon or, sometimes, represented by it. The baboon seems an enigmatic metaphor. On the one hand, the baboon was traditionally connected with the rising sun in the Egyptian cultural conception. On the other hand, the baboon was linked with speech, and associated with the ibis as a divine representative of the *mdw nṯr*. A few epithets of Thoth highlight our observations: 𓇋𓏺𓁟, *wpt*, 'messenger', sometimes with the determinative of the sitting baboon or the divine standard (*nṯr*). Similarly we find 𓇋𓁟, which can mean *iḳr ḏd*, 'splendid of speech', 𓍖𓁟, 𓊃𓁟, and the ***bnwt(y)***-ape of Denderah (Boylan 1922, 185). The sitting position of the hieroglyphic baboon is remarkable. It is the same as that of the carved baboons found in the deposits at Nekhen/Hierakonpolis (Quibell and Green 1902) and Tell el Farkha (Chlodnicki and Cialowicz 2006). It is remarkable that the baboon, sometimes associated with the other metaphor of Thoth, the ibis, is so closely associated with speech.

Therefore can we assume that the sacred baboon is the most ancient metaphor of a 'Lord of the Speech', and the basis for the progressive and speculative elaboration of the classical divine figure of Thoth, Lord of Speech, Lord of Divine Words, Lord of the Script? If we look for contemporary terms of comparison, we can find it in the Omo area, where many pastoralist cultures of Cushitic-speakers (Daaseneč, Arbore), Omotic-speakers (Hamar) or Nilotic-speakers (Nyangatom) co-exist. In the culture of the Hamar, for instance, the baboon represents superior knowledge: 'Let the people go like baboons' says one of their oral texts (Anselin 2009c). 'The picture of people going like baboons', Strecker comments, 'is a marvellous example of rhetorical creativity and competence. It remains strange and cryptic, however, until we know that the Hamar attribute superior knowledge to the baboon, especially an ability to sense danger from afar' (Strecker 1979, 2-5; see also, unpublished, 3-4).

Immaterial Culture: Some Basic Words of the Mind

The metaphorical, immaterial figure of speech as an activity of the mind is one thing, the words of the mind, another (Anselin 2009b). If we consider all languages as the archive of their civilisation, the Egyptian vocabulary reflects a lengthy ancient pooling of cultural features from Chadic-speakers and Nilo-Saharan-speakers, shepherds of the Western Sahara. Rather than focusing on the lexicon of material culture, or the significant corpus of the names of the body-parts, I will give a short overview of the immaterial culture through a comparative study of a few words of the mind, or concepts:

b3 < ****b-l***, 'soul' (Old Kingdom; *Wb* I, 411; on the identification of /3/ as /l/, see above and Anselin 2007a): West Chadic (Nigeria): Angas-sura: **běl**, 'reason, sense, to be wise, intelligence, understanding' (Takács 2004, 31); Central Chadic: Matakam (Cameroon): ****bl***, 'genius, spirit, mboko', **belbele-hay**, 'genius'; Niger-Congo: Fulfulde (Cameroon): ⁿ**beelu** (ⁿ**gu**), 'principe vital de l'homme – menacé d'être dévoré par les mangeurs d'âme' (Noye 1989, 40; see also, Anselin 2007b, 92); Semitic: ****bāl***, 'spirit, mind'; Aramaic: **bl**, 'spirit, intelligence'; Northern Syriac: **bālā**, 'reason, attention'; Arabic: **bāl**, 'attention, consciousness, mind' (Takács 2001, 6).

si3 <****s-r***, 'to understand, know > god of the knowledge' (Old Kingdom; *Wb* IV 30, 1-21), written with the hieroglyph of the cloth (Gardiner S32); *si3.t*, (Pyramid Texts; Coffin Texts variant, *sr3.t*, identifying /i/ as a reflex of /r/): Central Chadic: Mofu-gudur: **sər**, 'to know' (Barreteau 1988, 198); Merey: **sər**, 'to know' (Gravina *et al.* 2003); Udlam: **-sər**, 'to know' (Kinnaird and Oumate 2003); Muyang: **sər**, 'to get to know' (Smith 2003).

m33 < ****mVl***, 'to see, look, examine' (Old Kingdom; *Wb* II 7, 1-10, 7), phonetically written with the hieroglyph of the sickle (Gardiner U1), the phonetic complement of the vulture (Gardiner G1) or the determinative of the eye (Gardiner D4) (Kahl 2004, 166-7): Cushitic: Agaw: Bilin: **miliʔy-**, 'to look, examine'; Kemant: **mel-**, 'to examine, observe'; Eastern Cushitic: Oromo: **mal-**, 'to think'; Sidamo: **mal-**, 'to perceive, advise'; Somali: **mala**, 'thought'; Burji: **mala**, 'plan' (Anselin 2001). Omotic: Wolamo: **mil**, 'to believe'; Kafa: **mallet**, 'to observe' (Dolgopolsky 1973, 180).

ḫm, 'to know not, be ignorant of, be unconscious of', with the determinative of negation and the negative gesture (Gardiner D35) or, with the determinative of the seated man (Gardiner A1), meaning 'ignorant man' (*Wb* III 280, 6-8); *ḫmt*, 'to think, consider, intend' (*Wb* III 285, 5-11): Cushitic: Afar: **igim**, 'ignorant', **iggima**, 'ignorance', **eegeme**, 'to be ignorant' (Parker and Hayward 1985); Saho: **agam**; Beja: **gam**, 'to know not', **agim**, 'stupid'; Niger-Congo, West Atlantic: Fulfulde: **hiimago**, 'to reflect, think, plan, calculate', **kiim.ol**, 'calculation' (Noye 1989, 160), **hiim-**, 'to think, imagine' (Seydou 1998, 279); Wolof: **xam**, 'to know', **xam-xam**, 'knowledge', **ne xamm**, 'to be thoughtful', **ne xiim**, 'to be ignorant' (Anselin 2001; Fal 1990, 250, 259).

ip, 'to reckon, count, take a census'; Coptic: **wp (ⲱⲡ)** (Vycichl 1990, 128; *Wb* I 66, 1-21); *ipw*, 'inventory' (*Wb* I 67, 2): Central Chadic: ****l-p***, 'to reckon up'; Daba: **nif** <

*lif; Kola: **nof**. The same root is possible (with semantic shift): *ip* < *****lp**, 'to examine, investigate' (*Wb* I, 66): Western Chadic: Angas-sura: ***lap**, 'to investigate, look for'; Mupun: **yāp,** 'to look for something that is missing', **yàp**, 'to check' (Takács 1999, 88). Notice the later loanwords in Canaanite: **'ēpā**, 'to measure (capacity)'; Hebrew: **3ēfā**; Greek: οιφι, 'measure of corn', from the Egyptian *ip.t*, 'to measure'; Demotic: *ip, ipy.t, iyp.t*; Coptic: **ειοπε** (S), **οειπε** (Vycichl 1983, 15, 65, 155, 250). We don't know the consistent Semitic vocabulary of calculation in the Egyptian language, but for example, *ḥsb*, 'to count, calculate, reckon' (*Wb* III, 166, 11-167, 15; Kahl 2004, 326-7): Arabic: **hasab, yahsub** (Vycichl 1983, 193). The tool used for calculation, the 'calculus', could provide the pattern and the name: Arabic: **hṣb, hṣy**, pebbles; **hṣb**, to reckon. The Semitic word is as ancient as the Egyptian, and as old as the interactions between the Upper Egyptian kingdoms and Lower Egyptian polities, and between these and their Asiatic neighbors and partners – as ancient as the Palestinian wine-jars of the Tomb Uj of King Scorpion (Naqada IIIA; *c.* 3360-3200 BC). It entered the language in the same way and at the same time as the Semitic numerals 6, *sjs, srs*; 7, *sfḫ*; and 8, *ḫmnw* and it replaced original Chadic numerals based on a numerical anthropology whose vestiges are 4, *fdnw*, and 9, *psḏ* (Chadic: ***fʷad-**). On *psḏ* as a body-part mark in numerical anthropology, see *psḏ*: 'back'/*psḏ*: '9', with a body-part suffix -*ḏ* < *****g** (as in Beja: **fadig**, '4'), cf. Central Chadic: Logone: **pasē**, 'buttocks'; Omotic: ***p-s**, 'back'; Chara: **bizā**, '9'; Sezo: **bes'é** (see Anselin 2008). In relation to this, Takács suggested a relevant scenario that fits well with the archaeological data, characterised by the meeting of two waves of languages in the Nile Valley: one, the earlier, of which many vestiges survive in contemporary Chadic deriving from the Neolithic southern settlements and those of the Western Desert, and the other, later, from the northern Predynastic sites with their well-established oriental connections (Takács 1999, 47).

Similarly for the names of the key stars of the ancient Egyptian culture, this interpretation may be extended to the Nilotic domain for the key concept of the 'name': *rn* (*Wb* 425, 1-428, 19), one of the elements of the Egyptian person or self; in Coptic: **ran (ρλν)** (SBO), **ren (ρєν)** (AA²FO), **len (λєν)** (F), **rin (ριν)** (P), absolutely distinct from Berber: **ism**, pl. **ismawen**; Arabic: **ism** (P = 'Book of Proverbs; see Vychicl 1983, XII and 176) and Western Chadic: Angas-sura: ***ṣəm**, 'name'; Angas: **súm**, 'name, fame'; Sura, Goemy: **sum**; Mupun, **səm**, 'name, honor' (Takács 2004, 338). In Proto-Nilotic: **ka-Rin**; Western Nilotic (Luo, Nweer, Shilluk): ***rin**, 'name'; Dinka: **rin**, 'name, reputation'; West Chadic: Angas-sura: ***rin**, 'shadow, spirit', as an element of the personality, distinct from ***ṣəm**, 'name, honor, fame'; Mupun: **riin**, 'shadow of person, spirit'; Karekare: **rini**, 'shadow, one's senses, thinking clearly' (Takács 2004, 310); in Bokkos: **rin**, 'spirit'. The Angas-sura and the Bokkos (Ron family) share the root ***s-m**, 'name', with Berber and Semitic, and are active in a Benue-Congo linguistic environment. It is noteworthy that Angas-sura and Bokkos use the Nilotic root with the wide meaning of 'spirit' and not the strict meaning of 'name', which is always ***s-m**. This may signify that the Nilotic word, because of its basic place in the culture, was already shared by the time that the ancestors of Nilotics, Chadics and Egyptians came together, in the ancient pooling area of the Western Sahara desert, which came to constitute the standard of Egyptian culture.

Conclusion

It is possible from this overview of the data to conclude that the limited conceptual vocabulary shared by the ancestors of contemporary Chadic-speakers (therefore also contemporary Cushitic-speakers), contemporary Nilotic-speakers and Ancient Egyptian-speakers suggests that the earliest speakers of the Egyptian language could be located to the south of Upper Egypt (Diakonoff 1998) or, earlier, in the Sahara (Wendorf 2004), where Takács (1999, 47) suggests their 'long co-existence' can be found. In addition, it is consistent with this view to suggest that the northern border of their homeland was further than the Wadi Howar proposed by Blench (1999, 2001), which is actually its southern border. Neither Chadics nor Cushitics existed at this time, but their ancestors lived in a homeland further north than the peripheral countries that they inhabited thereafter, to the south-west, in a Niger-Congo environment, and to the south-east, in a Nilo-Saharan environment, where they interacted and innovated in terms of language. From this perspective, the Upper Egyptian cultures were an ancient North East African 'periphery at the crossroads', as suggested by Dahl and Hjort-af-Ornas of the Beja (Dahl and Hjort-af-Ornas 2006). The most likely scenario could be this: some of these Saharo-Nubian populations spread southwards to Wadi Howar, Ennedi and Darfur; some stayed in the actual oases where they joined the inhabitants; and others moved towards the Nile, directed by two geographic obstacles, the western Great Sand Sea and the southern Rock Belt. Their slow perambulations led them from the area of Sprinkle Mountain (Gebel Uweinat) to the east – Bir Sahara, Nabta Playa, Gebel Ramlah, and Nekhen/Hierakonpolis (Upper Egypt), and to the north-east by way of Dakhla Oasis to Abydos (Middle Egypt). This is important for the glottochronology of all these languages to which the first attestations of written words in Egyptian provide some chronological markers. This is also important in terms of the cultural anthropology of the languages. In a pool of cultures, a shared feature is never an accidental parallel; it is necessarily a concrete reality, a unique feature, an individual paradigm. From this perspective, the Western Egyptian Sahara, and the Nile Valley, was, from 6000 BC to 3500 BC, a true zone of linguistic compression, as defined by Jungraithmayr and Leger (1993). As well the conceptual names of the stars, we find many Chadic and Cushitic terms, and, already, Nilotic ones. In particular, the short conceptual vocabulary shared by contemporary Chadic-speakers, Nilotic-speakers and Ancient Egyptian-speakers suggests that the Western Egyptian Sahara was the northern region of this wider contact area that became a zone of linguistic and cultural compression following its desertification (Figure 14).

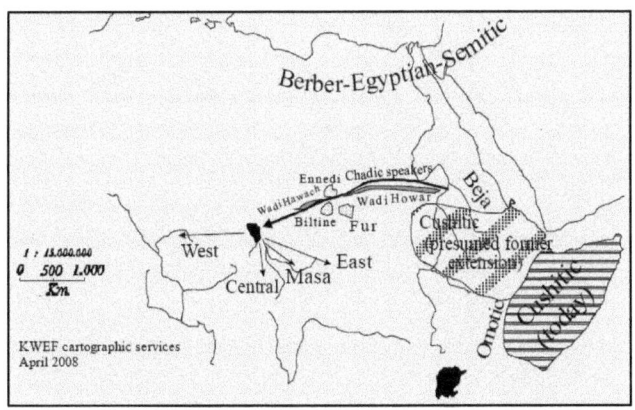

Figure 14. Maps of the distribution of the North-Eastern African populations (after Blench 2008, 124; Cerny 2006, 124) with proposed corrections (Anselin 2009a, 11a).

The distribution of these linguistic data, as well as the archaeological data, notably the artefact and the word for the Egyptian *w3s*-sceptre, is consistent with the first sets of genetic findings: on the one hand, in Upper Egypt, '... the Gurna population has conserved the trace of an ancestral genetic structure from an ancestral East African population, characterized by a high M1 haplogroup frequency. The current structure of the Egyptian population may be the result of further influence of neighbouring populations on this ancestral population' (Stevanovitch *et al.* 2004; for data on another (ancient) Upper Egyptian population, and its sub-Saharan affinities, see Crubezy 1992); on the other hand, '...the Chadic branch is linguistically close to the East African Cushitic branch (of Afro-Asiatic) although they are separated by 2000km of territory where different Semitic and Nilo-Saharan peoples live today. We show that only northern Cushitic groups from Ethiopia and Somalia are genetically close to Chadic populations' (Cerny *et al.* 2004). Therefore, on the one hand, marked grammatical and lexicographic affinities of the spongy Egyptian *vehicular* with Chadic are well-known (Diakonoff 1998; Takács 1999), and, on the other hand, consistent Nilotic cultural, religious and political patterns are detectable in the formation of the first Egyptian kingships (Anselin 2007b; Cervelló Autuori 2001; Ehret 2001). The question these data raise is the articulation between the languages and the cultural patterns of this pool of ancient African societies from which emerged Predynastic Egypt. These contradictory data could suggest a progressive pooling of various religious and cultural models through conflicts, alliances and integrations, and the common use of a progressively preeminent vehicular language (not a phylum) by various pastoralist societies, around ceremonial, funerary and political sites.

References

Anselin, A. 2001. Signes et mots de l'écriture en Égypte antique. *Archéo-Nil* 11, 21-43.

—2006a. Iconographie des rupestres sahariens et écriture hiéroglyphique. Signes et sens. *Cahiers de l'AARS (Association de l'Art Rupestre Saharien)* 10, 13-28.

—2006b. Les Mots de Geno. Fulbe, Couchites, Nilotes et Égyptiens anciens, in R. Confiant and R. Damoiseau (eds.), *Á L'arpenteur inspire. Mélanges offerts à Jean Bernabé*, 135-54. Matoury, Guyana, Ibis Rouge.

—2007a. Aegyptio-Graphica I. Note sur la valeur phonétique du hiéroglyphe du percnoptère translittéré /3/. *Cahiers Caribéens d'Egyptologie* 10, 29-42.

—2007b. Archéologie linguistique de la Vallée des Images. *Cahiers Caribéens d'Egyptologie* 10, 59-98.

—2008. Signes et mots des nombres en égyptien ancien: quelques éléments d'analyse et de réflexion, in B. Midant-Reynes and Y. Tristant (eds.), *Egypt at its Origins 2: Proceedings of the International Conference "Origin of the State: Predynastic and Early Dynastic Egypt," Toulouse (France), 5th–8th September 2005*. Orientalia Lovaniensia Analecta 172, 851–86. Leuven, Peeters.

—2009a. Un classificateur fossile en égyptien ancien. *Cahiers Caribéens d'Egyptologie* 12, 11-32.

—2009b. Some Egyptian Words of the Mind. *i-Medjat* 3, 8a-11a.

—2009c. Let the People go like Baboons. *i-Medjat* 3, 11a-b.

Arafa, N. 2005. Le dieu Igay. *Discussions in Egyptology* 63, 11-22.

Barreteau, D. 1988. *Description du Mofu-Gudur. Langue de la famille tchadique parlée au Cameroun*. Paris, Éditions de l'Orstrom.

Blench, R. M. 1999. The Westward Wanderings of Cushitic Pastoralists. Explorations in the Prehistory of Central Africa, in C. Baroin and K. Boutrais (eds.), *L'homme et l'animal dans le bassin du luc Tchad*. Actes du colloque du Réseau Méga-Tchad, Orléans, 15-17 Octobre 1997, 48 ff. Paris, Éditions de l'Orstrom.

—2001. Types of Language Spread and their Archaeological Correlates: The Example of Berber. *Origini. Preistoria et Protostoria delle Civiltà Antiche* 23, 169-89.

—2008/in press. Links between Cushitic, Omotic, Chadic and the Position of Kujarge. *Proceedings of the Fifth International Conference of Cushitic and Omotic Languages*.

Boylan, P. 1922. *Thoth, the Hermes of Egypt*. London, Milford.

Cerny, V., Hajek, M., Bruzek, J., Cmejla, R. and Brdicka, R. 2004. Relations génétiques des populations de langues tchadiques parmi les populations péri-sahariennes révélées par l'étude des séquences de l'ADN mitochondriale. *Antropo* 7, 123-31.

Cervelló Autuori, J. 2001. Monarchie pharaonique et royautés divines africaines. *Cahiers Caribéens d'Egyptologie* 2, 27-52.

Chlodnicki, M. and Cialowicz, K. 2006. *Tell El-Farkha 2006. Preliminary Report*. Polish Archaeology in the Mediterranean 18. Warsaw, Warsaw University Press.

Crazzolara, P. 1978. *A Study of the Pokot (Suk) Language, Grammar and Vocabulary*. Bologna, Editrice Missionaria Italiana.

Crubezy, E. 1992. De l'anthropologie physique à la paléo-éthnologie funéraire et à la paléo-biologie. *Archéo-Nil* 2, 7-19.

Dahl, G. and Hjort-af-Ornas, A. 2006. Precolonial Beja: A Periphery at the Crossroads. *Nordic Journal of African Studies* 15(4), 473–98.

Darnell, J. C. 2008. Rock Inscriptions and the Origin of Egyptian Writing, in R. F. Friedman, and L. McNamara (eds.), *Abstracts of Papers Presented at the Third International Colloquium on Predynastic and Early Dynastic Egypt*, 82-3. London, British Museum Press.

Diakonoff, I. 1998. The Earliest Semitic Society. Linguistic Data. *Journal of Semitic Studies* 43, 209-19.

Diouf, J.-L. 2003. *Dictionnaire wolof-français et français-wolof*. Paris, Karthala.

Ehret, C. 2001. The African Sources of Egyptian Culture and Language. In J. Cervelló Autuori (ed.), *África Antigua. El Antiguo Egipto, una Civilización Africana*. Actas de la IX Semana de Estudios Africanos del Centre d'Estudis Africans de Barcelona, 18-22 de Marzo de 1996. *Aula Aegyptiaca Studia* 1, 121-8.

Elfmann, P. 2005. *Women's Worlds in Dassanetch, Southern Ethiopia*. Arbeitspapiere des Instituts für Ethnologie und Afrikastudien der Johannes Gutenberg-Universität, Mainz, 53.

Erman, A. and Grapow, H. 1982 [1926-1953]. *Wörterbuch der ägyptischen Sprache*. Vols. I-XIII. Berlin, Akademie Verlag.

Fal, A., Santos, R. and Doneux J.-L. 1990. *Dictionnaire wolof-français*. Paris, Karthala.

Faulkner, R. O. 1994. *The Egyptian Book of the Dead*. San Franciso, Chronicle Books.

Frankfort, H. 1951. *La royauté et les dieux*. Paris, Payot.

Friedman, R. 1998. More Mummies: The 1998 Season at Hk43. *Nekhen News* 10, 4-5.

—2002a. The Predynastic Cemetery at Hk43: Excavations in 2002. *Nekhen News* 14, 9-10.

— (ed.) 2002b. *Egypt and Nubia. Gifts of the Desert*. London, British Museum Press.

—2003a. Hierakonpolis 2003: exhumer un éléphant. *Bulletin de la Société Française d'Égyptologie* 157, 9-22.

—2003b. Excavating an Elephant. *Nekhen News* 15, 9-10.

—2008. Hierakonpolis 2008 (April 2008-January 2009), Field Note 1. *Archaeology's InteractiveDig*. http://www.archaeology.org/interactive/hierakonpolis/field08/1.html

Gardiner, A. H. 1988 [1927]. *Egyptian Grammar*. Oxford, Griffith Institute.

Gadré, K. 2007. *Conception d'un modèle de visibilité d'étoile à l'œil nu. Application à l'identification des décans égyptiens*. Unpublished PhD thesis, University of Toulouse.

Gadré, K. and Roques, S. 2008. Catalogue d'étoiles peuplant le ciel de l'Égypte ancienne. *Cahiers Caribéens d'Égyptologie* 11, 5-14.

Gatto, M. 2003. Hunting the Elusive Nubian A-Group. *Nekhen News* 15, 14-15.

Gravina, R., Doumok, E. and Boydell, A. 2003. *Merey Provisional Lexicon*. Cameroon, SIL.

Hannig, R. 1995. *Die Sprache der Pharaonen. Grosses Handwörterbuch Ägyptisch-Deutsch*. Mainz, Philipp von Zabern.

Hartung, U. 2004. Excavations in the Predynastic Settlement of Maadi, in S. Hendrickx, R. Friedman, K. M. Cialowicz and M. Chlodnicki (eds.), *Egypt at its Origins. Studies in Memory of Barbara Adams*. Orientalia Lovaniensia Analecta 138, 337-56. Leuven, Peeters.

Hendrickx, S., Riemer, H., Förster, F. and Darnell, J. C. 2009. Late Predynastic/Early Dynastic Rock Art Scenes of Barbary Sheep Hunting in Egypt's Western Desert. From Capturing Wild Animals to the Women of the 'Acacia House', in H. Riemer, F. Förster, M. Herb and N. Pöllath (eds.), *Desert Animals in the Eastern Sahara. Status, Economic Significance and Cultural Reflection in Antiquity*. Proceedings of an Interdisciplinary ACACIA Workshop, University of Cologne, December 14-15, 2007. Colloquium Africanum 4, 189-244. Cologne, Heinrich Barth Institute.

Hollis, A. C. 1909. *The Nandi. Their Language and Folklore*. Oxford, Clarendon Press.

Huyge, D. 1998. Giraffes in Ancient Egypt. *Nekhen News* 10, 9-10.

Jungraithmayr, H. and Leger, R. 1993. The Benue-Gongola-Chad Basin. Zone of Ethnic and Linguistic Compression. *Berichte des Sonderforschungsbereichs* 268(2), 161-72. Frankfurt, Goethe Universität.

Kahl, J. 2004. *Frühägyptisches Wörterbuch unter Mitarbeit von Markus Bretschneider und Barbara Kneissler, Lieferung 3: h - ḫ*. Wiesbaden, Harrassowitz.

Keita, S. O. Y. and Boyce, A. J. 2005. Genetics, Egypt and History: Interpreting Geographical Patterns of a Y-Chromosome Variation. *History in Africa* 32, 221-46.

Kronenberg, A. 1959. Notes on the Religion of the Nyimang. *Kush* 7, 197-213.

Kuper, R. and Riemer, H. 2009. *The Gilf Kebir National Park. Challenge and Change for Archaeology*. Unpublished Conference Paper. Dakhleh Oasis Project

Sixth International Conference: New Perspectives on the Western Desert of Egypt, 20-24 September 2009, Università del Salenta, Lecce.

Lam, A. M. 2003. *L'Unité culturelle égypto-africaine à travers les formes et les fonctions de l'appui-tête*. Dakar, Presses Universitaires de Dakar.

Lefebvre, G. 1955. *Grammaire de l'égyptien classique*. Cairo, Institut Français d'Archéologie Orientale.

Le Quellec, J. L. 1993. *Symbolisme et art rupestre au Sahara*. Paris, L'Harmattan.

—2005. Une nouvelle approche des rapports Nil-Sahara d'après l'art rupestre. *ArchéoNil* 15, 67-74

—2008. Can One "Read" Rock Art? An Egyptian Example. In P. Taylor (ed.), *Iconography Without Texts*. Warburg Institute Colloquia 13, 25-42. London, Warburg Institute; Turin, Nino Aragno Editore.

Le Quellec, J. L. and Huyge, D. 2008. Rock Art Research in Egypt 2000-2004, in P. G. Bahn, M. Strecker and N. Franklin (eds.), *Rock Art Studies. News of the World* 3, 89-96. Oxford, Oxbow Books.

Mathieu, B. 2008. Les enfants d'Horus, théologie et astronomie. *Égypte Nilotique et Méditerranéenne* 1, 7-14.

Montet, P. Les boeufs égyptiens. *Kêmi* 13, 43-58.

Noye, D. 1989. *Dictionnaire foulfouldé-français. Dialecte peul du Diamaré, Nord-Cameroun*. Geuthner Dictionnaires. Paris, Geuthner.

Ohta, I. 1989. A Classified Vocabulary of the Turkana in Northwestern Kenya. *African Study Monographs Suppl.* 10, 1-104.

Parker, E. M. and Hayward, R. J. 1985. *An Afar-English-French Dictionary (with Grammatical Notes in English)*. London, School of Oriental and African Studies, University of London.

Payne, D. L. and Ole-Kotikash, L. 2008. *Maa Dictionary*. 2008 online version at: http://www.uoregon.edu/~maasai/

Quibell, J. E. and Green, F .W. 1902. *Hierakonpolis II*. London, Egypt Research Account.

Sadig, A. M. 2009. Preliminary Observation on the Neolithic Settlement Patterns in Central Sudan. *Sahara* 20, 31-56.

Seydou, C. 1998. *Dictionnaire pluri-dialectal des racines verbales du Peu. Peul-Français-Anglais*. Paris, Karthala.

Smith, T. 2003. *Muyang Provisional Lexicon*. Cameroon, SIL.

Strecker, I. 1979. *The Hamar of Southern Ethiopia. Vol. III. Conversations in Dambaiti*. Hohenschäftslarn, Renner.

—2000. Hamar Rhetoric in the Context of War, in B. Yimam, R. Pankhurst, D. Chapple, Y., Admassu, A., Pankhurst and B. Teferra (eds.), *Ethiopian Studies at the End of the Second Millenium. Proceedings of the XIVth International Conference of Ethiopian Studies, 6-11 November, 2000, Addis Ababa*. Addis Ababa, University of Addis Ababa.

Stevanovitch, A., Gilles, A., Bouzaid, E., Kefi, R., Paris, F., Gayraud, R. P, Spadoni, J. L., El-Chenawi, F. and Béraud-Colomb, E. 2004. Mitochondrial DNA Sequence Diversity in a Sedentary Population from Egypt. *Annals of Human Genetics* 68, 23-39.

Takács, G . 1995. Traces of Nominal Lexical Categories in Egyptian. *Lingua Posnaniensis* 37, 99-114.

—1999. *Etymological Dictionary of Egyptian. Vol. 1. A Phonological Introduction*. Leiden, E. J. Brill.

—2000. South Cushitic Consonant System in Afro-Asiatic Context. *Afrikanistiche Arbeitspapiere* 61 (Institut für Afrikanistik, University of Cologne), 69-117.

—2001. *Entymological Dictionary of Egyptian. Vol. 2. b-,p-,f-*. Leiden, E. J. Brill.

—2004. *Comparative Dictionary of the Angas-Sura Languages*. Berlin, Reimer.

Thubauville, S. (ed.) 2009. Handing Over Ceremony at SORC. *News from South Omo Research Center and Museum* 5, 1-2.

Tornay, S. 2001. *Les Fusils jaunes. Générations et politique en pays Nyangatom (Ethiopie)*. Nanterre, Société d'Ethnologie.

Trigger, B. G. 1983. The Rise of Egyptian Civilization, in B. G. Trigger, B. J. Kemp, D. O'Connor and A. B. Lloyd, *Ancient Egypt. A Social History*, 1-69. Cambridge, Cambridge University Press.

Vycichl, W. 1983. *Dictionnaire étymologique de la langue copte*. Leuven, Peeters.

—1990. *La Vocalisation de la langue égyptienne. Tome Ier. La Phonétique*. Cairo, Institut Français d'Archéologie Orientale.

Wendorf, F. and Schild, R. 2004. The Megaliths of Nabta Playa. *Focus on Archaeology. Academia* 1(1), 11-15.

Zboray, A. 2005. *Rock Art of the Libyan Desert*. Newbury, Fliegel Jezerniczky Expeditions Ltd. DVD.

Egypt in Afrika and Afrika in Egypt: The Example of Libation

Kimani S. K. Nehusi
University of East London

Abstract
This paper is a transdisciplinary reconstruction and analysis of the ritual of libation and its associated beliefs and practices, mainly through a focus on the sacred literature, language, social practice, myth, the creative imagination and popular culture in Kemet, modern Afrika and its Diaspora, i.e. the Afrikan world. The results reveal a tradition that has been alive in the Afrikan world from at least the time of Kemet to the present. Connection and continuity, though not without change, between Kemet and the modern Afrikan world is shown in the conception and practice of the ritual itself as well as the world view which instructs it. The founding myth of libation in Kemet is revealed to be logical and to make complete sense only if it is located in the Afrikan cultural context in which it was conceived and to which it has always belonged. This relationship is merely illustrative of a general cultural continuity between Kemet and the rest of Afrika that is increasingly being uncovered by scholarly investigation.

Keywords: Afrika, the Afrikan world, culture, Kemet, language, libation, myth, offerings.

Introduction
Scholarship has already established a symbiotic relationship between *Kmt*, Kemet (Ancient Egypt), the oldest Afrikan society about which we have much detailed knowledge, and the rest of Afrika. It is a relationship that was once denied by Western scholars, ultimately as a way of trying to justify the *Maafa* or Afrikan holocaust, the worst crime in history (Achebe 1990, 2000). The scholarship of James (1954), Diop (1974, 1989, 1991), Bernal (1987, 1991), Van Sertima (1989, 1994), Obenga (1992, 2004), Celenko (1996), and others has decisively overturned this unscientific theory. Today, scholars at the leading edge in the study of Afrika, in both the disciplines of Afrika Studies and Egyptology, recognise the irrefutable fact that Kemet is both in Afrika and of Afrika. The objective of this essay is therefore limited to extending and enriching our knowledge and understanding of Kemet in its Afrikan context specifically through an examination of the ritual of libation. This will be achieved by reconstructing the presence of libation in a time/space correlation that defines itself as the Afrikan world past and present, particularly through a focus on Kemet as a specific representation of that past, thereby adding to the growing links uncovered between Kemet and the rest of Afrika and further illustrating Kemet to be culturally one of the earliest known examples of the Afrikan world.

Definition
Libation is a highly distinctive combination of thought, word and gesture which together constitute a ritual drama that has been sacred to Afrikans for as long as humanity has counted time, and perhaps even before then. It is a powerful moment of profound significance in which divinity and ancestors are invoked, the environment acknowledged, and all the generations within the entire time/space correlation represented by the experience of living are united before the invoked forces. This unity is achieved simultaneously in both domains, for in terms of time there is a fusion of the past/present/future and in space that of the here/not here.

At this most potent moment of the ritual process a drink offering is made and favours sought. In the current historical era the offering is made with the right hand – to the Supreme Being, to lesser divinities, to the ancestors, to the absent living, to the unborn, and/or to the environment or aspects thereof. This is done in order to receive the support of these forces for the general well-being and/or for a specific purpose or purposes that the libationer seeks. This spiritual help is sought and normally secured through propitiating these forces or making reparations in order to ensure the repair and restoration of ruptured relations among the beings and things in the universe, or to affirm this good order (*Maat, asé*) if it is threatened, to give thanks for an achievement, to call down cosmic damnation on an enemy (i.e. issue a curse), or for any combination of these. The specific purpose(s) for which the support may be solicited would be made clear in each libation statement.

Throughout the vast sweep of Afrikan history the principle appears to have been that almost any liquid was good for the offering, though specific drinks have been favoured at particular places and times and sometimes even by a particular divinity. A wider variety of drink, including beer, wine, water and honey, was offered in Kemet. In more contemporary times beer has found foremost favour in East and Southern Afrika, while white spirits, more usually white rum, has been the main liquid of libation in West Afrika, the Caribbean and the Americas.

Time/Space Distribution
By virtue of their attestation of the ritual complex in which libation normally occurred, both the temple complex uncovered at Nabta Playa (Heratus 2007; Wilkinson 2000, 16) and an incense burner found at Qustul (Brunson 1991, 107-9; Williams 1985, 29-43; 1996, 95-7) may constitute indirect references to the practice of libation in organised political entities that existed before and beyond the state of Kemet. In these examples, the association of libation with the ritual complex that includes sacrifice and other offerings represent neither isolated instances nor a practice confined only to the distant Afrikan past. This very ritual complex is attested throughout the history of Afrika, though, like much else in culture, there have been a

number of variations and changes, including discontinuities. It is significant that both of these sites are to the south of Kemet. This is the direction from which Kemet inherited much of its people and heritage (Carruthers 1984, 19-23; DuBois 1965, 106; Finch 1994, 38-9; Williams 1976, 36, 110, 136).

Kemet provides much firmer ground for information and knowledge about libation as well as about much else in the study of Afrika. The evidence from this part of the Afrikan world is much more copious and much more decisive than so far recovered for earlier periods in the history of Afrika and so of the world. It is this profusion of details, from very early in its history, which helps to establish the importance of Kemet in the reconstruction of Afrika and its social history.

Much of this evidence about libation in Kemet exists in the form of artefacts, including libation vases, statues, temples and tombs that either directly attest to this ritual, or bear inscriptions that do so, or both. Much scholarly enquiry is based upon this particular group of sources. Examples abound, including the works of Assmann (2005), Gardiner (1903, 146), Guarnori and Chappaz (1983, 73-82), Schäfer (1898, 147-8) and Yellin (1982, 151-5).

One feature which distinguishes Kemet from the preceding historical eras is the possession of writing and literacy in the form of the 𓂋𓏤 *mdw nṯr* (*Medew Netjer*), the language of Kemet, which is commonly known in the West by the Greek term hieroglyphs. Writing and literacy were invented by the 𓂋𓏤 or 𓂋𓏤, the *rmṯ (n) Kmt* (*remetj (en) Kemet;* Coptic *remenkemi*), 'the people of Kemet' in the Predynastic era of that country. The written evidence of libation in Kemet therefore occurs in the earliest writings in the world, thus further illustrating the great antiquity of this ritual. The sacred literature of the land, a representative sample of which is contained in the writings now popularly known in the West as the Pyramid Texts (Faulkner 1969) and its successor texts, the Book of Vindication, called the Coffin Texts (Faulkner 1994a), the Book of Going Forth by Day, called The Egyptian Book of the Dead (Budge 1895; Allen 1974; Faulkner 1985; 1994b) and others, also provide some of the earliest recorded information on libation. Libation is so ancient and so important that there are libation utterances in the Pyramid Texts (Faulkner 1969), the oldest substantial writings in the world, and Utterance 598 in the Book of Vindication (the Coffin Texts; Faulkner 1994a, Vol. II, 193) may well be a libation ritual. Even more information on libation is contained in other, secular, documents as well as in artistic representations generated by the people of Kemet throughout the three thousand and more years that this state existed.

For example, in his 𓂋𓏤 *sbꜣyt* (*Sebayt*), 'teachings', 𓂋𓏤 *ꜣny*, Ani, an ancient wise man who lived during the New Kingdom (1550-1069 BC) of Kemet, commands us thus:

'Pour libation for your father and mother who rest in the valley of the dead. God will witness your action and accept it. Do not forget to do this even when you are away from home. For as you do for your parents, your children will do for you also.' (Karenga 1984, 53)

Language: 𓂋𓏤 The *Medew Netjer*

The very large number of lexical items pertaining to libation and its ritual context in the *Medew Netjer* announces a huge inventory of concepts, functionaries, paraphernalia and practices that were germane to the complex of offerings in which the ritual of libation occurred. Examples of such terms include 𓂋𓏤 (variations 𓂋𓏤 and 𓂋𓏤) *ḳbḥw* (*kebehew*), the noun for 'libation', and the verb 𓂋𓏤 *ḳb* (*keb*), which translates as 'pour a libation'. Another very important term is 𓂋𓏤 *ḥtp* (*hotep*), which has been translated as 'rest, go to rest, be at peace, pleased', 'make content', 'pacify' and so on (Erman and Grapow 1982, Vol. V; Faulkner 1962; Gardiner 1988). This is a key term for our understanding of libation, for it conveys the ultimate objective of this and related rituals such as censing, first fruits, sacrifice and prayers, which was to please the divinities and ensure peace among humanity, in the physical, social, ecological and spiritual environment in which we live and, indeed, in the entire cosmos. Its recurrences in the origin, structure and meanings of the vocabulary of the offering complex demonstrates how this concept is foundational to and permeates the rituals and paraphernalia through which and by which the entire devotional complex was articulated.

A few of the other terms should be mentioned here: 𓂋𓏤 *ḥtp(w)*, *ḥtpt* (*hetepew*, *hetepet*), 'offerings', 'food offerings'; 𓂋𓏤 *ḥnḳt* (*henket*); 'beer', and 𓂋𓏤 *mw* (*mu*), 'water', 'sometimes specified as *mw n r(n)py*' or '*mw rnp*: fresh water', meaning purifying and rejuvenating water (Smith 1993, 16, 41) or 'cool' water. Other words translate as wine, milk, altar, candle, censor, incense, ritually pure meat, invocation offerings and other articles, actions and personnel that further attest an elaborate complex.

It is important to ground our understanding of libation and associated ideas and practices at least partly in these lexical items in the language of Kemet, for a group of humans do not invent terms in their language to represent concepts that do not already exist in their physical, social and intellectual universe; that is, in their living reality. The fact, namely that these terms exist in the *Medew Netjer* and are indigenous to it, therefore must mean that the ideas and practices they represent existed in the social reality of the speech community of the people of Kemet, who were the inventors and users of the *Medew Netjer*. This presence of libation and other forms of offering also means that this entire behavioural complex existed in

Afrikan culture from very early times, certainly from the time of the people of Kemet, and most probably before then, as is indicated by the Nabta Playa temple complex (archaeological remains from 9,800 BP) and the Qustul incense burner (4th millennium BC). These terms therefore argue that this set of ideas and practices was of the greatest importance to the Afrikan people from as long as is known – and most likely even before then. They have remained so. This knowledge, with its related understandings, beliefs and practices, and the ritual of libation in which they find a specific expression, therefore comprise a most important part of Afrikan culture and, so, of Afrikan identity.

Legend, Myth and Divinity
The origins of the ritual of libation are so ancient that even to the people of the ancient Afrikan state of Kemet they were obscure, lost in the mists of time, and therefore accounted for in a particular myth. It is very likely that this account of things originated as an oral form before the invention of writing and the state of Kemet. It was probably handed down by word of mouth through an untold number of generations. It is certain, however, that this particular account was eventually committed to writing, first perhaps in the New Kingdom, as it is absent from the written literature of the preceding eras (the Old Kingdom, c. 2686-2181 BC and the Middle Kingdom, c. 2055-1650 BC). So far as is known, the earliest written account was inscribed on the largest of the gilded wooden shrines that enclosed the coffin of Pharaoh Tutankhamun. This text was also written on the walls of four other royal tombs in the Valley of the Kings during the New Kingdom, with the tombs of Seti I and Ramesses II housing the most complete accounts. Copies are also to be found in the tombs of Ramesses III and Ramesses IV.

In this account of the beginning of the ritual, the sun divinity Ra physically retreated in anger from humans and from the earth because of humanity's irreverence in plotting against him and ridiculing him because he had grown so old that he drooled. Ra sent his daughter, Hathor, to avenge his hurt. She decided to wipe out humanity and proceeded so well that Ra changed his mind and wanted to stop the slaughter. But Hathor's blood lust could not be easily quenched. Eventually she was stopped by a trick. She was served copious quantities of red beer. She drank, believing it to be blood, and became so drunk that she forgot about killing. And so humanity was saved. Libation was therefore so important to the people of Kemet that it was located in their sacred narratives, where it is to be found in the realm of divinity; that is, in the spiritual aspect of existence.

Egyptologists generally refer to this myth as 'The Destruction of Mankind' (Hart 1990, 46-9; Kaster 1995, 66-70; Lesko 1991, 110-11; Lichtheim 1976, Vol. II, 179-99; Thomas 2001; Tyldesley 2004, 9-15; Wilson 1969, 10-11). However, as the Afrikan-centred scholar, Théophile Obenga, points out, '[t]he ultimate theme of this narrative ... is salvation, not destruction' (Obenga 2004, 177). Further, most interpretations of this myth from within Egyptological circles miss its obvious reference to libation. Leonard H. Lesko provides a good example. He speculates that '[i]t may have been an attempt to rationalize plague as a divine punishment that had miscarried...' and asserts that this myth 'also provides an explanation for the origin of beer and for the drinking of beer, perhaps to excess, at the Festival of Hathor' (Lesko 1991, 111). It is another Afrikan-centred scholar, Ayi Kwei Armah, who provides the explanation of this legend or myth by relocating it within the Afrikan cultural universe. This is the only context in which this legend appears logical and makes complete sense, for this is the context in which it was conceived and to which it always belonged. 'This legend,' he asserts, 'explains the rise of a propitiatory custom found everywhere on the African continent: libation, the pouring of alcohol or other drinks as offerings to ancestors and divinities' (Armah 2006a, 207). To be very precise, the drink offering is also made to other beings and to things, and the custom is also found in Afrikan communities abroad. The restoration of libation to its Afrikan cultural context illustrates, once again, the connection and continuity between Kemet and the contemporary Afrikan world. It also suggests that on a general level, Kemet will not be properly understood unless it is placed in its Afrikan context and that the study of Afrika is incomplete and impoverished without this relocation of Kemet in Afrika.

Figure 1. The Pharaoh Taharqa offering libation to Hemen, the falcon divinity (Musée du Louvre, E.25276. © Des Robinson). Notice the use of both hands and his kneeling posture of humility.

The function of this myth is to provide the intellectual basis and the performance model for the ritual drama known as libation. This myth gives an origin and an explanation of the ritual. It also supplies a reference to the great importance to be attached to the ritual by locating it among the highest and most powerful category of beings in the Afrikan cosmology, the realm of divinity.

There are a number of extant representations of pharaohs

kneeling in performance of libation, making a liquid offering with both hands. The popularity of this representation indicates the importance attached to libation by the rulers of Kemet. The earliest known representation of this posture in the visual arts of Kemet is a green slate statue of Pepi I (c. 2321-2287 BC), now in the Brooklyn Museum (39.121). Taharqa, pharaoh in the 25th Dynasty (747-656 BC) of Kemet, is shown in exactly this posture (Figure 1). Many similar portrayals of other pharaohs are extant. It is evident that it became customary for the leader of the state to present the drink offering with two hands, one bowl in each, a format that clearly became predominant in Kemet during the Old Kingdom and was thereafter repeated for the remainder of that state's very long history, right down to the Late Period (747-332 BC; Clayton 1994, 65).

Figure 3. A priest pouring libation over Wasir.

Figure 2. Seti I pouring libation to Wasir (Osiris)

However, the foregoing does not mean that libation was always presented with both hands in Kemet. Figures 2-4 suggest that at least on some occasions, the pouring of a libation, and indeed the presentation of any offering, continued to be made either with one hand or with both hands (Budge 1973, 251-67, and *passim*). The reason for the eventual predominant use of both hands, especially on official occasions, is that it was a double offering by the leader of the Two Lands (Upper and Lower Kemet); one bowl and so one offering was made for each part of the state (see Figures 2-4). In the modern Afrikan world libation is made only with the right hand. This is a preference which, also like libation in Kemet, appears to find divine sanction, at least amongst the Igbo. Here, according to Awolalu and Dopamu (1979, 58), in the process of creation, Chukwu put his right hand into the pot to withdraw the first piece of white chalk, which became Otolo, the First Son.

Figure 4. Seti I making an offering of incense to Wasir – with the right hand.
(Figures 2, 3 and 4 after Budge 1911, 253; 255)

It seems that when Afrikans migrated from Kemet the powerful notion of the Two Lands ceased to hold sway over them, perhaps gradually. At present it is only to be imagined how the challenging conditions of migration and the increasing physical and emotional distance from the Two Lands loosened the bonds with this principle and lessened the need to give it dramatic effect in the ritual. In time, the new reality of a different environment was represented in a different way. Libation was now presented only with the right hand. Yet, again, this aspect of the ritual drama was a reflection of a social value and the social reality it instructed, for in modern Afrikan custom, the presentation of drink, like the eating of any food, falls into the sphere of those things that are done only with the right hand. This custom may indicate how in practice the presentation of the libation offering was changed so that the continuation of the ritual was assured.

Social History

The linguistic evidence for libation in Kemet obtained from content analysis of the language, the sacred literature and the myth of that land is corroborated by evidence from the social history of the people of Kemet. Janssen and Janssen show that the custom of 'pouring water' (i.e. libating, a linguistic formulation still widely distributed in Afrika today) for a deceased was widespread in Kemet throughout its very long history (Janssen and Janssen 1996, 50-1). Libating with water was also done for Imhotep, the deified architect of the Step Pyramid, and, more than likely, for the very few other outstanding private individuals who were elevated to divinity after their transition to the spirit world (Jacq 1985, 12). The sage Neferti, in a text dating to the Middle Kingdom, gives independent corroboration of this latter custom when he writes that '[t]he learned man will pour out water [i.e. make a libation] for me, when he sees what I have spoken come to pass' (Asante and Abarry 1996, 65).

Taken together these various pieces of evidence, from the language, the sacred literature, the founding myth of libation and social customs of Kemet, argue for the pervasive and extremely important presence of libation in the society of Kemet, ancient Egypt.

Figure 5. Ashurbanipal, King of Babylon (668-627 BC), pouring libation over dead lions in his palace to his god Ashur after a victory in battle (source: http://www.harvestfields.ca/ebook/02/053/013.htm)

It is also certain that Kemet-style libation, as well as the very idea and practice of this ritual, were passed on to Alexandrian Egypt, Greece, Carthage and Italy (Delia 1992). This piece of evidence confirms the more general conclusions about the transmission of knowledge and culture made in ancient times by Herodotus (trans. by A de Sélincourt 1972, 129-210 and *passim*) and in modern times by a growing number of scholars, including George G. M. James (1954), Cheikh Anta Diop (1974), Martin Bernal (1987, 1991) and Théophile Obenga (1989, 1992, 1995). It also illuminates the historical context of the references to offerings, including libation, made centuries ago by Homer (trans. by R. Fagles 1990). Libation was also extant in ancient Mesopotamia. The fact of the practice of the ritual in Mesopotamia, Greece and Rome is depicted and so confirmed by graphic representations taken from the art of the people who inhabited these places in ancient times (see Figures 5-7).

Figure 6. Libation in ancient Greece: the Greek god Apollo pours libation and plays music (interior of a white *kylix* found at Delphi, workshop of Sotades, *c.* 470-450 BC. The Archaeological Museum, Delphi, Greece).

Figure 7. Libation in ancient Rome: a Roman pouring libation into a living plant (source: http://www.vroma.org/images/flood_images/libation.jpg).

Figure 8. A Sem-priest pouring libation from an amphora or jug into a libation bowl held by a ministrant (after Budge 1909, 42).

Libation is also present in The Bible. There is a multitude of references to the ritual in this book. Here, the ritual is referenced both as 'libation' and as its synonym 'drink offering', and in both their singular and plural forms. Such references number at least 67, beginning at Genesis 35:14 (Osei-Bonsu, quoted in Sarpong 1996, 31). The references in The Bible occur over 2000 years after libation was first attested in Kemet (see, for example, Figure 8), and show the form and significance of libation to be derived from the pre-existing Afrikan tradition, much of which passed into the Eurochristian tradition through Moses, who is now considered by many to have been an ancient Egyptian or man of Kemet, and who gave to the Jews their religion and culture, which is essentially that of the people of Kemet (Assmann 1997; Freud 1985, 239-386).

In the study of Kemet and its relation to the Afrikan world – past, present as well as future – there are two observations which appear to reflect the relative under-development of the contemporary Afrikan world. The first is that despite an abundance of information on libation and a widespread living tradition, there is a paucity of academic and intellectual enquiry into this ritual. The second is that the study of Kemet has not yet been repositioned into the study of Afrika and the Afrikan world. The sole exception to the first observation appears to be the Right Reverend Dr. Peter Kwasi Sarpong's very brief text, of fifty pages (Sarpong 1996). It is the only scholarly work so far that makes libation its exclusive concern, though the ritual is attested by terms in Afrikan languages, numerous references in the sacred and secular literature – the oral and written texts of Afrika – as well as by the presence of this practice in contemporary Afrika and its world.

The popular presence of libation in the Afrikan world in historically recent times is reflected in the Afrikan creative imagination. A partial listing of Afrikan writers who wrote from a location on the continent should include Nwapa (1970), Ayi Kwei Armah (1975, 5-12, 136-7, 223, 263; 1979, 55-6, 161, 209-11), Elechi Amadi (1975), Flora Nwapa (1978), Chinua Achebe (1987) and Ben Okri (1991). The ritual also receives passing mention in numerous academic texts on Afrika and its communities abroad. A similar presence of libation in Afrikan communities abroad is registered in the work of such writers as Edward Kamau Brathwaite (1973, 89-99), Austin Clarke (2003, 337), Brenda Flanagan (2005, 178), Roy A. K. Heath (1978, 11) and, more recently, Lawrence Hill (2007, 360).

Libation is of course also present in the popular culture of Afrikans and so reflected in artistic works in other contemporary popular genres in the Afrikan world. In the process of socialising in Guyana and the Caribbean, sometimes someone may say 'Throw (or pour) one [i.e. a drink, a libation] for …', at which point is intoned the name of a loved one who has made her or his transition, or who is not physically present for some other reason, but who is present spiritually because they would have understood and agreed with the ritual and its meaning. Others who are around often join in these greetings to the Divinities, to the ancestors and to living relatives and friends who are absent, and to the symbolic orientation of the liquid. Sometimes, less often, the liquor is just poured out and consumed. In the villages and towns of Guyana, there will sometimes be threats to knock a drink of liquor out of the hand of anyone who dares to pour from a bottle that has not in this way been first offered to the Creator, the ancestors and others not physically present. Additionally, a spilt drink will invariably occasion enquiries about whether some of the liquor from that particular bottle had been poured (in libation) for 'unseen guests'. Sometimes the spilt liquor will occasion observations along the lines of 'Dem come foh dem own' – the unseen guests (i.e. the Spirits) have come to demand their drink (i.e. a libation). Unsurprisingly, the context and representation of this ritual in the living tradition of Afrikan Americans present striking similarities to its survival among Afrikans in the Caribbean.

This formula has been artfully extended in music to 'Play one for …', as in *kaisoes* such as 'Play One' (1979) by The Mighty Stalin (Leroy Caliste, later Black Stalin), a tribute to Winston Spree Simon, and the Mighty Sparrow's 'Tribute to Melody' (2000). Hip Hop from two of its leading exponents in inner city USA gives us, amongst others, 2Pac Shakur's deep and wonderfully descriptive 'Pour Out a Little Liquor' (2008) and the equally telling 'Just a Moment' from Nas (2008), which reflect the presence of libation in the folkways of Afrikans in the USA. Content analysis of the lyrics of these two songs establishes, without any doubt, that libation is an important part of the folk memory and popular culture of inner city USA. The following analysis is based upon the main elements identified in the definition of libation given above, that is, in the categories of thought, word and action.

The thought that instructed the audible word and visible

action is very clear. 2Pac mentions his best friend in jail, his cousin who died the year before, a death he still could not get over, and the 'so called Gs', that is, successful gangsters, who are heroes in the community. His purpose is to:

Reminisce about my niggaz, that's dead and gone
And now they buried, sometimes my eye still gets blurry
Cause I'm losin' all my homies and I worry.

Nas introduces this ritual in rap with a request for a moment of silence: 'Can we please have a moment of silence?' This request is in fact a demand for respect for the ritual and those whom he thereby memorialises. In effect, he creates a silent, peaceful space within the background of continuous violence against which the lyrics are set. This is a moment not merely of silence, but of power. Nas then goes on to invoke the spirit of absent beloved ones to whom the moment and the portions of liquor are dedicated:

That's for my niggaz doin' years in confinement
And for my soldiers who passed over, no longer living
That couldn't run whenever the reaper came to get 'em
Can we please pour out some liquor?
Symbolizin', let's take in time to consider that
Though our thugs ain't here, the love is here
And we gon' rep 'till slugs kill us here.

2Pac terms it reminiscing; Nas says that it is symbolising. In both lyrics the desire to remember and appreciate beloved ones who were not physically there, both dead and alive, but not physically present, give birth to the thoughts which instruct the word and the action. It is necessary to recall here, as we have seen above, that remembering and honouring those not there, both the dead and the absent living, is one of the expressed purposes of what we may call classical libation. The purpose of the ritual in Kemet five thousand years ago and the purpose in Afrikan American communities today is one and the same.

The word which announces these libations can hardly be separated from the ritual action. On the surface Nas' reference may be read as a respectful request, but in this context it has the power of a command. Hence, in both instances this word is a descriptive instruction. That instruction to pour out some liquor is repeatedly given throughout both lyrics, for in each case it is the emotional centre of the song and so a part of the refrain. Hence Nas asks, 'Can we please pour out some liquor?' and 2Pac instructs us to 'Pour out a little liquor!' 2Pac repeatedly contrasts the consumption of large amounts of liquor, of which he plainly disapproves, with this act of pouring out a little of the liquid in honour of those beloved not present, of which he certainly approves and promotes by repeatedly instructing us to do so.

Both lyrics contain the classic description of a libation in liquor, even though neither 2Pac nor Nas employs that term in a single instance. 'Pour out a little liquor' or 'pour out some liquor': not just any amount, but a little; not just anything, but liquor. These commands are strikingly similar to the ancient descriptive commands of 'pour libation' and 'pour water', which are frequently encountered in the literature of Kemet, and which are also popular currency among contemporary Afrikans on the continent. The vocabulary of libation displays a consistency from Ancient Egypt to modern Afrika and its enforced Diaspora.

The available evidence leads us to the conclusion that as enslaved Afrikans were transported abroad, chiefly to the Americas and the Caribbean, distance from the Afrikan wellspring grew and connections with the ritual and the diasporic understanding of it were generally lessened. We have seen that 2Pac and Nas do not have a name for the ritual. It is the same with Stalin and Sparrow and also informants in Dominica and Guyana (Blondel 2006; Nehusi 2006). Yet, in form and function they recall the ancient Afrikan practice of libation, of recognising and honouring the dead and others not physically present. This ritual is powerfully present in the folk memory and living tradition of the Diaspora. But it survives as a ritual which does not speak its name, or proclaim its origins too loudly. Yet even that is not the full picture, for the current movement towards reclamation of self-knowledge among Afrikans is a trend that embodies the very opposite to distance and loss of full understanding.

How did this ritual come to be distributed throughout the Afrikan world? It is not possible that this identical ritual has multiple origins among the innumerable places in which it has been attested. The facts point towards a common origin, most probably somewhere in the general area of the Nile Valley, with a known long residence in Kemet and eventual distribution mainly from this source, quite likely among others. Migrations to other parts of Afrika seem to be the chief candidate as the means of early distribution. Forced migration to the western hemisphere is certainly the means of distribution in the Americas and the Caribbean, for when a people migrate, or are forced to do so, they may be compelled to leave their material possessions behind. However, it is different with their cultural possessions. These cannot be easily separated from their owners; identity is not easily transformed (Nehusi 2001, 61).

World View
It was therefore not only the specific ritual of libation, or even only the offering complex of which it is a part, that Afrikans took with them on their migrations to people a continent and other parts of the world. There is abundant evidence that they also took a distinctive world view with them. It is a vision and explanation of the world that, like libation and much else, may be traced from ancient Kemet to modern Afrika. It is common in Afrikan communities throughout the world and constitutes one of the earliest statements of Pan Afrikanism. These cultural connections and continuities constitute a continuing testimony to this ideal and a powerful argument in the direction of the cultural unity of Afrika.

James Allen is quite explicit on how the people of Kemet

visualised their world:

'The ancient Egyptians divided their world into three classes of sentient beings: the gods (𓊹𓊹𓊹 *nṯrw*), the akhs (𓅜𓃀𓐍𓅱 *3ḫw*), and the living (𓋹𓈖𓐍𓅱 *ꜥnḫw*). The gods were the original forces and elements of nature, whose wills and actions governed all life. The akhs were the spirits of those who had died and made the successful transition to life after death. They do not live in some heavenly paradise, but in this world, among the living.' (Allen 2000, 31)

We may add here two other categories that were recognised, known and named by the people of Kemet – other animals besides humans, and inanimate things; in short, the physical environment. In this understanding of the cosmos, every being and thing in the universe, including lesser divinities, is brought into being by the Creator, 𓇋𓏏𓅓 *Itm(w)* (*Item(u)*), Atum (later variously Ra, Amun, Atum-Ra, Amun-Ra, Ptah, Khnum and the Aten), who is thus *nb tm* (*neb tem*), the 'Lord of Totality', and is at once both male and female (Allen 1988, 9-10, 60-3). Every being and thing was given a 𓂓 *k3* (*ka*), a 'life force', 'vital force' or 'energy' emanating from the Creator (Allen 1988, 14, 69; 2005, 11; Goelet 1994, 152).

This way of understanding and explaining the world arises directly from and is in fact a part of the creation stories of Kemet, perhaps the oldest known explanations of the universe. In this cosmology everything in the universe derived from the possibilities inherent in the 𓈖𓈖𓈖 *nnw* (*Nun*), or primordial waters, for the Nun is the oldest substance in the cosmos and contains all the possibilities of existence, that is, all reality everywhere that ever was, is and will be, all possible examples of anything; everything and its opposite as well as every possibility on the continuum between the two is included.

It should not surprise us that, with some developments and variations, the very same model of the cosmos exists among the contemporary successors of the people of Kemet, both on the continent of Afrika and in the numerous Afrikan communities abroad. Asante and Abarry assert that '[t]he ancient African along the Nile River was in contact with the spiritual world of the ancestors in ways that are similar to the expressions of ancestral relations found in African societies throughout the continent' (Asante and Abarry 1996, 12). To this we may add the many Afrikan communities abroad where this and other aspects of Afrika are lived today. The reason for this tremendous continuity is not difficult to discern. We turn again to Asante and Abarry, who explain that as Afrikan culture and society developed and became more complex and distant, in both space and time, from its ancient sources in the Nile Valley, 'new interpretations, revelations, and permutations occurred', but that 'in all cases the ideas of [Afrikan spirituality] kept the societies close to the fundamental principles of harmony between humans, humans and the environment, and humans and the spirit world' (Asante and Abarry 1996, 59).

The details vary among different groups of Afrikans, but all who retain Afrikan culture continue the ancient Egyptian concept of the world, which is clearly the model of John Mbiti's division of the contemporary Afrikan world into five categories:
1. God as the ultimate explanation of the genius and sustenance of both [hu]man[s] and all things;
2. Spirits being made up of superhuman beings and the spirits of [humans] who died a long time ago;
3. [Hu]man[s] including human beings who are alive and those about to be born;
4. Animals and plants, or the rest of biological life;
5. Phenomena and objects without biological life [i.e. the rest of the physical environment].
(Mbiti 1988, 16; see Figure 9)

The Creator (God)	The Spirit World or the Unseen World
Lesser Divinities (or Gods)	
	(Spiritual Relationships)
Ancestors and other Spirits	
Humans	The Natural World or the Seen World
Other Animals	

Figure 9. The divine cosmic order.

Mbiti goes further, telling us that 'in addition to the five categories, there seems to be a force, power or energy permeating the whole universe'. God is the origin and 'ultimate controller' of this force, but the spirits and certain humans also have access to it' (Mbiti 1988, 16). Sarpong's explanation of this arrangement is irresistible: 'The divinities and the ancestors exercise executive powers only in as far as he permits them' (Sarpong 1996, 2). This 'force, power or energy' that is in everything is the same as the *ka* of Kemet (Allen 2005, 11; Faulkner 1969, 247), the *kra* of the Akans in Ghana and Ivory Coast and most Afrikans in Suriname, and also the same as the *asé* of the *Orisas* (Orishas) that are propitiated by Afrikans (and sometimes by non-Afrikans) in Yorubaland. This very spiritual system, which features the Orishas, is called Orisha in Trinidad, where the same force is also propitiated, as it is among adherents to *Voodoo*, *Candomblé* and *Santería* in Haiti, Cuba, Jamaica, Brasil, the USA and other places, and to Kumina in Jamaica. It is also the same as the *ike* and *chi* of the Igbos (Achebe 1998, 67-72) and *ntu* of Afrikans in central and southern parts of the continent, the so-called Bantu, from whom this concept has been translated as 'vital force' (Temples 1998, 429-34). Odudoye provides even further evidence of these connections, showing a linguistic link between this *ka* in the *Medew Netjer* and *chi* in Igbo, and noting that the likely influence is from the Ancient Egyptians to the Igbos, not *vice versa* (Odudoye 1996, 129).

Further close similarities and continuities, in both form

and function, may be noted with the ancient Nile Valley spiritual system, though it is not appropriate to burden this text with much of the details. For example, like Atum, then Ra and Atum-Ra of Kemet, who are the sole source of *ka*, Olodumare, also known as Olorun, the supreme divinity of the Yorubas, is the sole source of *asé*, which s/he parcels out to the *Orisas*. Again like Atum, Ra and Atum-Ra, Olodumare is both male and female, dwells in a place that is remote from human habitation, and is the Creator of the world (Canizares 1993; Tyldesley 2004, 11, 13). Among the Igbos the Creator is *Chukwu* (Great Chi) or *Chineke* (*chi[nke]naeke*, i.e. *chi* who creates) who also dwells far away from humanity (Awolalu and Dopamu 1979, 56-64, 214-5; Ogbaa 1992, 10) and is a gender neutral divinity. The archetype of the supreme divinity that dwells in a place remote from humans, a retreat from the human world usually brought about as a direct result of some human weakness, may be encountered in the Myth of Libation examined above. The lesser divinities in each of these three expressions of the Afrikan spiritual system are each a specific aspect of the Creator, either as a personification of a principle or a natural force or, less often, a deified ancestor. The same or very similar conceptualisation of the world is extant among Afrikans everywhere and is either clearly stated or clearly implied in studies of the Afrikan world (see for example, Awolalu and Dopamu 1979, 70-4; Lucas 1948, 34, 119; Sarpong 1996, 1-5, amongst numerous others). Ayi Kwei Armah, a foremost spokesperson of the Afrikan story, says definitively that '[t]his outlook is common to African society everywhere' (Armah 2006a, 195) and that '[n]o African society anywhere could find this outlook anything but familiar' (Armah 2006b, 12).

In Kemet the maintenance of cosmic relations by each individual was examined at death. The soul of the deceased was required to make a series of forty-two declarations affirming that while on earth it did not infringe any of these relations among the Creator, the lesser divinities, humans past, present and future, and the environment. These are known today as the Declarations of Innocence, which may be found in Chapter 125 of The Book of Going Forth by Day. The Declarations are the intellectual basis of both the good moral life in Kemet and the Ten Commandments in Christianity. Hence the very world view which influenced Afrikans in Kemet still holds sway in many parts of the Afrikan world today, directly through its continuation among Afrikans who practice their culture, and in some ways indirectly through Christianity.

In this world view it was, it is and it will always be necessary to maintain this divine cosmic order, or (variation) *mꜣꜥt* (*maat*), a concept first encountered and articulated in Kemet, where it was also rendered as the feather and personified as the female divinity of the same name: , also rendered . Interpretations vary. This concept has been variously translated as truth, justice, righteousness, order, balance, harmony and reciprocity (Adams 1994; Allen 1988, 25-7; Carruthers 1984, 54-6; Karenga 1991, 352-95; 2004; Obenga 2004 189-93, 203, 220-2). However, these terms merely describe some of the parameters of the concept, which is elastic and simultaneously inclusive of all of them (Karenga 2004). The opposite of Maat is (variation) *isft* (*isfet*). Logically, this is the absence of Maat, the lack of truth, balance, justice, righteousness, harmony or reciprocity. Such a condition must mean wrongdoing, evil, disorder and chaos.

The maintenance of this order, that is, all these relationships, has always been achieved by a periodic show of this respect – or by making appeasement and restoration when something has gone wrong. And things go wrong usually through some inappropriate action by humans. Respect and appeasement of the divine forces were both achieved through making offerings, by sacrifice and by pouring libation (see Abarry 1996, 92-3; Armah 2006a, 23-4; 2006b, 14; Asante and Abarry 1996, 61; Mbiti 1988, 9, amongst others).

Hence everyone who has poured libation or will pour libation, whether in Kemet five thousand years ago or anywhere else in the Afrikan world then or since, has done so and will do so ultimately for the identical reason: the maintenance of order and balance within individual selves, families, clans, communities, nation and the cosmos. Respect for and understanding of this cosmic order confers order, meaning, purpose, value and motivation on the Afrikan way of life. It was the same in Kemet. It is the same today. It will be the same wherever Afrikans practice Afrikan culture.

Conclusion
The earliest evidence of libation is via its ritual context of offerings at Nabta Playa and Qustul. Both of these are to the south of Kemet, the direction of inner Afrika from which Kemet received most of its people and its culture. But it is in Kemet that details of this ritual begin to abound and our understanding of it increases. Today this ritual is distributed throughout the Afrikan world. The same may be said of the offering complex to which it belongs and the world view that instructed these rituals. These facts announce a symbiotic relationship between Kemet (Ancient Egypt) and the rest of the Afrikan world, from ancient to modern times. Consideration of the ritual of libation adds to our growing knowledge and understanding of the true nature of Kemet and its connections and continuities with the Afrikan world of which it has been a part. Kemet is in Afrika as well as of Afrika; that is, Kemet is an intimate aspect of Afrika geographically as well as culturally.

Libation seems logical and makes complete sense only within the Afrikan cultural context. The reason for this is not difficult to discern, for libation was conceived within this cultural context and always belonged there. There is an abundance of evidence which shows that this ritual was widely practiced in Kemet. This evidence includes indigenous terms in the language, the sacred literature of the land, the foundation myth of the ritual, the social custom of the people of Kemet, and the specific professional ritual practice of scribes in honour and remembrance of Imhotep, one of the greatest of their fraternity. Further, libation and the general complex of offerings to which it belongs were instructed by a specific world view that was evident in Kemet and is evident in the contemporary Afrikan world. The inescapable conclusion must be that Kemet belongs to the identical cultural context and world view as the Afrikan world that exists today.

Another conclusion is therefore logical and so necessary. Kemet cannot be properly understood, or understood at all, except in its Afrikan cultural context, and our understanding of Afrika itself, its true achievements and its future possibilities, will be incomplete – and impoverished – without an understanding of Kemet as an example of humanity's achievement in Afrikan skin. The study of Kemet must be repositioned into the study of Afrika and the Afrikan world if any of these entities – Kemet, Afrika or the Afrikan world – is to be properly understood.

References

Achebe, C. 1987 [1958]. *Things Fall Apart*. London, Heinemann.

—1998. 'Chi' in Igbo Cosmology. In E. C. Eze (ed.), *African Philosophy: An Anthology*, 67-72. Malden, Mass. and Oxford, Blackwell Publishers.

—1990. The Song of Ourselves. *New Statesman and Society* (9th February), 30-2.

—2000. Africa's Tarnished Name, in H. Wylie and B. Lindfors (eds.), 13-24. *Multiculturalism and Hybridity in African Literatures. Selected Proceedings from the 1998 African Literature Association Conference*. Trenton, N.J., Africa World Press.

Allen, J. P. 1988. *Genesis in Egypt: The Philosophy of Ancient Egyptian Creation Accounts*. Yale Egyptological Studies 2. New Haven, Connecticut, Yale University Press.

—2000. *Middle Egyptian: An Introduction to the Language and Culture of Hieroglyphs*. Cambridge and New York, Cambridge University Press.

—2005. Introduction. In R. O. Faulkner. *The Ancient Egyptian Book of the Dead: The Book of Going Forth by Day*, 11-16. New York, Barnes and Noble.

Allen, T. G. 1974. *The Book of the Dead or Going Forth by Day: Ideas of the Ancient Egyptians Concerning the Hereafter as Expressed In their Own Terms*. Studies in Ancient Oriental Civilization 37. Chicago, University of Chicago Press.

Amadi, E. 1975. *The Great Pond*. London, Heinemann.

Armah, A. K. 1975. *Fragments*. London, Heinemann.

—1979. *The Healers*. London, Heinemann.

—2006a. *The Eloquence of the Scribes: A Memoir on the Sources and Resources of African Literature*. Popenguine, Senegal, Per Ankh.

—2006b. Who Were the Ancient Egyptians? *New African* 450 (April), 19.

Asante, M. K. and Abarry, A. S. (eds.) 1996. *African Intellectual Heritage: A Book of Sources*. Philadelphia, Temple University Press.

Assmann, J. 1997. *Moses the Egyptian: The Memory of Egypt in Western Monotheism*. Cambridge, Mass. and London, Harvard University Press.

—2005 (trans. D. Lorton). *Death and Salvation in Ancient Egypt*. Ithaca and London, Cornell University Press.

Awolalu, J. O. and Dopamu, P. A. 1979. *West African Traditional Religion*. Ibadan, Nigeria, Onibonoje Press and Book Industries (Nig.) Ltd.

Bernal, M. 1987, 1991. *Black Athena: The Afroasiatic Roots of Classical Civilization*. Vols. I and II. London, Free Association Books.

Blondel, E. 2006 (9th October). Interview with Mr Sion Adams (100 years old). Colihaut, Dominica.

—2006 (9th October). Interview with Mr Albert Severin (87 years old). Colihaut, Dominica.

—2006 (9th October). Interview with Mr Radcliffe St. Louis (91 years old). Colihaut, Dominica.

—2006 (10th October). Interview with Ms Sylvia Thomas (76 years old). Colihaut, Dominica.

DuBois, W. E. B. 1965. *The World and Africa: An Enquiry into the Part which Africa has played in World History*. New York, International Publishers.

Brathwaite, E. K. 1973. *The Arrivants*. Oxford, Oxford University Press.

Brunson, J. E. 1991. *Before the Unification: Predynastic Egypt. An African-centric View*. DeKalb, IL., The Author.

Budge, E. A. Wallis. 1909. *The Liturgy of Funerary Offerings*. Manchester, Ayer Publishing.

—1911. *Osiris and the Egyptian Resurrection. Illustrated after Drawings from Egyptian Papyri and Monuments*. London, P. L. Warner.

—1967. *The Egyptian Book of the Dead (The Papyrus of Ani)*. New York, Dover Publications.

—1973. *Osiris and the Egyptian Resurrection*. Vol. I. New York, Dover Publications.

Caliste, L. (The Mighty Stalin, later Black Stalin) 1979. Play One. *To The Caribbean Man*. LP. Wizards MCR-147, Makossa M2342.

—1979. Play One. *Play One/Caribbean Unity*. Wizards MCR-147.

—1991. Play One. *Roots, Rock, Soca*. Rounder C-5038.

Canizares, R. 1993. *Walking with the Night: The Afro-Cuban World of Santeria.* Rochester, Vermont, Destiny Books.

Carruthers, J. 1984. *Essays in Ancient Egyptian Studies.* Los Angeles, University of Sankore Press.

Celenko, T. (ed.) 1996. *Egypt in Africa.* Bloomington, Indiana, Indianapolis Museum of Art/Indiana University Press.

Chappaz, J.-L. and Guarnori, S. 1983. Deux tables d'offrandes et un bassin à libations au Musée d'Art et d'Historie à Genève. *Chronique d'Égypte* 58, Fascicule 115-6, 73-82.

Clarke, A. 2003. *The Polished Hoe.* Kingston, Jamaica, Ian Randle Publishers.

Clayton, P. A. 1994. *Chronicle of the Pharaohs.* London, Thames and Hudson.

Delia, D. 1992. The Refreshing Water of Osiris. *Journal of the American Research Center in Egypt* 29, 181-90.

Diop, C. A. 1974. *The African Origin of Civilization: Myth or Reality?* New York, Lawrence Hill and Company.

Erman, A. and Grapow, H. 1982 [1926-1953]. *Wörterbuch der ägyptischen Sprache.* Vols. I-V. Berlin, Akademie Verlag.

Faulkner, R. O. 1962. *A Concise Dictionary of Middle Egyptian.* Oxford, Griffith Institute.

—1969. *The Ancient Egyptian Pyramid Texts.* Warminster, Aris and Phillips.

—1994a. *The Ancient Egyptian Coffin Texts.* Vols. I-III. Warminster, Aris and Phillips.

—1994b. *The Egyptian Book of the Dead: The Book of Going Forth by Day.* San Francisco, Chronicle Books.

—2005. *The Ancient Egyptian Book of the Dead.* London, British Museum Press; New York, Barnes and Noble.

Finch, C. 1994. Nile Genesis: Continuity of Culture from the Great Lakes to the Delta. In I. Van Sertima (ed.), *Egypt, Child of Africa. Journal of African Civilizations* 12, 34-54. New Brunswick, Transaction Publishers.

Flanagan, B. 2005. *You Alone Are Dancing.* Ann Arbor, Michigan, University of Michigan Press.

Francisco, S. (The Mighty Sparrow) 2000 (Re-issue). 'Play One for Melo', Track 6 in *Down Memory Lane.* Millennium Series.

Freud, S. 1985. *The Origins of Religion: Totem and Taboo, Moses and Monotheism and Other Works.* The Penguin Freud Library, Vol. 13. London, Penguin.

Gardiner, A. 1902-03. Imhotep and the Scribe's Libation. *Zeitschrift für ägyptische Sprache und Altertümskunde* 40, 146.

Goelet, O. Jr. 1994. A Commentary on the Corpus of Literature and Tradition which constitutes *The Book of Going Forth by Day.* In R. O. Faulkner, *The Egyptian Book of the Dead: The Book of Going Forth by Day*, 137-71. San Francisco, Chronicle Books.

Hart, G. 1990. *Egyptian Myths.* London, British Museum Press.

Heath, R. A. K. 1978. *The Murderer.* London, Allison and Busby Ltd.

Herodotus. 1972 (trans. A de Sélincourt, rev. A. R. Burn). *The Histories.* London, Penguin Classics.

Hertaus, J. "Nabta Playa", http://www.mnsu.edu/emuseum/archaeology/sites/africa/nabtaplaya.html [Accessed 6th April, 2007]

Hill, L. 2007. *The Book of Negroes.* Toronto, HarperCollins.

Homer. 1990 (trans. R. Fagles). *The Iliad.* London, Penguin Classics.

Jacq, C. 1985 (trans. J. M. Davis). *Egyptian Magic.* Warminster, Aris and Phillips.

James, G. G. M. 1954. *Stolen Legacy.* New York, The Philosophical Library.

Janssen, R. M and Janssen, J. J. 1996. *Getting Old in Ancient Egypt.* London, Rubicon Press.

Karenga, M. (ed.) 1984. *Selections from the Husia: Sacred Wisdom of Ancient Egypt.* Los Angeles, Kawaida Publications.

—1989. Towards a Sociology of Maatian Ethics: Literature and Context. In I. Van Sertima (ed.), *Egypt Revisited. Journal of African Civilizations* 10, 352-95. New Brunswick, Transaction Publishers.—2004. *Maat: The Moral Ideal in Ancient Egypt: A Study in Classical African Ethics.* New York and London, Routledge.

Kaster, J. 1995. *The Wisdom of Ancient Egypt: Writings from the Time of the Pharaoh.* London, Michael O'Mara Books.

Lesko, L. H. 1991. Ancient Egyptian Cosmogonies and Cosmology. In B. E. Shafer (ed.), *Religion in Ancient Egypt: Gods, Myths and Personal Practice*, 88-122. Ithaca and London, University of Cornell Press.

Lichtheim, M. 1976. *Ancient Egyptian Literature, Vol. II: The New Kingdom.* Berkeley, Los Angeles and London, University of California Press.

Lucas, J. O. 1948. *The Religion of the Yorubas.* Lagos, CMS Bookshop.

Mbiti, J. 1988. *African Religions and Philosophy.* London, Heinemann.

Nas. 'Just a Moment', *Street's Disciple.* anysonglyrics@hotmail.com [Accessed 1st May 2008].

Nehusi, K. 2001. From 𓏏𓏤𓊹 *Medew Netjer* To Ebonics. In C. Crawford (ed.), *Ebonics and Language Education of African Ancestry Students,* 56-122. New York and London, Sankofa World Publishers.

—2006 (6th May). Telephone Interview with Ms. Patsy Russell (54 years old). Toronto, Canada.

—2006 (7th October). Telephone Interview with Mrs. Vera Venture (82 years old). New York, USA.

—2006 (19th November). Telephone Interview with Ms. Lorine James (44 years old). New York, USA.

—2006 (20th November). Telephone Interview with Ms. Voi James (68 years old). Queenstown Village, Essequibo Coast, Guyana.

—2006 (20th November). Telephone Interview with Ms. Evelyn James (40 years old). New York, USA.

—2006 (22nd November). Telephone Interview with Ms. Eunice Walcott (72 years old). Queenstown Village, Essequibo Coast, Guyana.

Nwapa, F. 1970. *Idu.* London, Heinemann.

—1978. *Efuru.* London, Heinemann.

—1992. *Never Again.* Trenton, N.J., Africa World Press.

Obenga, T. 1989. African Philosophy of the Pharaonic Period (2780-330 B.C.). In I. Van Sertima (ed.), *Egypt Revisited. Journal of African Civilizations* 10, 286-324. New Brunswick, Transaction Publishers.

—1992 (trans. A. Sheik). *Ancient Egypt and Black Africa: A Student's Handbook for the Study of Ancient Egypt in Philosophy, Linguistics and Gender Relations.* London, Karnak House.

—1995-1996. La parenté égyptienne: considérations sociologiques. *Ankh: Revue d'Egyptologie et des Civilisations Africaines* 4-5, 139-83.

—2004 (trans. A. K. Armah). *African Philosophy: The Pharaonic Period: 2780-330 BC.* Popenguine, Senegal, Per Ankh.

Oduyoye, M. 1996. *Words and Meaning in Yoruba Religion.* London, Karnak House.

Ogbaa, K. 1992. *Gods, Oracles and Divination: Folkways in Chinua Achebe's Novels.* Trenton, N.J., Africa World Press.

Okri, B. 1991. *The Famished Road.* London, Vintage.

Sarpong, Rt. Rev. Dr. P. K. 1996. *Libation.* Accra, Anansesem Publications.

Schäfer, H. 1898. Eine altägyptische Schreibersitte. *Zeitschrift für ägyptische Sprache und Altertümskunde* 36, 147-8.

Shakur, 2Pac. 'Pour Out A Little Liquor', on www.youtube.com [Accessed 10th May 2008].

Smith, M. 1993. *The Liturgy of Opening the Mouth for Breathing.* Oxford, Griffith Institute.

Tempels, P. 1998. Bantu Ontology. In E. C. Eze (ed.), *African Philosophy: An Anthology*, 429-34. Malden, Mass. and Oxford, Blackwell Publishers.

Thomas, A. P. 2001. *Egyptian Gods and Myths.* Princes Risborough, Shire Publications.

Tyldesley, J. 2004. *Tales from Ancient Egypt.* Bolton (UK), Rutherford Press.

Van Sertima, I. (ed.) 1989. *Egypt Revisited. Journal of African Civilizations* 10. New Brunswick, Transaction Publishers.

—(ed.) 1994. *Egypt, Child of Africa. Journal of African Civilizations* 12. New Brunswick, Transaction Publishers.

Wilkinson, J. G. 1994. *The Ancient Egyptians: Their Life and Customs.* Vol. I. London, Senate.

Wilkinson, R. H. 2000. *The Complete Temples of Ancient Egypt.* London, Thames and Hudson.

Williams, B. 1985. The Lost Pharaohs of Nubia. In I. Van Sertima (ed.), *Nile Valley Civilizations: Proceedings of the Nile Valley Conference, Atlanta, Sept. 26-30. Journal of African Civilizations* 6, 90-104. New Brunswick, Transaction Publishers.

—1996. The Qustul Incense Burner and the Case for a Nubian Origin of Ancient Egyptian Kingship. In T. Celenko (ed.), *Egypt in Africa*, 95-7. Bloomington, Indiana, Indianapolis Museum of Art/Indiana University Press.

Williams, C. 1976. *The Destruction of Black Civilization: Great Issues of a Race from 4500 B.C. to 2000 A.D.* Chicago, Third World Press.

Wilson, J. A. 1969 (Third Edition). Deliverance of Mankind from Destruction. In J. B. Pritchard (ed.), *Ancient Near Eastern Texts Relating to the Old Testament 10.* Princeton, N.J., University of Princeton Press.

Yellin, J. W. 1982. Abaton-Style Milk Libation at Meroe, in N. B. Millet and A. L. Kelley (eds.), *Proceedings of the Third International Meroitic Conference, Toronto, 1977. Meroitica* 6, 151-5.

Meroitic Worship of Isis at Philae

Solange Bumbaugh
University of Chicago

Abstract
This paper will explore Meroitic pilgrimage and worship at the Temple of Isis, located on Philae Island in Upper Egypt. Unlike most Egyptian temples, the temple on Philae is oriented towards the south, towards Nubia. Philae temple seems to have been constructed with Nubian worshippers in mind. Later, Meroites (the kingdom flourished from *c.* 300 BC-AD 300) came as pilgrims to worship Isis. This paper will consider the inscriptions left on the walls of the temples on Philae. The inscriptions span the period from the 1st to the 3rd century AD. The Meroites left their inscriptions in three languages: Demotic, Greek and Meroitic. They mention the festivals in which the Meroites participated as well as the rich gifts of gold that they brought from their king. The principal festivals mentioned were Khoiak, the celebration of Osiris' resurrection, as well as Isis' Feast of Entry. Taken together, the Demotic and Meroitic inscriptions describe a way of worship that not only preserved traditional Egyptian forms of piety but also expressed other traditions, those of the peoples further south in Africa. While Egypt began its slow conversion to Christianity, the Meroites preserved and maintained traditional worship of the great Goddess Isis in her pre-eminent temple at Philae.

Keywords: Ancient Egyptian religion, Festival of Entry, Isis, inscriptions, Khoiak, Meroë, Meroitic religion, Osiris, Philae.

Introduction
Unlike most Egyptian temples, the temple of Isis on Philae Island is oriented towards the south, towards Nubia. It is located at the First Cataract that has served as the border between Egypt and Nubia for most of Egypt's history. This extraordinary temple has a documented history of pre-Christian pilgrimage that spans a period of 700 years – from the Ptolemaic period (332-30 BC) to the 5th century AD. Worshippers from Nubia came to Philae as pilgrims throughout the entire period. This paper will consider the significance of Philae and the cult of Isis for the Nubians who were actively involved as priests, worshippers and financial supporters of the traditional cult well into the early Christian period. Through the numerous inscriptions carved by the Nubian worshippers on the temple walls at Philae, we can discern an African perspective on the cult of Isis, a unique perspective that is often neglected in general studies of the temples of Philae.

While the existing Isis temple at Philae was constructed under Ptolemy II (285-246 BC), blocks from a small kiosk built under Psamtek II (595-589 BC) have been recovered. Blocks from a temple built under Amasis/Ahmose II (570-526 BC) were discovered reused in the lower courses of some columns and in the second pylon. Archaeological remains have been recovered that indicate that an earlier community predated any of these constructions. Its pottery is unlike that found elsewhere in Egypt and shows the greatest affinity to Kushite pottery (Haeny 1985, 201). Possibly associated with this community is the granite altar dedicated to Amun of Takompso (Maharraga, the southern limit of the Dodecaschoenus 'border region' located between Egyptian and Meroitic territory) and decorated with the cartouches of Taharqa (690-664 BC). The altar is the earliest evidence of religious activity at Philae and stood in the southeast corner of the forecourt of the temple of Isis (Griffith 1931, 128). King Taharqa was the penultimate ruler of Egypt's 25th Dynasty, known as the Kushite period. A Kushite presence is next attested at Philae when the Kushite king Arqamani seized Philae during the Upper Egyptian rebellion against Ptolemy V at the end of the 3rd century BC. His cartouches can be found in the temple of Arensnuphis also located on the island. The Meroites ruled the Middle Nile region from their capital at Meroë. Their empire stretched from the south of the Sixth Cataract (near present-day Khartoum) north to the border with Egypt at Aswan and lasted from approximately 300 BC until AD 300. The Meroitic Empire coincided with foreign rule in Egypt, first by the Ptolemaic kings and then by Rome. The area of the Dodecaschoenus, the 12 *schoeni* or 120 kilometres from Philae to Maharraga, served as a buffer zone between the sometimes friendly, sometimes antagonistic rulers of Roman Egypt and Meroë.

This paper will focus on pilgrimage to Philae as it is documented in the adoration graffiti, or *proskynema*, left by the Meroites. Meroitic pilgrims left inscriptions in a variety of languages throughout the Dodecaschoenus, primarily in Demotic, but also in Greek, and Meroitic (Griffith 1912a). These pilgrims came to Philae as priest and 'agents'[1] of Isis, but also as political envoys who served as diplomats for their king in Meroë in his dealings with the Roman rulers of Egypt. Inscriptions attributed to Meroites comprise twenty-seven written in Demotic, two in Greek and thirty-one inscribed in the Meroitic cursive script.

The Meroites at Philae Temple
The two Meroitic scripts were based on Egyptian scripts: formal hieroglyphs as well as a cursive script based on Demotic. Both the hieroglyphic and cursive Meroitic scripts were alphabetic. It was the cursive script that was used to inscribe prayers of the faithful on the walls of the

---

[1] The Meroite title 'perite' (Egyptian *prt*) designated a financial representative of the temple estate. This title was often combined with priestly titles, most frequently with that of 'qeren' for which we have no exact translation, but which may indicate that it was a royal appointment.

temples of the Dodecaschoenus. Cursive Meroitic consists of 15 consonant signs, four syllabic signs and four vowel signs (Figure 1). Because this writing system was alphabetic, it appears that literacy was quite widespread amongst the large ruling class. Meroitic inscriptions have been found throughout the Kingdom of Meroë.

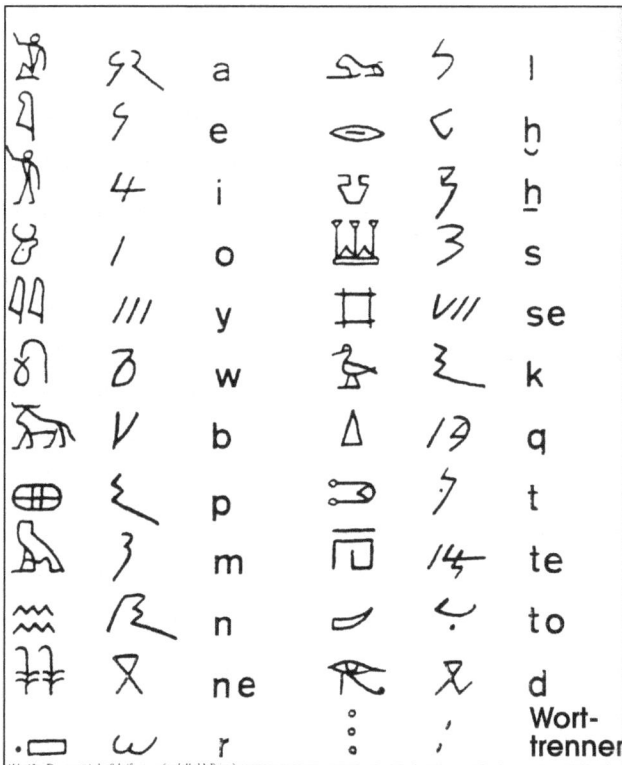

Figure 1. Hieroglyphic and cursive Meroitic script (after Hintze 1978, 93).

In the temple complex at Philae, the bulk of graffiti inscribed by Meroites is clustered in three areas: inscriptions in both Demotic and Meroitic are concentrated in the Birth House and on the Gate of Hadrian (Figure 2). This gate, located to the west of the temple of Isis, led from the Osiris chapel toward the point of departure for Biga Island, the burial site of Osiris, Isis' consort or 'husband'. The third important group of inscriptions is located in the Meroitic Chamber opposite the Birth House and between the two pylons.

While Meroites are clearly designated as prophets and agents of Isis, Meroitic pilgrims seem to have made annual visits to Philae timed to coincide with two festivals. The dated graffiti left by Meroites were dedicated either in the month of Khoiak or during the Festival of Entry. Khoiak was the fourth month of the season of inundation and lasted from the 27th November to the 26th December. This month marked the end of the Nile flood and so the end of the period of sowing crops. Because the Osiris cult was intimately linked with the fertility of the land, Osiris' funeral and triumphant rebirth were celebrated at this time with the hope that it would ensure the continued fertility of the land. The rites performed in this period re-enacted the funeral of Osiris.

The culmination of the Khoiak festival was the ferrying over of Isis to Biga Island on the 22nd day of Khoiak to bury her husband. Osiris was revived eight days later and this victory over death was celebrated by the ceremonial erecting of the Djed pillar, a symbol of eternity.

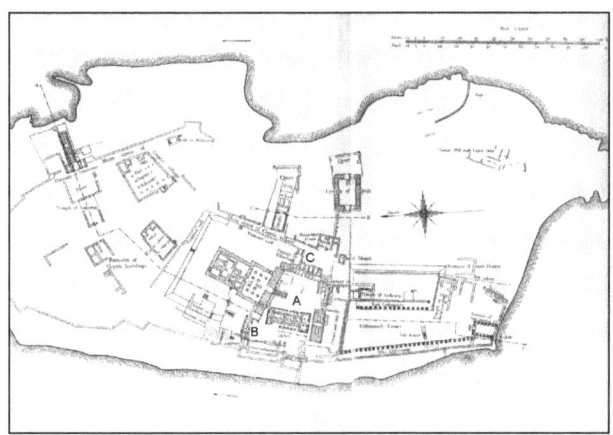

Figure 2. Map of Philae, showing the Birth House (A), the Gate of Hadrian (B) and the location of the Meroitic Chamber (C) (after Griffith 1912b, pl. XVII).

Three of the inscriptions left by Meroites are dated during this month. Philae Inscription 403, found in the temple of Imhotep, contains the prayer of Weyegete, a seventh generation member of the Meroitic priestly family, Wayekiye. He served as both a priest and an official at Philae as well as serving as an official of the king at Meroë. This inscription is dated to day 11 of Khoiak, states his titles and requests the blessing of Isis.

Philae Inscription 449, found on a loose block, appears to have sustained much damage and contains numerous lacunae. The author, Pakhom, mentions celebrating a 'feast' (wme.t) on day nine of Khoiak. He prays to Isis to grant him strength so that he may perform his services of work. Pakhom mentions that he has come together with others and that they have made the 'payment', as Griffith translates šty. This is the one instance of this word found in the Demotic inscriptions, according to Griffith's index of the inscription vocabulary. In Erichsen's *Glossar* (1954, 528) we find that šty is a late form of šd that has the meaning 'to feed, nourish, support', along with the additional meaning of 'to suckle' that was found in earlier New Kingdom usage (*Wb* IV, 564). This verb would have been used to describe the way a wet nurse suckled a child or a goddess suckled the king; it also conveyed the concept of support that a child would receive from an adoptive parent. It seems that the term 'payment' might misconstrue the actions of the Meroites by portraying them as offering tribute when they may instead have viewed themselves as the caretakers or financial supporters of the traditional religion celebrated at Philae. This fact is certainly borne out by the next inscription. Philae Inscription 416 was also dedicated in the month of Khoiak. It is the longest known Demotic inscription and describes two separate visits made by Pasan, an envoy of the Meroitic king to Rome, *c*. AD 253. Pasan's inscription also mentions that a feast was held. This lengthy graffito enumerates all of the costly offerings brought by the Meroites to the goddess of Philae. Pasan tells us that his king ordered him to measure out 10 talents (money) for the local priests and their daughters. The king also ordered that a party, consisting of festivals and banquets, be thrown for the entire district. On Pasan's second mission to Philae, also described in the graffito, he mentions the 'honours' the temple priests did for him upon his arrival. Next he says, 'We made our 'collections' (*swhe.w*) in exchange for the breath of life for our Lord'. This word Griffith translates with a questions mark and notes in his index of inscription vocabulary that it only appears in this text and in Philae Inscription 411, also left by a Meroite. The many pounds of gold brought by the highest officials of the Meroitic kingdom were fashioned into gold cult objects including a sistrum for Isis, and the *wšb*-cup, or situla, of gold sent by King Tequereramani. These cult objects would have been used during the celebration of Khoiak as well as during the Feast of Entry.

Because the bulk of the dated demotic inscriptions left by Egyptians at Philae were dedicated in the month of Khoiak, we know that the Meroites would not have been the only visitors to the temple at this time. This would have made Khoiak an important time to convene with Egyptians for political negotiations. The busy annual festivities period would also have allowed the Meroites to display their wealth and powerful support of the priesthood at Philae. This might explain why Pasan, the envoy of Meroë to Rome, would have been present in Philae at this time.

Another rite that held great importance for the Meroites was the Festival of Entry. The festival enacted a visit by Isis to the Abaton ('forbidden place') on Biga Island in order to pour milk and water libations for her husband Osiris. Two Ptolemaic decrees carved on Hadrian's Gate describe the milk libations to be offered to Osiris (Junker 1913). The importance of the milk offerings is underscored by the numerous reliefs and inscriptions dealing with milk that have been carved on the walls of the temple near these decrees. The Festival of Entry would have consisted of transporting the cult statue of Isis over to Biga Island at the start of each of the three 10-day weeks where the goddess could witness the presentation of offerings and milk libations for her dead husband. This celebration does not appear frequently in Demotic inscriptions, but seems to have been particularly important for the Meroites. A reference to the festival appears in two Philae graffiti located on the Gate of Hadrian. It also appears in two inscriptions (Dakka 30 and 33) left by members of the Wayekiye family at the temple of Dakka, located further south in the Dodecaschoenus. The two Philae inscriptions are Philae 411 and Philae 421. Both these inscriptions describe ferrying the shrine of Isis across the river to Biga Island to perform many acts of piety. These inscriptions were dedicated in the early to mid 3rd century AD, at the height of Meroitic involvement at Philae.

The author of Philae Inscription 421, Wayekiye A, happens to be the father of Hornakhtyotef II who is the author of Dakka 30, the other inscription to mention the Festival of Entry. Both men served as royal astronomer and magician and performed the Festival of Entry for Isis at Dakka. Here we see clearly the hereditary nature of the position of Meroitic royal astronomer in Nubia. Hornakhtyotef I accompanied his son, Wayekiye A to perform the rites of the Festival of Entry for Isis at Philae. Wayekiye A's son, Hornakhtyotef II later performed a similar rite for Isis in the temple of Dakka further south in the Dodecaschoenus. Another similarity between the inscriptions is that they are carved on a west-facing wall of the temple overlooking a body of water. At Philae this body of water separates the island of Philae from the island of Biga, the burial place of Osiris. Although the festival was to be performed at the beginning of every week, it appears that the Meroites came once a year to perform its rites. Most likely, the gilding of the statue of Isis would have happened during the Meroites' annual celebration of the festival. The presentation of gold along with the working of it by Meroitic gold workers seems to comprise a large part of the offerings made by these priests and pilgrims. Several inscriptions mention working the gold offerings into libation vessels and cult instruments, as well as the gilding of divine statues. In Philae Inscription 416, the Meroitic envoy Pasan records a total donation of 16.5 pounds of gold that were then fashioned into cult objects for Isis!

Other religious rites are described in the graffito of Tami, a Meroitic tax collector at the temple of Isis. He states that he measured oil for the illumination of Isis, presumably for lamps. He procured oil, loaves of bread and incense for the festival procession. In addition, Tami planted persea trees on the Abaton on Biga Island, on Philae and outside the town. Additionally, he applied pitch to the bark of Isis in order to re-caulk it. All of these duties can be seen to relate to the annual Festival of Entry that included the procession of Isis to the Abaton to offer libations to Osiris.

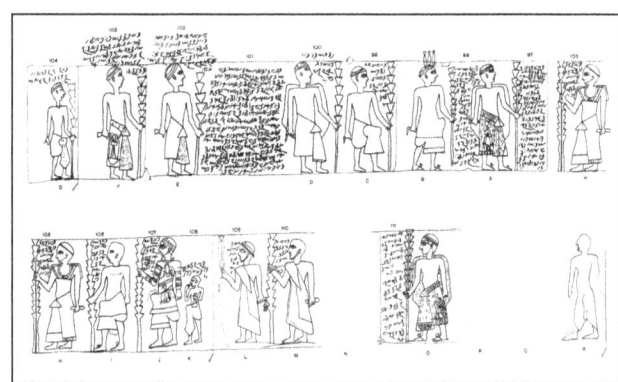

Figure 3. Images and inscriptions from the Meroitic Chamber at Philae (Griffith 1912b, pl. XVIII).

Among the 31 inscriptions in the Meroitic script found at Philae, the largest concentration by far is found in the Meroitic Chamber. This chamber is located behind the

Eastern Colonnade between the two pylons and directly opposite the Birth House, where a series of small rooms runs from north to south. The Meroitic Chamber is located within the second room, formerly a purification chamber. A combination of figures and texts written in the cursive Meroitic script cover three walls of the dimly lit chamber (Figure 3; Griffith 1912b). Two processions face each other meeting at the north wall. Procession I consists of seven figures facing right. They cover the north wall and continue around to the west wall, ending at the entrance to the chamber. Procession II included 11 figures, of which eight figures have survived. Procession I depicts Manitawawi followed by Bekemete who is in turn followed by four representations of Mastaraqye and, finally, Apamalo. Procession II depicts the same three people: Manitawawi, Bekemete and Mastaraqye. This time a small child follows Bekemete. The two primary figures depicted in the Meroitic Chamber are part of the Wayekiye family that served as priests of Isis and administrators for the Meroitic king in Lower Nubia. Each figure carries a palm branch that often appears in Egyptian as well as Meroitic scenes of Isis worship. Some scholars have called this the Isis flower (Roeder 1910, 120), although others argue that it is a stylised palm branch. Palm branches can be found in inscriptions at Kalabsha, Dakka and Elephantine. In the early 20th century they continued to be used in Nubian ceremonies (Blackman 1916, 32). At Nubian funerals, a palm rib, stripped of its leaves, was stuck into the ground or laid upon the grave itself. Women regularly carried palm ribs, stripped of their foliage in wedding processions of certain Nubian towns (Blackman 1916, 31-2). Although the precise cultic significance of the palm branch has not been determined, clearly it holds importance for the people of Nubia.

Manitawawi's titles include 'Strategus of the Water'. Bekemete holds the titles 'Strategus of the Land' and 'King's Son', meaning that he was the Governor of Lower Nubia, the northern province of Meroë. Mastaraqye is a ≈b≈n, an unknown Meroitic title, an 'Agent of Isis' and a 'Qeren' of Isis. The titles of Manitawawi and Bekemete are civic in nature while Mastaraqye's are priestly. The embassy depicted here is dated to the first half of the AD 260s. Although the texts indicate numbers and most likely refer to quantities of offerings made to the temple, the primary reason for the embassy appears to have been political negotiations with Roman authorities similar to the mission of Pasan, as envoy to Rome, undertaken 10 years previously. As is typical of the Meroitic *proskynema*, this over-sized *proskynema* seems to combine religious pilgrimage with political negotiation.

Conclusion

In conclusion, Meroitic pilgrimage to Philae may prove to be very old. The block and shrine attributed to King Taharqa of the 25th Dynasty attests to a Kushite presence on the island of Philae as early as 690 BC. Temple construction undertaken by King Arqamani who reigned from 270-260 BC testifies to active participation by Meroites at Philae during the Ptolemaic period. Although there are no inscriptions that predate the Ptolemaic period, older inscriptions may well have been obliterated when the Ptolemaic kings dismantled and rebuilt the older sanctuaries on the island. It is possible that we have a thousand-year tradition of Kushite/Meroitic pilgrimage to the Island of Philae beginning in the early 7th century BC during the Kushite period and lasting up until the fall of Meroë in the early 4th century AD. Ample evidence appears in the graffiti left by the Meroites that they conceived of Isis as a 'helper' deity, a sign of personal religion. She is often referred to as 'the one who hears the petitions of those who are far off' and 'the giver of wealth'. In contrast to the brief and unemotional graffiti left in Greek and the short and formulaic graffiti left by Egyptians in Demotic, the graffiti left by the Meroites display an intense personal piety linked with a great concern to enumerate the family relationships of the worshipper. The detail included in the inscriptions left by Meroitic pilgrims gives us a glimpse into the intensity of feeling they held for the great goddess as well as the communal nature of their worship and long-lived devotion to the traditional rites as celebrated in the month of Khoiak and Isis' Festival of Entry.

References

Blackman, A. M. 1916. Libations to the Dead in Modern Nubia and Ancient Egypt. *Journal of Egyptian Archaeology* 3 (1), 31-4.

Erichsen, W. 1954. *Demotisches Glossar*. Copenhagen, E. Munksgaard.

Erman, A. and Grapow, H. 1982 [1926-1953]. *Wörterbuch der ägyptischen Sprache*. Vols. I-V. Berlin, Akademie Verlag.

Griffith, F. Ll. 1912a. *Demotic Graffiti of the Dodecaschoenus. Les temples immergés de la Nubie: Documents*. Edited by G. Maspero. Vols. 19 and 20 (plates). Cairo, Institut Français d'Archéologie Orientale.

—1912b. *Meroitic Inscriptions, Part II. Napata to Philae and Miscellaneous*. Archaeological Survey of Egypt 20. London and Boston, Egypt Exploration Fund.

—1931. Four Granite Stands at Philae. *Bulletin de l'Institut Français d'Archéologie Orientale* 30, 127-30.

Heany, G. 1985. A Short Architectural History of Philae. *Bulletin de l'Institut Française d'Archéologie Orientale* 85, 197-233.

Hintze, F. 1979. *Africa in Antiquity: The Arts of Ancient Nubia and the Sudan*. Proceedings of the Symposium held in Conjunction with the Exhibition, Brooklyn, Sept. 29-Oct. 1, 1978. *Meroitica* 5.

Junker, H. 1913. *Das Götterdekret über das Abaton*. Denkschriften der kaiserlichen Akademie der Wissenschaften in Wien, philosophisch-historische Klasse 56/1. Vienna, Hölder.

Roeder, G. 1910. Die Blumen der Isis von Philae. *Zeitschrift für ägyptische Sprache und Altertumskunde* 48, 115-23.

Part 2: Interpreting Ancient Egypt

Introduction: Critical Comments on Essays on Interpreting Ancient Egypt presented at the Egypt in its African Context Conference

Charles A. Grantham
Northeastern Illinois University

I was asked to read four essays* to be included as chapters in the publication of the proceedings of the Egypt in African Context conference held at the Manchester Museum, University of Manchester, UK in October 2009, which I attended. The four essays are 'Curating Kemet, Fear of a Black Land?' by Sally-Ann Ashton; 'Petrie's Revolutions: The Case of the Qurneh Queen' by Bill Manley; 'Contesting Egypt: Facts, Rhetoric or Sentiments?' by C. A. Folorunso and 'Public Understandings of Ancient Egypt in the Formation of Dalit and Afro-American Identities and History Curriculum' by Clyde Ahmad Winters. Following are my comments on each of these essays.

I began with 'Curating Kemet, Fear of a Black a Land?' Sally-Ann Ashton is the curator of the Egyptian collections at the Fitzwilliam Museum, Cambridge (UK) and states that in that position at the Museum she has undertaken to present Egypt in its African context using the Museum's collection and drawing upon the 'results of qualitative research, community engagement and individual research' (p. 105). Ashton immediately separates herself from a number of her formally trained Egyptological colleagues by acknowledging and using the name Kemet when referring to Ancient Egypt and stating boldly and unapologetically that not only does she recognise the Ancient Egyptians as being African but that they were 'Black'. She goes on to state that she uses the term in the current racialised way to 'identify a universal political association of all those who experienced racism and were non-White' (p. 106)

The other way Ashton distinguishes herself from her colleagues is by engaging the Black community and being open to interpretations and research presented by individuals who have been labelled as African-centred and thus marginalised by individuals who have specialised knowledge that comes from having been formally trained in the discipline. In this paper Ashton successfully demonstrates how museum personnel, community members and African-centred scholars can come together around a museum's Egyptian collection and present a factual and objective view of Kemet that shows that the people of Ancient Egypt were not only African but were 'what we would consider today Black Africans' (p. 111). Her view is that the role of museums should be to challenge people's perspectives and stereotypes of cultures created by racism and indifference.

The second paper I read was 'Petrie's Revolutions: The Case of the Qurneh Queen' by Bill Manley. Anyone remotely familiar with Ancient Egyptian history and the early pioneers of Ancient Egyptian archaeology has read something about Sir Flinders Petrie. He was considered a giant in the rediscovery of Ancient Egypt's splendour and to this day, his meticulous collection of discarded pot sherds, stone vessels and ceramics grace many museums' Ancient Egyptian collections. This is the view most averagely informed people have of Petrie. However, what Manley does in this paper is to expose another side of Petrie by using what should have been the most spectacular discovery of its day (1908) from Ancient Egypt: a rich burial uncovered by Petrie dating to the 16th century BC, containing the mummified remains of a woman and a child, as well as Nubian pottery, who in all likelihood had familial ties with Nubia. Manley states that 'the grave indicates "a level of wealth that would be notable in any period" (Roehrig 2005, 16) and yielded "the largest group of goldwork that had left Egypt" (Petrie 1932, 212)' (p. 93).

This was fourteen years before the rediscovery of King Tutankhamun's tomb in 1922 by Howard Carter and yet Petrie deliberately chose to ignore the importance and significance of the find by downplaying it and selling it to the Royal Scottish Museum (a precursor of National Museums Scotland). In his essay, Manley does an excellent job revealing why this was done by Petrie – discussing what we would regard today as Petrie's racist agenda – and exposing Petrie's true sentiments about Egypt, the Ancient Egyptians and Nubia.

In the essay 'Contesting Egypt: Facts, Rhetoric or Sentiments', C. A. Folorunso states in his abstract that one of his objectives in presenting this paper is to demonstrate that views held by both Afrocentrists and Eurocentrists, as they pertain to Ancient Egypt, can both be faulty. To be fair to Folorunso, his exact words are: 'European views are usually not supported with hard facts while the Afrocentric interpretations of the evidence are also equally faulty, particularly in the establishment of relations between Ancient Egypt and tropical Africa' (p. 73). Folorunso starts his paper by explaining what he means by facts, rhetoric and sentiments and how these terms will be used in his essay. Although Folorunso points out some interesting discussions that have taken place between individuals over the 'Ancient' and 'Aryan Models' and contentions over the racial construction of the Ancient Egyptians, when it comes to the question of whether the Ancient Egyptians were Black or White in the racialised sense of the words, specifically between contemporary Eurocentric and Afrocentric

---
* Editor's note: as noted in the Preface, José Lingna-Nafafé's paper was a late submission and therefore was omitted from the discussions in the introductory sections.

interpretations, the essay, in my opinion, falls a little short. While it purports to show interpretations of evidence presented by Afrocentrists as faulty, it omits to mention any of the key players, with the exception of Théophile Obenga, who have been proponents of a Black Egypt.

In his essay 'Public Understandings of Ancient Egypt in the Formation of Dalit and Afro-American Identities and History Curriculum', Clyde Ahmad Winters draws some interesting parallels between the two groups and uncovers a relationship that apparently links them biologically, but is seldom discussed. Underpinning both of these group's ancestral heritage, as the title suggests, is Ancient Egypt. Winters looks at the writings of some of the earlier proponents of a Black Egypt in the United States to see how those writings were used to counter the opposing argument being trumpeted by White scholars of that era who denied the very existence of civilisations in Africa, unless of course they had been created at the behest of White European intervention (see Manley, *Petrie's Revolutions*). Turning to India and the 'Dalits', pejoratively known as the 'untouchables', Winters looks at East Indian scholars who acknowledge a connection between East Indians and enslaved Africans in the Americas dating back to the Atlantic slave trade and who, in more recent years, have attached their liberation movement in India to those of the Civil Rights movement of Blacks in the United States during the late fifties and sixties.

The conference brought together an array of scholars presenting papers that demonstrated the continued interest in Ancient Egypt (Kemet) and its place in African historiography. It also highlighted the need for further discussions and dialogue on Ancient Egypt in its African Context to help dispel opinions that have morphed into myths and have become popularised in the eyes of the general population.

Contesting Egypt: Facts, Rhetoric or Sentiments?

C. A. Folorunso
University of Ibadan

Abstract

This paper attempts to review claims and counter-claims about the Ancient Egyptian civilisation, using the chapters in the 2003 edited volume, *Ancient Egypt in Africa* (London, UCL Press), as a starting point for much of the discussion. The paper suggests that many of the claims are not supported by hard evidence but rather based on rhetoric and sentiments to achieve preconceived objectives. It also suggests that the main contention has been on the racial/cultural (biological, linguistic, institutional, material) status of the Ancient Egyptians and the cultural relations of Ancient Egypt to Greece and tropical Africa. This study accepts the explanation that the 'ancient European' world recognised Ancient Egypt as an African civilisation and acknowledged its influence. It also agrees with the view that the interpretation of Egypt as peripheral has its roots in the 19th century desire to deny an African Egypt its contributions to European civilisation, which were not consistent with the prevailing view of Africa as a dark continent. The views of Eurocentrists and Afrocentrists on Ancient Egypt are considered with the observation that Eurocentric views are usually not supported with hard facts while the Afrocentric interpretations of the evidence are also equally faulty, particularly in the establishment of relations between Ancient Egypt and tropical Africa. The study concludes that Ancient Egyptian and tropical African cultural developments might have shared common origins in the Prehistoric (Neolithic) period.

Keywords: Africa, Ancient Egypt, Greeks, Hamites, language, Nubians, racial, sub-Sahara.

Introduction

As an opening remark, it should be noted that the author of this chapter is not an Egyptologist nor an expert of any subject on Egypt, but an archaeologist who, over the years from his student days to the period of his professional career, has encountered Egypt in the interpretations and explanations of cultural developments in parts of Africa, specifically sub-Saharan Africa. These experiences have led me to reflect on the claims of Ancient Egyptian cultural influence on developments in West Africa (Folorunso 2003). The title of this presentation has been framed as a question because I believe that there are just too many unanswered questions on the subject of Ancient Egypt in the varied perspectives from which it has been studied. Whichever way, it is an incontestable fact that Ancient Egypt was an early centre of civilisation in world history, and still remains today an important subject of discourse.

It is of course not difficult to pick out from those contesting Ancient Egypt, facts, rhetoric and sentiments. It might be useful here to explain what I consider to be facts, rhetoric and sentiments as used in this paper, rather than defining them in any formal way. Facts, rhetoric and sentiments are used here for statements made about Ancient Egypt which, when evaluated against the available evidence, one could judge as to the level of their accuracy or otherwise. Though accuracy may be relative, facts are regarded as claims based on the indisputable interpretation of material and non-material evidence. To us, facts may not be absolute but would not also change in any significant form to alter their value and substance. For instance, Ancient Egypt existed as a cultural entity in the past and it is not a fictional construct; what may be contestable is whether it was a civilisation or not. In contesting the claim of being a civilisation or not, material and non-material evidence would be sought, some factual, some non-factual. Facts are equally contestable but they are expected to stand and be reinforced in the light of any new method of investigation and evidence. Rhetoric is defined as a method of discourse which utilises unsubstantiated claims based on faulty or biased interpretation of the available evidence, which evidence is generally very weak in the light of the claims being made. For instance, the claim that cultural developments in sub-Saharan Africa had their origins in Ancient Egypt is not based on proven material and/or non-material evidence. Usually, rhetoric is the product of imaginative thinking arising from very weak lines of evidence. Although it is possible that rhetoric (unsubstantiated claims) could turn out to be facts if they are invariably substantiated with incontrovertible evidence, they generally fall flat in the light of new methods of investigation and evidence. Sentiments are considered as preconceived claims made for reasons other than for scientific study, or as a social therapy to satisfy ego. Sentiments are based on flimsy, unverifiable material and non-material evidence. Sentiments may arise against unpalatable fact which must be subdued at all cost, and forgery of data may not be out of place in order to sustain sentiments. Sentiments are therefore the complete opposite of facts, and they have no scientific value as they can never change under any situation.

Some Facts about Ancient Egypt

To a non-partisan observer of the debate on Ancient Egypt, one may ask the question, so what? Why are enlightened debates desirable, and rhetoric and sentiments in academic and scientific debates uncalled for? What is at stake? Would such a stance change anything significant in the present material well-being of those contesting the opposing views on Ancient Egypt? Martin Bernal's *Black Athena* (1991) is probably the one single significant publication on Ancient Egypt that narrates its relationship with other parts of the ancient world. As North (2003, 30) puts it, '*Black Athena* places the contention that the Egyptians were black Africans, and that the Greeks were culturally indebted to them, at the very heart of the debate Bernal was trying to evoke'. One therefore does not need to hide from the question, which simply put is, were the Ancient Egyptians black or white? A follow-up question would be, did the Ancient Egyptian civilisation have any influence on the Greeks? Therefore, to contest Bernal's propositions could mean saying on the one hand that the Ancient Egyptians were not black Africans but that they had cultural influence on the Greeks, or that they were Blacks but had no significant cultural influence on the Greeks. My interest here is to examine the elements in the arguments to see if they are based on facts, rhetoric or sentiments.

It seems that Bernal (2003) appears to claim that he was not stating anything new but only saying, lest we forget, that these issues had long been settled. Bernal was therefore reacting against what he saw as a deliberate and progressive misappropriation of the Ancient Egyptian civilisation. He stated two important facts embedded in the two distinct versions of the early history of Greece: the Ancient and the Aryan Models. By the Ancient Model, Bernal established that 'until the beginning of the 19th century, scholars had accepted the ideas of the writers of Classical, Hellenistic and Roman periods (500 BC-AD 250) on Greece's distant past' which 'was that the ancestors of the Greeks had lived in idyllic simplicity until the arrival of Egyptian and the Phoenician leaders' and that 'Greeks had continued to learn from the Egyptians, through study in Egypt, and that many, if not most, of the greatest Greek statesmen, philosophers and scientists had visited the Nile Valley' (Bernal 2003, 23). He therefore advocated what he called 'a return to older scholarly beliefs' (Bernal 1991, 522). Bernal has stated a fact which no one seems to have contradicted.

The second fact has to do with the origin of the Aryan Model of the early history of Greece, which according to Bernal was only developed in the 1830s and 1840s. As Bernal describes it, the Aryan Model, which is 'still generally dominant today, sees Classical Greek civilization as the result of a conquest of present-day Greece from the north by the "Hellenes"', who were Indo-European speakers, or 'Aryans', while the indigenous Caucasian population of the Aegean, who did not speak an Indo-European language and were definitely not Semitic speakers or Egyptians, are simply labelled as 'Pre-Hellenes' (Bernal 2003, 23). According to North (2003), 'it still is a widely accepted proposition that the Greeks originated almost all the great cultural achievements of "the West"... without any suggestions that this attribution of credit is at all contested or problematic'. He explains further that 'this was in some sense a racial construction, emphasising the role of those perceived as co-race-members and eliminating the apparent influence of those who were not' (North 2003, 32). Bernal therefore observed that 'for several decades, the new image of Greek origins co-existed uneasily with the traditional belief that Phoenicians – though not the Egyptians – had played a significant role' (Bernal 2003, 27). It appears therefore that the motive behind the Aryan Model that expunges any Egyptian influence on the Greek civilisation was born out of sentiment and has been sustained by rhetoric.

Bernal also provides the contextual background to the development of the Aryan Model of the early history of Greece. He states that it has its root in the racism that had become 'an obsession in northern Europe by the end of the 17th century, with the establishment of racial slavery in America' (Bernal 2003, 24). As Reid has pointed out, 'Ancient Egypt had long been known to Europeans, principally because of its appearance in the Bible and its perceived peripheral location in the Classical and Medieval worlds.... In the late 18th century, Ancient Egypt was readily perceived as African and as a minor polity of little significance' (2003, 58). However, with Napoleon's expedition to Egypt demonstrating that Ancient Egypt went beyond this peripheral status, this 'implied, under prevailing perceptions, that Ancient Egypt was highly sophisticated and African. Not surprisingly, thought changed rapidly to describe Ancient Egypt as a "white" civilization' (Reid 2003, 58), and, throughout the 19th century, the Egyptian civilisation was increasingly perceived to be incompatible with an African origin (Reid 2003, 66). 'By the 19th century, Europeans had constructed elaborate evolutionary frameworks representing Africans as the lowest form of human development' (Reid 2003, 58). As Bernal notes, Central and West Africans were portrayed 'as animals or devils and as the epitome of barbarism', and as Africans were treated inhumanely and dehumanised by Europeans; 'the role of Egypt as the foundation of western civilization was difficult to fit into this picture as Egypt was inconveniently situated on the African continent' (Bernal 2003, 24). The solution was either to see Egypt as 'civilized and white', or 'uncivilized and black' (Bernal 2003, 24). Reid puts the dilemma this way: it was 'whether Ancient Egypt was African and not so sophisticated, or non-African and highly civilized', adding, 'a third possible option, that it was African and highly civilized, was unthinkable' (Reid 2003, 55). Therefore, 'during the 19th century the notion of Hamites was resurrected by a subtle shift in biblical interpretation, which allowed Hamites to be considered as Caucasoid; as such they could then be considered capable of civilization' (Reid 2003, 66).

As expected, Bernal's views on the Aryan origin for Greek civilisation were subtly criticised. North states that Bernal had created 'the impression that departing from the norm of the beliefs held by earlier generations requires some special and probably sinister explanation', and is of the view that such a departure is the very foundation of the work of the historian (2003, 33). It follows therefore that Bernal's call for 'a return to older scholarly beliefs' is misplaced and against the norms of historical research. North expresses the opinion that it is normal for older views to be tested and challenged no matter how long-established, and that new hypotheses be formulated and new evidence sought. He states further that Bernal's attack is in line with 'the whole method on which historical research currently rests' (North 2003, 34).

North's argument is interesting in that he seems to have earlier accepted the fact that the Aryan Model was 'a racial construction' which 'cannot be separated from the process through which European nations were simultaneously establishing imperial domination over other parts of the world' (2003, 32). One cannot really find any new elements introduced into the debate by North except the point that all knowledge should be subjected to scrutiny no matter how long-established. Although this point is also true for all subjects of scientific enquiry, knowledge cannot be jettisoned simply because it has become too ancient, and unfashionable, for the social, economic and political realities of an era. The circumstances surrounding the development of the Aryan Model – that the continent of Africa which hosted Ancient Egypt could not have been civilised – as described by Bernal have not been disputed. While it is legitimate to explore alternative explanations for whatever reason, such explanations should be able to dismantle existing explanation through new evidence. Unfortunately, this has not been the case in the subject of Ancient Egypt and the foundation of the Greek civilisation. North also counters Bernal's argument that 'the Greeks are exceptional among the Indo-European groups because their language was more heavily affected by non Indo-European linguistic influences' by stating that Georges Dumézil (1898-1986), the French comparative philologist, had 'found that he could not absorb them into his theoretical structures and explained this as resulting from their greater creativity, [and] their rejection of older traditions of behaviour often retained by more conservative groups' (North 2003, 36).

North does not fault Bernal's claim that 'less than 40 percent of the Greek vocabulary and very few Greek proper names can be explained in terms of other members of the Indo-European linguistic family' (Bernal 2003, 23), but presents an alternative explanation which is based on mere speculation rather than on facts and data. How was the explanation of 'their greater creativity' and 'their rejection of older traditions of behaviour' arrived at? These are the signs of rhetoric and sentiment rather than science. In any case it has been demonstrated that other parts of the world that had relations with Ancient Egypt did show admiration for it.

The chapters in the volume *Ancient Perspectives on Egypt* (London, UCL Press, 2003), edited by Roger Matthews and Cornelia Roemer, beautifully illustrate relations between Ancient Egypt and the ancient world. It has been demonstrated that Herodotus showed his curiosity for the preciousness of the materials and the finesse of their elaboration by the Egyptian craftsmen and for the monumentality of the buildings: 'The pyramids and the labyrinth are admired especially for the countless workmen involved in the construction of the chambers they contain' (Matthews and Roemer 2003, 14). Walker, in the same volume, demonstrates that 'surviving works of art made in the 1st century AD to celebrate Roman interest in Egyptian culture' show some caricatures, which, in conjunction with 'opinions voiced in ancient literature suggest a continued tension in Roman attitudes towards Egypt, even a century after the defeat of Cleopatra VII and the resultant conquest of Egypt in 30 BC' (2003, 191). The caricatures show black pygmies fighting with hippopotami and making love to white women in boats floating between these exotic animals (Matthews and Roemer 2003, 18). Whichever way Ancient Egypt was conceived by the ancient world, it is obvious that it could not then, and can still not now, be ignored.

The Ancient Egyptians

Were the Ancient Egyptians black or white? This may appear to be a difficult question to answer by scholars working on Ancient Egypt as incontrovertible evidence may be hard to come by. So far all the claims regarding the racial affiliation of the Ancient Egyptians consist more of rhetoric than hard facts. However, one can safely state that they were Africans, though this in itself depends on what we mean by 'African'. Is it location-bound, cultural or racial? It is obvious and very evident that Ancient Egypt, even when it is not directly implied, has been viewed mainly from its racial perspective. When Ancient Egyptian influence is vehemently denied or insidiously claimed on the basis of very doubtful evidence, racial considerations become the determining factor in such interpretations and explanations. The geographical location of Ancient Egypt in northeastern Africa has complicated matters for those contesting Egypt. I can imagine that were Ancient Egypt located in the Niger delta of Nigeria and not on the Nile, the arguments would be very different. Of course, for some, location would always have been irrelevant – the Ife civilisation in Nigeria was once assigned to a lost Hamitic race (see Frobenius 1913). The geographical location has led to various interpretations as to the origin and character of the Egyptian civilisation.

The first chapter of Stephen Gardiner's book, *Introduction à l'Architecture* (1984), is entitled 'Egypt and Primitive Civilizations', in a sense recognising Egypt as a very early centre of civilisation. However, with the influence of diffusionist ideas which had been a 'well-regarded explanation of cultural change' since the late 19th century (Reid 2003, 61), Gardiner traces the origin of the Egyptian pyramids to Mesopotamia. He asserts that, between the 1st and 2nd Dynasty, Egypt had established contact with Mesopotamia, and that the first pyramid in Egypt, the Step Pyramid at Saqqara, constructed between 2667 and 2648 BC, was inspired by the White Temple of Anu at Uruk, dating to the 4th millennium BC. However, Gardiner recognises the striking differences between the White Temple of Anu and the Step Pyramid, in structure, fineness and building materials – for example, the Sumerians used sun-dried mud bricks while the Egyptians used stone (Gardiner 1984, 8-9). Whatever influence Anu might have had on the Step Pyramid, it is obvious that there had been experimentation over a long period at Saqqara as there are several precedents in the area. The most relevant precedent is found in Saqqara mastaba 3038. The substructure lies in a 4m deep rectangular pit, and has mud brick walls rising to 6m. Three sides were extended and built out to create eight shallow steps rising at an angle of 49 degrees. This would have been an elongated step pyramid if the remaining side hadn't been left uncovered (Lehner 1997, 80-93). In any case, Gardiner did not infer that the Egyptian civilisation was as whole influenced by the Sumerians.

The Ancient Egyptian language has been classified as belonging to the Afro-asiatic language family (formerly Hamito-Semitic), therefore sharing affinities with modern Berbers of North Africa, Omotic speakers of Ethiopia, Chadic speakers of the Lake Chad Basin, Cushitic speakers of eastern Africa, and the Hebrew and Arabic Languages. The assignment of the ancient Egyptian language to Afro-asiatic has been challenged by Diagne who argued that 'the lexicon, the structure and the essential principle of written Egyptian ... are closer to corresponding phenomena in languages such as Wolof or Hausa, or to the Dahomeyan graphic tradition, than to the Hamito-Semitic systems to which they had been uncautiously assimilated' (Diagne 1981, 246; see Anselin, this volume). It has also been argued that 'the Egyptian language could not be isolated from its African context and its origin could not be fully explained in terms of Semitic; it was thus quite normal to expect to find related languages in Africa' (Devisse 1981, 75-6). Obenga has noted that a fundamental problem 'is to find appropriate techniques for comparing Ancient Egyptian with contemporary black African languages, in order, so far as possible, to reconstruct, on the basis of morphological, lexicological and phonetic analogies and affinities, their common ancestors' (Obenga 1981, 80). Obenga (2001) has consistently claimed that Semitic, Berber and Egyptian languages are not genetically related and that science has been sacrificed to achieve preconceived objectives.

Evidence for the biological relationship of the Ancient Egyptians to 'Africans' is probably the most contested and manipulated, as has been demonstrated in the work of Shomarka Keita on this subject. Reviewing works done on morphological and morphotypological, morphometric/metric, metric, non-metric, limb ratio, blood typing, hair morphology and dental studies that date from the 19th century, Keita (1993) has shown that there exist racial prejudices in the interpretations of the evidence by certain researchers. He has been shown that while some scholars have rightly recognised the 'Africanness' of the Ancient Egyptians, others, such as Morton (1844), on the basis of racial prejudice, were of the view that the ancient Egyptians could not have been of African origin because '...civilization...could not spring from Negroes, or from Berbers and never did...' (cf. Keita 1993, 142). Keita in his study has demonstrated clearly that in all the various kinds of biological studies the Ancient Egyptians have been revealed to have close biological affinities to African populations of the south. He states that 'in most cases the morphological descriptions of early southern "Egyptian" crania clearly fall within Broad to Elongated Saharo-tropical African ranges of variation' and that 'more recent metric and morphometric studies largely confirmed the overlap of early southern Egyptians with more southern, especially East African' populations (Keita 1993, 149). He further asserts that the non-metric studies show 'a Nubian-Sudanese relationship for the Egyptians' and concludes that 'the morphological metric, morphometric, and non-metric studies demonstrate immense overlap with tropical variants' (Keita 1993, 150).

Egypt's Relationships within the African Continent
Egypt was certainly not an island located in the northeastern part of the African continent, as has often been implied, but had relationships with other parts of Africa, though the nature and character of the relationships are poorly understood. As a result, various claims have been made as to the cultural links of Ancient Egypt to sub-Saharan Africa in ways not sufficiently explained, or superfluous and unsubstantiated. O'Connor (1983) was of the view that 'Egyptian contact with and knowledge of Africa was relatively shallow, partly because of severe natural restrictions on access such as the Sahara and the difficulty of movement along the Upper Nile' (O'Connor 1983, 252). However, O'Connor and Reid draw attention to the fact that there 'was the circumnavigation of Africa carried out by Phoenicians commissioned to do so by a native Egyptian pharaoh, Necho II (610-595 BC), which is generally accepted as a historical event' and as 'an expression of Egyptian interest in parts of Africa relatively remote from Egypt' (O'Connor and Reid 2003, 17). O'Connor and Reid further state that historic Egypt's contact with areas in Africa was 'structured by a fundamental climatic reality, the extreme aridity of the Sahara for most of the historic period' and this has been responsible for the paucity of information on the relationship between Ancient Egypt and West and Central Africa, 'except insofar as Egyptian influence was mediated via Nubia' (O'Connor and Reid 2003, 17).

Linguistic and archaeological evidence has been adduced by McDonald (2003) to indicate that there were probable contacts across the Sahara in prehistoric times long before the rise of Ancient Egypt, and that this might also explain the genesis of the kingdom. McDonald has suggested that 'during the Holocene optimum (*ca.* 7000-6000 BP), Afro-Asiatic speakers were probably entering the Lower Nile region from the south and the east, assimilating and displacing local speakers of Nilo-Saharan and Niger-Congo languages' (McDonald 2003, 97). He further explains that 'the lack of Niger-Congo/Nilo-Saharan words or grammatical borrowings in Egyptian itself (cf. Greenberg 1955) ... would seem to indicate minimal interaction of early Egyptians with speakers of these "inner African" language phyla, and the rapid displacement and / or acculturation of speakers of these languages along the Lower Nile before Predynastic times' (McDonald 2003, 98).

Wengrow (2003) expresses the view that the Neolithic pastoral cultures of Middle Egypt and of Central Sudan show some fundamental similarities that would suggest the Neolithic pastoral communities extending from Middle Egypt to modern Khartoum were probably responsible for the political developments that led ultimately to the pharaonic state. O'Connor and Reid consider that 'this "African" model of social evolution fits the circumstances better than others based primarily on the archaeological record of South West Asia' (2003, 18).

McDonald draws attention to 'a possible tenuous linkage between Inner Africa and Nubia, not Dynastic Egypt' on the basis of the existence of 'a Trans-Saharan Pastoral Techno complex dating to between 3800 and 1000 BC, which ultimately stretched from Kerma (Sudan) in the east to Dhar Tichitt (Mauritania) in the West' (2003, 104). He therefore wonders why cultural connections between the Egyptian state and Inner Africa have been almost ignored, if, on the one hand there was a connection between Egypt and Nubia, and on the other hand contacts have been documented between Nubia (Kerma and Kush) and the interior, particularly Carthage, with apparent trade-links spanning the Sahara (McDonald 2003, 104).

To properly understand whatever contact might have existed in the past between Egypt and sub-Saharan Africa we should seriously consider the view of Rowlands (2003) that there is a challenge as to 'whether it is possible for academics to discuss a more inclusive notion of Africa that will respond to the perception that a certain unity of cultural form not only exists but has an historical origin' (2003, 40). Rowlands further observes that sub-Saharan Africa and Ancient Egypt seem to 'share certain commonalities in substantive images and ideas, yet whose cultural forms display differences consistent with perhaps millennia of historical divergence and institutionalization' (Rowlands 2003, 43). Earlier in the same chapter Rowlands states that the overwhelming Egyptocentrism of many past researches has 'obscured the more central question of whether a shared repertoire of cultural forms can really be identified for Sub-Saharan Africa' (Rowlands 2003, 41). These 'commonalities' with other African cultures may therefore suggest an African origin for major aspects of the Egyptian civilisation (O'Connor and Reid 2003, 18). It therefore seems that the semblance of the unity of cultural form has been wrongly interpreted in the various claims of Ancient Egyptian influences on sub-Saharan Africa.

Rowlands (2003, 41) discusses Seligman's ideas that ancient Egyptian kingship had a sub-Saharan origin, in a part of prehistoric Nubia, and that in cultural historical terms the 'flow' had been south to north (Seligman 1934), as well as Seligman's understanding that the Ancient Egyptians were an offshoot of the Hamitic race (Seligman 1930). Reid also discusses Frankfort's ethnographic interpretation of Ancient Egyptian kingship (1948) in which he claims that there are living groups of people in Africa today who are the survivors of the 'great East African substratum out of which Egyptian culture arose' and that 'cultural ties could be shown to link Egypt with people such as the Buganda; people who are related to the Ancient Egyptians at least in their Hamitic traits' (Reid 2003, 70). Wengrow explains that the Hamites, often characterised as part of an 'African substratum', were considered 'on what now appear entirely spurious grounds, to be linguistically and racially affiliated to "Mediterranean" rather than "Negroid" peoples and some scholars even considered possible distant relationship with "Indo-European" pastoralists of the inner Asiatic steppes' (2003, 123).

Despite the earlier view of Seligman (1930) that the Ancient Egyptians were originally of the Hamitic race, his later view (1934) that the cultural 'flow' had been south to north and Frankfort's 1948 view that the Ancient Egyptian culture arose out of an East African substratum are significant because they are ways of explaining the commonalities between Ancient Egypt and the African interior which the proponents of the Hamitic hypothesis and the Egyptocentric scholars have not considered. In this context, O'Connor and Reid note that 'there is a relative abundance of ancient materials relevant to contact and influence, as well as striking correlations between ancient Egyptian and the ethnography of recent and current Sub-Saharan communities, chiefdoms and states' (2003, 21). They are however not unmindful of the 'considerable theoretical problems in comparing the two, not the least those imposed by chronology' (2003, 21).

Claims of Egyptian Influence in Sub-Saharan Africa
The claims of Egyptian influence on cultural development in sub-Saharan Africa are based on 'ideas generated by explorers, missionaries and administrators in the late 19th century' and have been behind many of the academic interpretations of African history in the 20th century (Reid 2003, 55). According to Reid, most European writers on the Great Lakes found it unthinkable that states could have arisen there without external stimuli and were 'unanimous in looking for what they considered to be non-African elements' – the scope of the external stimuli included, but was not restricted to, Ancient Egypt. 'Various items of material culture and elements of cultural practice were drawn upon to demonstrate the connection between Ancient Egypt and the Great Lakes. These links were made on an extremely casual and often contradictory basis' (Reid 2003, 62). Reid further states that 'there is no single piece of archaeological evidence to indicate direct contact between the Great Lakes and Egypt' and that the Meroitic furnaces that 'were thought to provide proof for the diffusion of iron smelting technology into Africa' had been 'discovered to be later, relating to the Roman occupation of Egypt' (2003, 71-2). Schmidt's investigation of iron smelting in Buhaya, on the western shores of Lake Victoria, suggests 'early dates and a distinct technology, possibly indicating an independent innovation of iron smelting' (Schmidt 1981; Reid 2003, 72). Reid concludes that the 'elements of material culture cited as evidence for contact between Egypt and Great Lakes Africa can be dismissed as superficial similarities, based on causal, uncritical comparisons', and 'where more detailed investigations of these similarities have subsequently been made, these have demonstrated significant differences' (2003, 73-4).

Bennett, discussing claimed Egyptian connections with South Africa, explains that '[m]issionaries, believing in a common human cultural origin, automatically looked for diffusion from the world of the early Old Testament' (2003, 111) and that faint but detectable cultural links had been cited to infer that the Bantu peoples of southern Africa have connections with Egypt and also with Israel, a logical interpretation in view of the missionaries' belief in 'human diffusion from the single source described in Genesis' (Bennett 2003, 114). He further states that missionaries and secular scholars have drawn varied parallels to establish the perceived links, the former drawing 'parallels both with Semitic cultures and with Ancient Egypt, the latter especially with reference to the Sotho-Tswana animal totems, but also sometimes with reference to circumcision' (Bennett 2003, 118).

In my chapter in the volume *Ancient Egypt in Africa* (2003), I discuss the weaknesses of the Hamitic explanations of cultural developments in West Africa which directly or indirectly link West Africa to Egypt (p. 87). I also address the claims of connections to Ancient Egypt on the basis of certain ethnographic cultural forms, concluding that the claims cannot be substantiated and can be explained according to Zachernuk's theory that many of these myths of external origins emerged under colonialism, and served to proclaim a common origin for all the people and cultures of the sub-region as a rhetorical strategy for political unity (Zachernuk 1994, 451). Accordingly, the late colonial period witnessed growing regional-ethnic antagonisms in Nigeria and led amateur local historians to adopt the 'Hamitic Hypothesis' tradition in the search for historical primacy and cultural superiority over other Nigerian groups.

Conclusion
In the *Ancient Egypt in Africa* volume Reid seems to be in a dilemma over the proper interpretation of the elements of influences, contacts and connections in African archaeology and history as they relate to Egypt. In his conclusion he states that 'whilst it is easy to understand why archaeologists and historians would now want to avoid north-south models of development, there are some unintended consequences of such a position'. For him, 'rejecting Egyptian and general northern influences on sub-Saharan Africa', would appear to confirm that 'Ancient Egypt was in Africa, but not *of* Africa' and conversely, acceptance of 'African connections for Ancient Egypt would appear to side with the view that sub-Saharan Africa was incapable of its own development and sat inert over 5,000 years without being able to create political change'. He concludes that 'there are some items, such as domesticated plants and animals, which, on present evidence, are understood to have diffused southwards' and are indications of 'a historical process of diffusion which does require investigation' (Reid 2003, 76).

The above issues raised by Reid become unnecessary if we attempt a better understanding of the commonalities shared between Ancient Egypt and sub-Saharan Africa. Egypt did not have to influence sub-Saharan Africa before it could be *of* Africa. As earlier noted, the views of Seligman (1934) and Frankfort (1948) that cultural 'flow' had been south to north have remained unexplored by researchers. Why is it unthinkable to consider a south-north flow of influence, when, despite the establishment of some commonalities, north-south influence has not been supported by facts and data? It has been shown in this paper that there were contacts between Egypt and Nubia on the one hand, and between Nubia and inner Africa on the other. This means that there could have been indirect exchanges between Egypt and sub-Saharan Africa which could not and were not necessarily uni-directional (north-south) as proponents of the Hamitic hypothesis and Egyptocentric scholars would want us to believe. As O'Connor and Reid put it, 'the fact that commonalities do exist suggests that, because of the great time depth and different organization, these commonalities may result from inherent African processes' (O'Connor and Reid 2003, 21).

As Reid has explained, viewed from a historiographical perspective, we can begin to understand why and how all the essentially unsubstantiated conclusions about an Egyptian influence on sub-Saharan Africa was readily accepted in the past. The same historiographical perspective demonstrates how such ideas were rooted in 19th century racism and colonialism (Reid 2003, 76). It could be stated that Ancient Egypt has been and probably continues to be interpreted to achieve preconceived objectives. It is obvious that some would want to see Ancient Egypt as a non-African civilisation that served as the conduit of diffusion of cultural developments to tropical Africa. Unfortunately, those who argue for Ancient Egypt as an African civilisation tend to accept an unwholesome Egyptian influence on other parts of Africa, thus portraying these areas as a backwater of civilisation. The available evidence does not support such a position, but rather indicates cultural developments that were quite independent of Ancient Egypt. It has therefore been suggested that the commonalities that existed between Ancient Egypt and tropical Africa could be explained in terms of shared origins and contacts in Prehistoric times, during the Neolithic, and that there could not have been a uni-directional influence from north to south.

References

Bennett, B. S. 2003. Ancient Egypt, Missionaries and Christianity in Southern Africa, in D. O'Connor and A. Reid (eds.), *Ancient Egypt in Africa*, 107-19. London, UCL Press.

Bernal, M. 1991. *Black Athena: The Afroasiatic Roots of Classical Civilization, Volume II. The Documentary and Archaeological Evidence*. New Brunswick, N.J, Rutgers University Press.

—2003. Afrocentrism and Historical Models for the Foundation of Ancient Greece, in D. O'Connor and A. Reid (eds.), *Ancient Egypt in Africa*, 23-9. Walnut Creek, CA. and London, Left Coast Press/University College London.

Diagne, P. 1981. History and Linguistics. In J. Ki-Zerbo (ed.), *UNESCO General History of Africa I:*

Methodology and African Prehistory, 233-60. Berkeley, University of California Press/UNESCO/Heinemann.

Devisse, J. 1981. Annex to Chapter 1: Report of the Symposium on 'The Peopling of Ancient Egypt and the Deciphering of the Meroitic Script', Cairo, 28 January - 3 February 1974, in G. Mokhtar (ed.), UNESCO *General History of Africa II: Ancient Civilizations of Africa*, 58-82. Berkeley, University of California Press/UNESCO.

Edwards, D. N. 2003. Ancient Egypt in the Sudanese Middle Nile: A Case of Mistaken Identity? in D. O'Connor and A. Reid (eds.), *Ancient Egypt in Africa*, 137-50. Walnut Creek, CA. and London, Left Coast Press/University College London.

Folorunso, C. A. 2003. Views of Ancient Egypt from a West African Perspective, in D. O'Connor and A. Reid (eds.), *Ancient Egypt in Africa*, 77-92. Walnut Creek, CA. and London, Left Coast Press/University College London.

Frankfort, H. 1948. *Kingship and the Gods. A Study of Ancient Near Eastern Religion as the Integration of Society and Nature*. Chicago, University of Chicago Press.

Frobenius, L. 1913. *The Voice of Africa*. Vol. 1. London, Hutchinson.

Gardiner, S. 1984. *Introduction à l'Architecture*. Editions du Club France Loisirs, Paris, avec l'autorisation des Éditions Aimery Somogy. [Original English edition: Oxford, Equinox Ltd., 1983]

Greenberg, J. H. 1955. *Studies in African Linguistic Classification*. New Haven, Compass.

Keita, S. O. Y. 1993. Studies and Comments on Ancient Egyptian Biological Relationships. *History in Africa* 20, 129-54.

Lehner, M. 1997. *The Complete Pyramids: Solving the Ancient Mysteries*. New York, Thames and Hudson.

MacDonald, K. C. 2003. Cheikh Anta Diop and Ancient Egypt in Africa, in D. O'Connor and A. Reid (eds.), *Ancient Egypt in Africa*, 93-105. Walnut Creek, CA. and London, Left Coast Press/University College London.

Matthews, R. and Roemer, C. (eds.) 2003. *Ancient Perspectives on Egypt*. London, UCL Press.

—2003. Introduction. The Worlds of Ancient Egypt: Aspects, Sources, Interactions, in R. Matthews and C. Roemer (eds.), *Ancient Perspectives on Egypt*, 1-20. London, UCL Press.

Morton, S. G. 1844. *Crania Aegyptiaca, or, Observations on Egyptian Ethnography, Derived from Anatomy, History and the Monuments*. Philadelphia, J. Pennington.

North, J. A. 2003. Attributing Colour to the Ancient Egyptians: Reflections on *Black Athena*, in D. O'Connor and A. Reid (eds.), *Ancient Egypt in Africa*, 31-8. Walnut Creek, CA. and London, Left Coast Press/University College London.

Obenga, T. 1981. Sources and Specific Techniques used in African History: General Outline. In J. Ki-Zerbo (ed.), *UNESCO General History of Africa*. Vol. 1, 72-86. California, Heinemann.

—2001. *Le sens de la lute contre l'Africanisme eurocentriste*. Paris, L'Harmattan.

O'Connor, D. and Reid, A. 2003 Introduction. Locating Ancient Egypt in Africa: Modern Theories, Past Realities, in D. O'Connor and A. Reid (eds.), *Ancient Egypt in Africa*, 1-21. Walnut Creek, CA. and London, Left Coast Press/University College London.

Reid, A. 2003. Ancient Egypt and the Source of the Nile, in D. O'Connor and A. Reid (eds.), *Ancient Egypt in Africa*, 55-76. Walnut Creek, CA. and London, Left Coast Press/University College London.

Rowlands, M. 2003. The Unity of Africa, in D. O'Connor and A. Reid (eds.), *Ancient Egypt in Africa*, 39-54. Walnut Creek, CA. and London, Left Coast Press/University College London.

Schmidt, P. R. 1981. *The Origins of Iron Smelting in Africa: A Complex Technology in Tanzania*. Providence, R.I., Brown University Press.

Seligman, C. G. 1930. *The Races of Africa*. Oxford, Oxford University Press.

—1934. *Egypt and Negro Africa: A Study of Divine Kingship*. London, Routledge.

Walker, S. 2003. Carry-On at Canopus: The Nilotic Mosaic from Palestrina and Roman Attitudes to Egypt, in R. Matthews and C. Roemer (eds.), *Ancient Perspectives on Egypt*, 191-202. London, UCL Press.

Wengrow, D. 2003. Landscapes of Knowledge, Idioms of Power: The African Foundations of Ancient Egyptian Civilization Reconsidered, in D. O'Connor and A. Reid (eds.), *Ancient Egypt in Africa*, 121-35. Walnut Creek, CA. and London, Left Coast Press/University College London.

Zachernuk, P. S. 1994. Of Origins and Colonial Order: Southern Nigerian Historians and the 'Hamitic Hypothesis' c. 1870-1970. *Journal of African History* 35, 427-55.

West African Perspectives on Ancient Egypt: African Renaissance

José Lingna-Nafafé
University of Birmingham

Abstract
Debate about issues pertaining to Ancient Egyptian historical influence on West Africa or *vice versa* has been overshadowed by modern discourses such as colonialism, post-colonialism, Eurocentrism and Afrocentrism. This chapter is an attempt to retrieve from the first European – that is, Portuguese – encounter with West Africa, the absence and significance of Egyptian relations with West Africa and their implications for West African identity politics. The focus of the chapter is on the *Catalan Atlas* and the Hereford *Mappa Mundi*, in order to examine issues raised by recent African Renaissance debates on identity, nationalism, inhumanity of Africans, racial stereotyping and power. The chapter will first examine the *Catalan Atlas* representation of West Africa, then the Hereford *Mappa Mundi*'s ideological representation of the African continent and its relationship to Egypt, and finally it will critically examine the African Renaissance model for an inclusive understanding of Egypt and its place in West Africa in the light of the new Afrocentrism debate.

Keywords
Africa, Afrocentrism, *Catalan Atlas*, colonial, Egypt, Eurocentrism, Europe, *Mappa Mundi*, Portuguese.

Introduction
The introduction of Black African slaves to Western Europe as early as the 15th century, and the need to justify the European domination that then followed, has marked and locked the debate concerning Ancient Egyptian cultural interaction with sub-Saharan Africa or Western Europe in a binary opposition mode of representation (Bernal 2001; Devisse 1979; Mudimbe 1988; Palmberg 1978). This Ancient Egyptian historical influence on West Africa or *vice versa* has also been overshadowed by modern discourses such as the colonial, post-colonial, Eurocentric and Afrocentric. This chapter is an attempt to retrieve from the first European encounter with West Africa, the absence and significance of Ancient Egyptian relations with West Africa and their implications for current West African identity politics. The focus of the chapter is on the *Catalan Atlas* (Figure 1) and the Hereford *Mappa Mundi* (Figure 2) representation, in order to examine issues raised by recent African Renaissance debates on identity, nationalism, inhumanity of Africans, racial stereotyping and power.

The notion 'Egypt-Africa or Africa-Egypt' has been predicated on racial prejudice (Devisse 1979; Mudimbe 1988; Pieterse 1992; Snowden 1983). A land of Black African, sub-Saharan regions has traditionally been associated with backwardness, and, later in the 18th and 19th centuries, enveloped within interrelated discourses, particularly those concerning 'race' and 'racism'. Land becomes associated with a particular representation of the people who inhabit it. As Burns argues, 'colour is the most obvious outward manifestation of race, the criterion [by] which men are judged' (1948, 16).

Thus, colour prejudice has been a prominent mode of differentiation, possessing a vital position and means of justification within the the debate about Ancient Egypt and its geographical relationship to the rest of sub-Saharan Africa. Therefore, in this chapter I intend to consider political and cultural discussions concerning the new Afrocentrism and its theoretical positioning within a posited 'African Renaissance' in general, in order to ascertain the influence of Egypt in Africa and its minor influence in the representation of both the *Catalan Atlas* and the Hereford *Mappa Mundi*. In order to interrogate critical debates about the place of Ancient Egypt in West Africa, such as its influences on cultures and history, I aim to examine the ideological representations of the *Catalan Atlas* and Hereford *Mappa Mundi* in the 13th and 14th centuries respectively, then interrogate Appiah's contestation of new Afrocentrism (1997).

It is therefore the primary concern of this chapter to examine in some detail the socio-cultural and political impact brought about by the 20th century debate. Such an undertaking, however, poses particular challenges. The principal problem for anyone engaged in writing about Ancient Egypt and its cultural influences on sub-Saharan Africa lies in the fragmentation of sources and the unsystematic way in which they have been preserved, although this is not particularly the concern of this study. The chapter intends to situate this discussion around 'Africa' and 'Egypt', focusing particularly within the context of African modern identity and history, as this has traditionally been the most bifurcated. In addition, I intend to provide images which form 'an essential part of the process by which meaning is produced and exchanged' (Hall 1997, 15) of the two maps, to help elucidate how sub-Saharan Africa is conceived within the modern period and how Egypt has been excluded as part of Africa.

The chapter will first examine the *Catalan Atlas* representation of West Africa and its relationship to Egypt, and then will critically examine the *Mappa Mundi*'s ideological representation of Africa; thirdly, the Portuguese expansion and their representation of Egypt in relation to the wider West African perspective will be addressed, before, finally, arguing for an inclusive understanding of Egypt in the Egypt-West Africa relationship using the African Renaissance model.

The *Catalan Atlas* and the Hereford *Mappa Mundi* Representation of West Africa
The *Catalan Atlas* or Cresques' *Atlas*, completed in 1375, was commissioned by Prince John of Aragon and made by Abraham Cresques, a Majorcan Jew who lived in

Catalonia (Cresques 1375).[1] It is now in France in the Bibliothèque Nationale. It was originally titled 'Mappa Mundi, image of the world and of the regions there are on Earth and the various peoples which inhabit it'. This atlas incorporated Africa – West Africa. It is included in the chapter because of its representation of the West African people and landscape. I use it to make a contrast with the Hereford *Mappa Mundi*.

The *Catalan Atlas*, or Cresques' *Atlas*, is worthy of being renamed *Atlas Africana*, since it was a great source of information which aided Europeans in plotting their sea routes to explore the West African coast and indeed Africa as a whole.[2] Cresques' *Atlas* was probably drawn from a combination of knowledge obtained from the Jews and from Arab travellers, who had already been to the African continent three hundred years before the first Europeans arrived (Lydon 2009). Petersen states that:

'The means by which Islam penetrated into West Africa was via the trade routes from North Africa. The main goods involved in the trade included gold, slaves, ivory and gum from West Africa and manufactured goods from the Mediterranean area. This trade was a continuation of pre-Islamic Roman and Byzantine trade routes and was in the hands of the Berber tribes of the Sahara. Already by the end of the seventh century there are accounts of Muslim traders from North Africa and Egypt in the markets of the Sudan. By the end of the eighth century the northern part of the trade was controlled by the semi-independent Berber dynasties of the Rustamids in Morocco and the Idrisids in western Algeria. These dynasties controlled the northern termini of the West African routes at Sijimassa and Tahert and were able to collect taxes from this lucrative trade.' (Petersen 1996, 302-3)

Sources relating to Arab travels to Africa, from the North to the West African coast, belong to an important phase prior to European African exploration but are highly relevant to it. Mansa Musa, mentioned in the *Atlas* by Cresques, made his 'legendary pilgrimage' to Mecca in 1325, accompanied on his return by Abu Ishaq al-Saheli, an Andalusian poet. Although following closely in the footsteps of earlier kings of Mali, the most noteworthy aspect of Mansa Musa's outward journey was the way in which he dispensed large quantities of gold; so much so that a contemporary account recorded that the value of gold in Egypt was considerably depreciated after his arrival (Hopkins and Levtzion 1981). Mansa Musa's fame and that of his kingdom of Mali spread all over the Islamic world, to the extent that Mali appeared on contemporary European maps of the time (Petersen 1996, 170-3; Whitfield 1994, 28-9).

Mansa Musa had acquired his great wealth as a consequence of the unification of the empire and the subordination of neighbouring states such as Ghana, Gagaran and Bambuko, which were areas rich in gold (Hopkins and Levtzion 1981). Cresques was aware of this history, for in his *Atlas*, particularly in leaf six, there is a vivid image of Africa as the wealthiest continent in the world (as part of leaf five also indicates). Mansa Musa, the king of Meli (Mali), was depicted by Cresques as the richest and noblest man in this entire region as he received his Saharan merchant. Cresques said: 'This Negro Lord is called Musa Melly, the Lord of the Negroes of this Guinea, this king is very rich and noblest Lord of all this region for the abundance of wealth that is in his land' (Cresques 1375, 30).[3] In this work Cresques showed a balanced appreciation of African civilisations and of the empire of Mali in particular. His wide-ranging interest enabled him to take a reflective approach, providing a positive representation of the African continent which was subsequently treated in the 18th and 19th centuries in a rather negative fashion (Lorimer 1978, 131-255; Palmberg 2001, 7-74).

It would seem unreasonable to suppose that Cresques had not intentionally imposed some of his own understanding of Africa on his *Catalan Atlas* (Cresques 1375, 30). Certainly he had ample justification for representing Africa in its true light. His portrait of African economy, culture and war-ready strength was endorsed by later writers (Donelhas 1625). It was in this positive frame of reference that Cresques deliberately set out to represent Africa. According to him, Mansa Musa was a truly regal king, to be depicted wearing a crown of gold on his head and holding in his left hand a gold sceptre and in the right hand a gold nugget. He saw the continent of Africa surrounded by a column of mountains broken by Arabs at a place called 'Vall de Darha', thus indicating their commercial activities in the interior of Africa (including Egypt). The column of mountains also signified the political and commercial control by the succession of Mali's kings, particularly Mansa Kanka Musa, simply known as Mansa Musa. Cresques indicates the extent of the knowledge that was available to him from merchant travels to Africa and in particular their trading with Mali's ruling class. Cresques states that:

'En aqueſt loch paſſen los merchaders q[ue] entren en le terra dels negres de gineua lo qual pas es appellat vall de darba' ('Merchants pass through this place if they wish to enter the land of the Negroes of Guinea. This pass is called Vall de Darha [Valley of Darha]'; Cresques 1375, leaf 6).

---

[1] Abraham Cresques' *Atlas* is in the Bibliothèque Nationale, Paris, France, in the Département des Manuscrits Division Occidentale, catalogued as *El Atlas Catalan*, Espagnol 30, 1375. The *Atlas* was given to Charles V of France, perhaps by the King of Aragon, as a gift. Since then it has been kept in the Bibliothèque Nationale, probably since 1380. The original author is disputed; there is no doubt, however, that Cresques was the final author of this important work, if not the original author.

[2] Cresques' son Jafudà Cresques, known as Jaume Ribes, was appointed by Henry the Navigator as the coordinator of Portuguese cartography at the naval school of Sagres in the 1420s (see Diffie and Winius 1977, 116-7; Pacheco Pereira 1954, chapter 33).

[3] *El Atlas Catalan*, folio 6 [my translation]: 'Aqueſt ſenyor negre es appellat Musse Melly ſenyor dels negre de gineua aqueſt rey es pus rich el pus noble ſenyor de tota eſta partida per l'abondãçia de la qual feraull en la suua terra'.

Figure 1. Representation of Africa, in Abraham Cresques' *El Atlas Catalan* (Espagnol 30, folio 6, 1375). The West African cities and towns mentioned in leaf six of Cresques' map are: 'Tenbuch' (Timbuktu), 'ciuitado Mellj' (The City of Melli), '*f*udam' (Sudan), 'Tagaza' and the entire region of West Africa – GUNYIA (Guinea).

Cresques surely showed the passage to the interior of Africa which was the main route to the main markets of the continent, through which all the merchants going to and fro passed, giving the precise name of the valley as the Valley of Darha, although there were several different trans-Saharan routes at the time, including that of Sijilmassa. It was through this valley that merchants returned from the great commercial sites such as Timbuktu, Gadja (Gao) and Tagaza, which were centres of enormous mercantile interest. Thus, Darha was the gateway providing a link between the Mediterranean world, Egypt, Spain and Italy and Timbuktu, as Leo Africanus, the early 16th century Arab traveller and scholar who visited the region was to discover a century later:

'This Prouince beginning at mount Atlas extendeth it selfe southward by the deserts of Lybia almost two hundred and fiftie miles, and the bredth thereof is verie narrow. All the inhabitans dwell upon a certain riuer which is called by the name of the Prouince... [T]heir castles are inhabited by goldsmiths and other artificers, and so are all the regions lying in the way from Tombuto to Fez: in this prouince also there are three or fower proper townes, frequented by merchants and strangers, and containing many shops and temples... [A] merchant they will most courteously entertaine a whole yeere together, and then friendly dismissing him, they will require nought at his hands, but will accept such liberalitie as he thinkes good to bestow vpon them.' (Leo Africanus 1632, 778-9)

Consequently, Cresques presents a wealthy Africa that Europeans coveted, not the poor and backward continent that later Portuguese historians led us to believe (Terra 1964). Further, Cresques' description of Africa in his *Atlas* appears to be North Africa geographically (North Africa including West Africa) but his location of the main cities indicates that he was dealing with West African urban centres. Among the West African cities and towns mentioned in leaf six of Cresques' map were: 'Tenbuch' (Timbuktu), 'ciuitado Mellj' (The City of Melli), '*f*udam' (Sudan), 'Tagaza' and the entire region of West Africa – GUNYIA (Guinea). Cresques' ideology is clearly shown in this little known atlas, for it contains not only maps and geographical references, but also cosmology. Cresques showed the importance of Egypt to the rest of Africa, but in particular West Africa through commercial routes and it was via these routes that West Africa connected with Egypt culturally (Figure 1).

Cresques' *Atlas* differs from those of other Medieval cartographers, for he depicted Africans as full human beings, not in the fashion of a distorted image of half-body and half-animal to be seen, for example, in Hereford's 13th century *Mappa Mundi* drawn by Richard of Haldingham (Figure 2).[4] The ideology found in the Haldingham's *Mappa Mundi* was later used in the 18th century by the machinery of the slave trade in order to justify its own cause (Costa 2004, 63-72; Lorimer 1978).

---

[4] Richard Haldingham, also known as Holdingham (*d.* 1278?), was a cartographic patron and probably a map-maker. He is believed to be the author of the Hereford *Mappa Mundi*. Haldingham was a hamlet in the parish of Lafford, Lincolnshire. Lafford was a prebend of Lincoln Cathedral. Haldingham refers to this in this map as a way of marking his identity. In 1265 Haldingham was a canon of Lincoln, and he also held the office of treasurer of Lincoln Cathedral from October 1270 to April 1278. He died on 4th November 1278. There may be more than one author to this map. For detailed discussion on the authorship of this map, see Ramsay 2004; see also Harvey 2002.

Figure 2. Richard of Haldingham's *Mappa Mundi* (1290) in Hereford Cathedral, depicting a T-shape map with three continents: Africa, Asia and Europe.

When considering the Hereford *Mappa Mundi*, we need to juxtapose it with Herodotus' accounts of travel in the ancient world outside his homeland Greece, with which it has many points in common. In his *Histories*, Herodotus describes the peoples and places he observed ethnographically but there is also a sense of mythology about them. He writes of the Egyptians that, 'not only is the Egyptian climate peculiar to that country, and the Nile different in its behaviour from other rivers elsewhere, but the Egyptians themselves in their manners and customs seem to have reversed the ordinary practices of mankind. For instance, women attend market and are employed in trade, while men stay at home and do the weaving' (Herodotus, *Histories*, trans. Sélincourt 1996, 98). Here Herodotus is suggesting that the manners and customs of which he is a part are the way of mankind and what he has encountered in Egypt is of course 'other' (Pieterse 1992, 29; Snowden 1983).

Pliny represents his 'others' as monstrous: they are portrayed as more closely resembling animals than humans, a discourse with lasting momentum that would culminate in the European expansion and colonisation of the lands these people supposedly inhabit. Furthermore Richard of Haldingham's Hereford *Mappa Mundi* shows images of the 'other' similar to the ones described by Pliny (Figures 3-6; Harvey 2002; Oxford Dictionary of National Biography 2004). Crone suggests a reason for these representations as being 'partly mythical and partly based on misunderstood or distorted characteristics' (Crone 1949, 14). It is a presentation encoded in the medieval mentality of the time about the people who live in a distant land beyond the known world of Europe, who are believed to be affected by the conditions of their climates. Strickland states that:

'Medieval authorities believed that climates, time and place of birth, balance of bodily fluids and physical appearance were all related to each other, and if properly interpreted could be used to gauge a person's character... [T]he universe was believed to be composed of the four basic elements of air, water, fire, and earth. The varying balance of these elements produced the different world climates and determined whether a given place was habitable or not. Therefore, the first step in the analysis of a person's physical form was assessment of environmental influences, the most important of which was climate.' (Strickland 2003, 30)

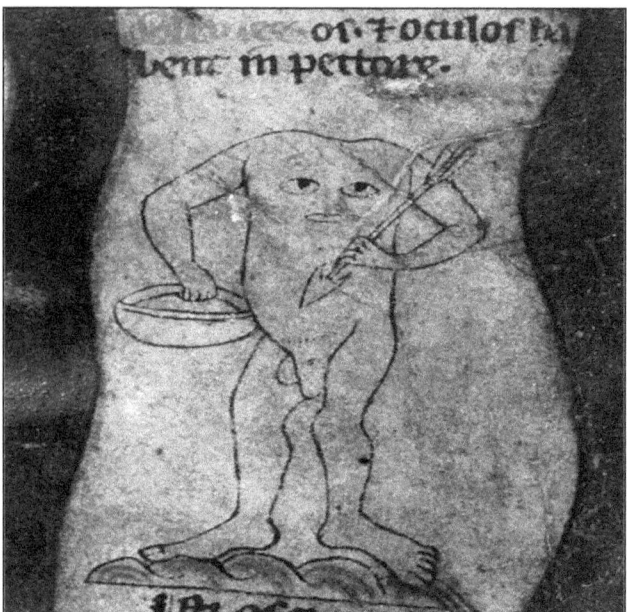

Figure 3. Headless male Blemy holding his weapon – an arrow, from the Hereford *Mappa Mundi* (1290), described as: 'Blemee: os et oculos habent in pectore' ('The Blemmyes have their mouth and their eyes in their chest').

Figure 4. Headless female Blemy holding her weapon, from the Hereford *Mappa Mundi* (1290), described as: 'Isti os et oculos hnt ī humeris' ('These ones have mouth and eyes in their shoulders').

The *Mappa Mundi* is concerned with the geography of the world as was understood in the West and its worldview which includes mental representation. Lagerlund explains how medieval representation operates:

'(R1) The mental representation and the thing represented have the same form.
(R2) The mental representation resembles, or is a likeness of, the thing represented.
(R3) The mental representation is caused by the thing represented.
(R4) The mental representation signifies the thing represented.'
(Lagerlund 2004, 14-16)

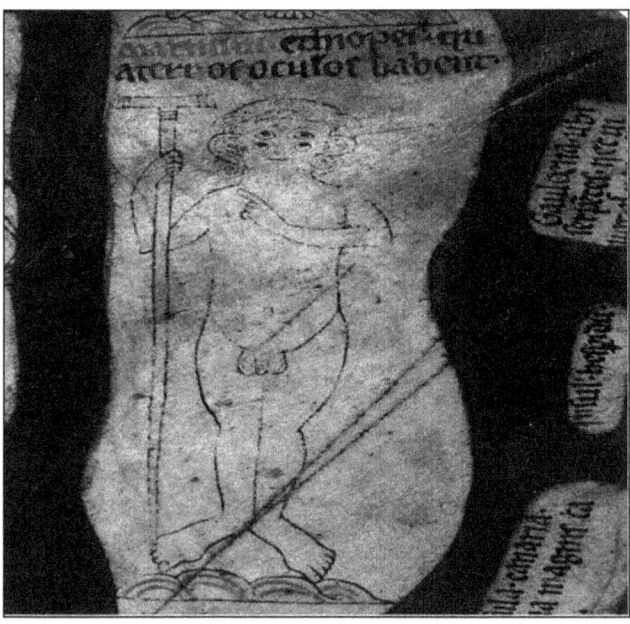

Figure 5. Marnumi Ethiopian holding his weapon, from the Hereford *Mappa Mundi* (1290), described as: 'Marnumi Ethiopes quaternos oculos habent' ('Marnumi Ethiopians have four eyes').

Figure 6. From the Hereford *Mappa Mundi* (1290): Gens ore concreto calamo cibatur' ('A people with a sealed mouth who take food through a straw').

The representation of monsters in the Hereford map is an expression of power and it is also an enquiry into the private and public dimensions of the perversity of the Other, whose complexion, practices and deviances break the acceptable rules of civilisation, namely of Europe (Lagerlund 2004). Religion – Christianity – was used as a yardstick by which to measure the mental capacity of the others to govern themselves. Non-Christians were generally thought of as 'barbarians' and 'uncivilised'. The people who lived furthest from the centre of civilisation, including Christianity, were viewed as monstrous races (Lagerlund 2004). These persons represented disorder, a major fear in the mind of medieval Europe (Friedman 1981, 30-55). This psychology is implied and coded in the headless Blemyes with two eyes in their chests and shoulders respectively, Sciapods who possess a single large foot, four-eyed Ethiopian men and three-faced Ambaris. Apart from their strange practices and distorted anatomies, the Blemyes' political system was flawed, hence acephalous, that is with no head (Hawthorne 1998, 2) – acephalous means a stateless society or an ethnic group that does not have a king. Thus the Blemyes represented political fragmentation, without a legal system to govern them. They also represented the other side of humanity: emotional and incapable of controlling its own destiny (Liddell and Robert 1901, 301, 744, 821, 1003). As headless people they were inclined to strong sexual urges, social upheaval and religiously superstition in need of Christianity. They were depicted as people in constant inter-ethnic conflicts (Figure 7).

Figure 7. Gangines Ethiopians at war with each other, from the Hereford *Mappa Mundi* (1290), described as: 'Gangines ethiopes amicia cum eis non eft' ('Gangines Ethiopians: with them there is no friendship').

The *Mappa Mundi* also depicted Egypt through the Red Sea and connected Egypt with sub-Saharan Africa via the River Nile which ran through the entire continent (Figure 8). The importance of Egypt to West Africa was later inferred by the Portuguese explorers in the 16th century, but these links remained seminal rather than historical (Almada 1594; Cadamosto 1944; Donelhas 1625; Hair and Mota 1977). Almada claimed that the pattern of agriculture used in West Africa was similar to that of Egypt and that the River Nile was an important source of irrigation in West Africa: 'usaren nas suas searas e lavouras, como usão os do Egypto com as crescentes do Rio Nilo' ('They did in their harvests and farming, as they do in Egypt, with the rising of the River Nile'; Almada 1594, chapter I)

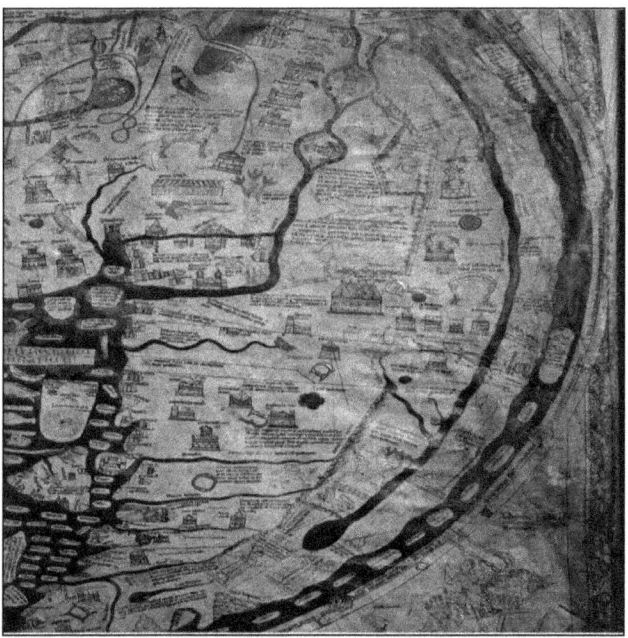

Figure 8. Representation of Africa in Richard of Haldingham's *Mappa Mundi* (1290).

The fundamental differences between these two maps lie in their ideological content and also their practical knowledge. Haldingham's map was based on the scant knowledge that was available at this time; Africa (without Egypt) was still considered an old world by Europeans even though so little was known about it. The depiction of Africa on maps such as this betrayed contemporary ignorance as well as knowledge. In fact, what little knowledge existed was based mainly on that acquired from the Romans (Crone 1954; Harvey 2002, 22; Westrem 2001, xiv-xlvi).

According to the medieval world-view, the world was in the shape of a **T** with only three continents: Africa, Asia and Europe (Figure 2). Africans and Asians were portrayed as cannibals with a distorted anatomy, half-human and half-animal and they were involved in inhumane acts, practices which were condemned by the Church, whereas Cresques' representations of Africans were very different, for he depicted Africans as fully human and engaged in the affairs of their time, producers of culture and masters of their own destiny. Cresques' *Atlas* was a precursor to the Portuguese expedition to Africa; it provided detailed knowledge available at the time, indicating clearly names of towns and cities. It also showed the economic strength of the Africans.

Portuguese Expansion and Representation of Africa

The Portuguese or 'Western' encounter with the people and traditions of West Africa occurred in the second half of the 15th century. The term 'Western' is used here in its fullest sense to refer to Europeans and others from different countries – Portugal, Spain, Holland, France, England, Palestine, Italy, Greece and Germany – who had established contact in one form or another with West Africa. While North and East Africa as far as the Sahara had been penetrated by Westerners since Roman times, by the 15th century West Africa was also very much on their maps. However, Egypt as part of Africa was largely excluded, hence 'Africa invented' (Mudimbe 1988). In fact the entire West African coast was known as austral Ethiopia (Aethiopia australis) or inferior Libya (Libia inferior). The ancient geographer and astronomer Ptolemy had called the region Agizimba, though later it was called Guinea.[5] Thus, Münzer confidently stated the vastness of the area in the following terms:

'Indeed Ethiopia is very wide and long, as is seen in Ptolemy's map, because in the equatorial regions, and in respect of its great length [it] corresponds with its width, as astronomers know, and [it is] very marshy. And it sustains the tallest trees, to say the least.' (Münzer 1494/1958, fols. 280-8)

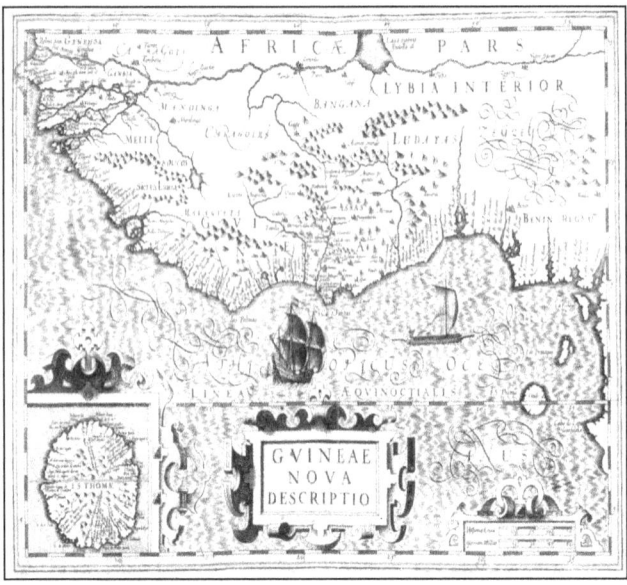

Figure 9. Gvineae Nova Descriptio, *Atlas Mercator* (1609). Collection of the Centre for the Study of History and Ancient Cartography, Instituto de Investigação Científica Tropical, Portugal. The map shows the region of the Upper Guinea Coast.

By the time Portuguese interest became focused on this region and not on Egypt and its relation to West Africa, map makers and scholars had introduced significant terms of differentiation. The area of West Africa from Cape Verde to Cape Mount was known by the Portuguese as Guiné do Cabo Verde, Rios de Guiné do Cabo Verde, Senegâmbia de Cabo Verde, by the French as Rivières du Sud and by the English as the Upper Guinea Coast (Rodney 1972, 1-6). At the same time, the region as a whole was called by the Moorish name Guinauha (Guinea), meaning a land inhabited by Negroes, a name probably adopted by the Portuguese (see Figure 9).

Portuguese exploration during the 15th century came about largely as the culmination of long established and familiar aims and skills: tracing the source of gold and spices which for centuries had been obtained from the ports of North Africa and the Eastern Mediterranean. Although European merchants had already crossed the Sahara and ventured overland to China, by the end of the 14th century it had become clear that resources could only be tapped profitably by sea. Long sea voyages therefore became commonplace by the 15th century. Venetian traders turned up regularly in English ports, while Baltic traders plied their trade in the ports of Spain. The Portuguese too were ready to take advantage of the existing culture of overseas exploration and trade.

The Portuguese interest in the region was not entirely motivated by Christianity, but by their perceived need for commerce and trade. Spies returning from North Africa gave a greater incentive for the government's decision to mount the expedition to the West African coast.[6] This expedition was undertaken on the basis of up-to-date knowledge emanating from the schools of cartography, such as that in Catalonia. In particular, the work of Abraham Cresques – the *Catalan Atlas* – may have been one the major catalysts of Portuguese interest in trading with the interior of Africa.[7] This Portuguese overseas expansion project began under Dom Henrique (better known to the English-speaking world as Henry the Navigator)[8] and took many years to complete. However,

---

[5] See Gomes 1900, fol. 270, p. 187. Of this region, Gomes has given the following description: 'qualiter fuit inuenta Aethiopia australis quae Libia inferior nuncupatur vltra descriptionem Ptolomei quae Agizimba nominabatur nunc vero Guinea ab inuentoribus Portugalensibus nuncupata est vsque hodiernum diem'; 'Just as Ethiopia austral was discovered from what was called inferior Libya which Ptolemy also described as Agizimba, now, assuredly, it is called Guinea by the Portuguese discoverers, up to the present day' (author's translation).

[6] Spies were sent by João II to North Africa to find out about what was going on in the interior of Africa. The source of information at this time was the Arab merchants who had been going to the region many years before the Portuguese, so when the spies returned they gave positive information to the Portuguese Crown about African commerce. It must also be noted that spies were an integral part of Portuguese political and commercial activities with foreign lands. Spying was not an activity confined to the Portuguese alone, but also the Spaniards. Ferdinand, King of Spain, made effective use of diplomacy and was assisted by a cadre of diplomats, agents and spies. For detailed information on this topic, see Payne 1973; Thomas and Cortesão 1938.

[7] Obviously this was not the only map of the period, there are many others such as: *North Atlantic Atlas* (1546) by João Freire, and *Universal Atlas* (1560) by unknown author in *Livro de Marinharia, de João de Lisboa*. For detailed information, see Souto 1973; see also Diffie and Winius 1977.

[8] Henry the Navigator was the son of João I of Portugal. Born in 1394, he was in charge of the voyages of discovery that he organised and financed, which led to the 'discovery' of Africa and the sea routes to India. Henry was also a very devout man, and was Governor of the Order of Christ from 1420 until his death in 1460. By the time of his death the Portuguese had explored as far as Sierra Leone in West

it was the Perfect Prince (Princípe Perfeito), João II, who made it what it was. His meticulous organisation and dealings with African kings, directly paying them taxes in order to gain trade licences, established the project on a relatively firm footing (Rodney 1972).

Portuguese cultural exchange that took place soon after the European contact with West Africa from 1446 and its cultural relation to Egypt remains peripheral in scholarly debate, rarely discussed in literature or at international academic gatherings – in particular the impact of Egypt on West African history and the human interaction and the exploration of the common humanity in the continent. Sources emerging from Portuguese expansion rarely mention or express the importance of Egypt to the West; even where it is mentioned, its apparent historical significance is not stated.

Fundamentally there has been little attempt to establish the place of Egypt in Africa in terms of human relations, whether between rulers and nobles or at grass roots, from a socio-religious, diplomatic, political and economic perspective. This lack of scholarly engagement with sub-Saharan Africa has led to debate about Eurocentrism and New Afrocentrism, and in particular to debate about the African Renaissance. The notion 'Egypt-Africa or Africa-Egypt' has been predicated on racial prejudice (Snowden 1983). Black African, sub-Saharan regions have traditionally been associated with backwardness and, later in the 18th and 19th centuries, enveloped within interrelated discourses, particularly those concerning 'race' and 'racism' (Snowden 1983).

The African Renaissance Model
Egypt and its influences on the rest of the continent have been debated around the issue of African pride, hence 'Renaissance'. Njeza recently stated that it has become fashionable in certain circles of contemporary discourse to talk about *Afrocentrism*. At the socio-political level the debate is centred around the concept of African Renaissance, whereas the religio-theological dimensions of the discourse are concerned with African Christianity (1997, 47). It is the former that is the concern of this chapter and I will examine the socio-political aspect of that debate, interrogating particularly the contention of Appiah (1997). But, first, we need to look at the Mbeke's claim (1998) about African Renaissance.

The political hypothesis is that the African root of Egyptian civilisation must be accepted as given. Egypt is in Africa, for this reason historiography must give preferential treatment to its value and influence for African identity formation (Mudimbe 1988). The concern is a political and a cultural one, that African identity must bypass European influences and return to the values that have been neglected and under-reported by Europeans. The cry is to African identity and Egypt as a source for its political development and positive representation (Njeza 1997).

An African Renaissance from this point of view is to contest the basic tenets of European modes of representation and produce an alternative to its dominant consensual discourse. African Renaissance rejects at face value the European model of knowing reality, hence ontology. It also challenges Western epistemology, that is, in terms of knowing African reality and not only knowing, but also setting a specific form of knowledge about how to know Africa. This contestation is to demonstrate critically that knowing is parochial and a representation of the known reality, and, in the case of Africa, is ideologically driven. African Renaissance raises fundamental questions of identity, nationalism, the inhumanity of Africans, racial stereotyping and power. The contention is to question the absence of Egypt in the representation of Africa; for Mbeke, Egypt plays an important part so far as African identities are concerned, that is, Egypt is an important part of ideologies of culture for Africa. The task of African intellectuals, according to Mbeke, is to denaturalise Eurocentric representational texts on African history and culture, by demonstrating that its commonsense meanings are not a given, but broadly a product of ideological coding. Mbeke states:

'I speak of African works of art in South Africa that are a thousand years old. I speak of the continuum in the fine arts that encompasses the varied artistic creations of the Nubians and the Egyptians, the Benin bronzes of Nigeria and the intricate sculptures of the Makonde of Tanzania and Mozambique. I speak of the centuries-old contributions to the evolution of religious thought made by the Christians of Ethiopia and the Muslims of Nigeria.'
(Mbeke: http://www.unu.edu/unupress/mbeki.html)

Mbeke's attempt is to revitalise the African image by claiming its authenticity in an African glorious past, hence a critical engagement with the past text and representation, providing Africans with tools to work towards demythologising stereotypical discourses about the continent. African Renaissance is fundamental in reverting negative images of Africa and connecting its current identity with that of antiquity. Mbeke goes further:

'[A]n essential and necessary element of the African Renaissance is that we all must take it as our task to encourage she, who carries this leaden weight, to rebel, to assert the principality of her humanity – the fact that she, in the first instance, is not a beast of burden, but a human and African being.'
(Mbeke: http://www.unu.edu/unupress/mbeki.html)

Mbeke's statement demonstrates the complexity of colonial representation and its aftermath, *viz.* postcolonial engagement towards the possibilities of cultural 'recovery' or 'return to the source'; his rationale problematises terms and concepts such as African identity and history, which are often characterised by fixity of language and imaginative space. Notwithstanding, Mbeke is calling for a new reading of the African past that involves revising its history. He argues for a rejection of

---
Africa. For more detailed information, see Livermore 1976, 107-38; Russell 1995.

representation of that which dismisses or omits African identities and ways of belonging to a human race. Let us return to Appiah's contention on the question of Egypt and its sub-Saharan African influence, hence African Renaissance. I will use terms such as African Renaissance, New Afrocentrism and 'Kemetism' simultaneously in this chapter.

A major issue for the articulation of the African Renaissance and New Afrocentrism experience lies in the question about Egypt and its relations with the rest of Africa, which pertains to the apparent inescapability of structures of imperial domination, allowing that all anti-colonial struggles inevitably involve an acknowledgement of regimes of colonial power and control. Appiah indicates that tensions between Afrocentrism and Eurocentrism are posited on false premises. For Appiah, both Afrocentrism and Eurocentrism are ethnocentric, because they are fought on the basis of the superiority of a particular race or ethnic groups, hence Europeans and Africans. Appiah terms this 'the Greek and African miracle' (1997, 47), acknowledging that any sort of resistance attained by the post-colonial subject will still be permeated by discursive reminders of their colonial history. As such, Afrocentrism's approach to the theorisation of this complex project of moving beyond Egypt or 'Kemetism' of identity and value, of locating subject-positions, fails, because of its obsession with Egypt. Afrocentrism for Appiah is 'Europe upside down', in that it mimics Eurocentric claims of authenticity which go back to Greece as a centre of Western civilisation. Ella Shohat and Robert Stam classify Eurocentrism in five discourses, but I will only use the first one:

'Eurocentric discourse projects a linear historical trajectory leading from classical Greece (constructed as 'pure', 'Western', and 'democratic') to imperial Rome and then to metropolitan capitals of Europe and the US. It renders history as sequences of empires: Pax Romana, Pax Hispanica, Pax Britannica, Pax Americana. In all cases, Europe, alone and unaided, is seen as the 'motor' for progressive historical change: it invents class society, feudalism, capitalism, the industrial revolution.' (Shohat and Stam 1994, 2)

This particularity of Greece is taken up by Afrocentrism to claim that Egypt is the centre of African civilisation. For Appiah, Egypt must have a meaning outside of Eurocentric hierarchical discourse. Appiah argues for different views of 'Kemetism' theory and that there are varieties of perspectives and positions available with which to engage with ideas about the potential scope of strategies of resisting colonial ideology and representation. He states:

'Like most cultural movements at full flood, this Afrocentric turn is a composite of truth and error, insight and illusion, moral generosity and meanness. But if there is one thing that strikes me more about it than any other it is how thoroughly at home it is in the frameworks of nineteenth century European thought. (One of the symptomatic features of much Afrocentric writing is that the antagonists it identifies are largely dead.) Afrocentrism, in short, seems very much to share the presuppositions of the Victorian ideologies against which it is reacting.' (Appiah 1997, 49)

Appiah's main argument is based on the inadequacy of Afrocentrism's rationale to underwrite any Eurocentric concept of unique origin. The flaw of Afrocentrism in this instance is its direct borrowing of Eurocentric model of superior versus inferior, which is enshrined in difference. For Appiah such difference is detrimental to the rest of the content, because it fails to acknowledge the history and cultural values of sub-Saharan Africa. Afrocentric interest in Egypt contains within it a system of inequality and distorted types of knowledge which negates, dismisses and omits African identities and ways of belonging. Legitimising the centrality of Egypt for Africa is inherently Eurocentric, that is, Afrocentric historiography is to see Ancient Egypt containing political, social and religious structures equal to that of Greece, and complex architectural and literate systems. For Appiah this model represents a Eurocentric regime of power used to measure successful historical achievements and in so doing excluding other civilisations. As Shohat states:

'Europe is seen as the unique source of meaning, as the world's center of gravity, as ontological "reality" to the rest of the world's shadow. Eurocentric thinking attributes to the "West" an almost providential sense of historical destiny. Eurocentrism, like Renaissance perspectives in painting, envisions the world from a single privileged point. It maps the world in a cartography that centralizes and augments Europe while literally "belittling" Africa.' (Shohat 1994, 1-2)

The Afrocentric point of reference has been to give preferential treatment to Egypt as the centre of civilisation, which in turn gives a positive image for Africa and becomes the seat for African cultural unity. Appiah remarks, '[i]t is surely *prima facie* preposterous to suppose that there is an African culture, shared by everyone from the civilizations of the upper Nile thousands of years ago to the thousand or so language-zones of contemporary Africa?' (1997, 49). For Appiah, to centralise debate on Egypt without engaging with the rest of Africa is 'simply Eurocentrism turned upside down' (1997, 49).

Appiah, however, has been critised recently for his stance on African Afrocentrism by Njeza. For Njeza, Afrocentrism is essential in understanding Egypt and its place in Africa and in the construction of African identity politics. He contends that:

'Afrocentrism is not about replacing white with black Egypt, or *vice-versa*. It is not the pigmentation thereof, but the geo-cultural location of Egypt that concerns us. In fact, evidence indicates that ancient Egyptians varied in skin colour from very dark to light brown and, significantly, that they were culturally African… [I]t is...the symbolism of Egypt as part of the continent of Africa and ancient Egypt as a symbol of African pride and initiative that places it at the centre of Afrocentrist discourse. Afrocentrism is not about black totalitarianism; rather it is about making a claim for Africa in world history.' (Njeza 1997, 53)

According to Njeza, Appiah's argument is flawed on the grounds that Afrocentrism is not a direct substitute for Eurocentrism. He contends that the aim of Afrocentrism is not to engage critically with historiography of Egypt, 'but rather to promote a more authentic view of the world as the product of all human cultures, broadly defined and valued in their many hues, not least of which is black. In so doing, Afrocentrism...challenges Eurocentric claims to superiority' (Njeza 1997, 53). Allowing that Ancient Egyptian history and its role in constructing African identities is still being overshadowed by Eurocentric discourses and representations, this makes Afrocentrism an indispensable tool in defusing these negatives claims. Njeza states that, 'Africa's claim is necessary in connecting contemporary African identity with that of the past, even antiquity. We need to continue to relate the past to the present even if only to demonstrate evolutions of modern Africa and the modern African' (1997, 53). Past colonial domination provoked a re-reading and re-writing of African history and its relation to classical Greek civilisation. The historiography of Africa has been Eurocentric in tone, favouring Western dominant discourse:

'[It] was recast to conform to colonialist norms, in the name of an eternal West unique since its moment of conception. From the African Renaissance point of view, their claim is not merely reactionism, it is not a reaction to Eurocentrism but rather to Eurocentric *racialism*. African Renaissance simply challenges the basis of the Aryan model and reasserts the claims of the ancient model in a revised form if necessary.' (Njeza 1997, 53)

Challenges to the Eurocentric discourse, however, are not new. At the heart of Martin Bernal's thesis is an attempt to revise the interpretation of the place of Egypt in Africa and to argue for an acknowledgement of the African roots of, and influences on, classical Greek civilisation. Bernal contends that 'Greece derived its civilization from Egypt' (2001, 38). The debate here is for recognition that Africa has played a major role in influencing European civilisation. Notwithstanding, philosophers such as Hegel rejected from the outset any Egyptian influence on Greek culture, *viz*. religion and philosophy. For Hegel, 'Egypt belongs to the history of the Persian Empire, rather than to the history of Africa' (Bernasconi 1998, 43). This particular debate is beyond the remit of this paper. Afrocentrism in Jana's words has a wider agenda than that envisaged by Appiah. For Jana 'the African Renaissance vision is an all-embracing concept that draws its inspiration from the rich and diverse history and cultures of Africa. It acknowledges Africa as the cradle of humanity, whilst providing a framework for the modern Africa to re-emerge as a significant partner in the New World order' (2001, 38). However to do justice to Appiah, his critique is not entirely about philosophical thinking emanating from Africa about the place and the relationship of Egypt to rest of Africa, but that of American intellectuals.

Concluding remarks

Afrocentrism is an attempt to reverse representations of Africa and it aims are to place Africa at the centre of the world history debate, which should be inclusive about the continent. Thus, the pre-colonial Africa represented in the *Catalan Atlas*, particularly with regard to Ancient Egypt, did not receive the attention that was required to map out African identity and its culture. It appears more of an appendix and the Black Africans that are represented in the *Mappa Mundi* appear to be caricatures. Evidence for the Portuguese view of Egypt and its importance to West Africa from the period between 1446 and 1800 in terms of culture and identity is even slighter. Sources from this period are scant; even the extant reports from the later period are disjointed and incoherent. These reports appear uninterested in historical connections between Egypt and West Africa in terms of identity or culture and for the most part, appear as little more than historical anecdotes which make it virtually impossible to offer any reliable reading, except those of 20th century scholarship that have attempted to make such historical links. The scholar is thus faced with a great deal of hard work requiring considerable caution in order to attempt to reconstruct individual events. Certainly, the accounts that have come down to us are far from providing adequate evidence for the reconstruction of Ancient Egypt and its connection with West Africa.

The *Catalan Atlas* representation of the West Africa is significant for making an attempt to reconstruct the African past, but even in this atlas particular attention is not given to Egypt and its particular place in the history of West Africa. For this reason the claim of Afrocentrism in constructing African identities from Egypt is not farfetched and nor can it be seen as attempt to replace the Eurocentric claim with that of an African one. It must be understood as political claim about the cultural and historical location of Egypt that is pertinent to the rest of African identity.

References

Almada, A. Á. 1594. *Tratados Breue dos Rejnos Deguine Docaboverde*. Lisbon, Biblioteca Nacional de Lisboa.

Appiah, K. A. 1997. Europe Upside Down: Fallacies of the New Afrocentrism, in R. R. Grinker and C. S. Steiner (eds.), *Perspectives on Africa*, 48-54. London, Blackwell Publishers.

Barros, J. 1932. *Década I*. Lisbon, Sá da Costa.

Bernal, M. 2001. European Images of Africa – Tale of Two Names: Ethiopia and N---. In D. M. Mengara (ed.), *Images of Africa: Stereotypes and Realities*, 23-45. Trento, Africa World Press.

Bernasconi, R. 1998. Hegel at the Court of the Ashanti.

In Barnett, S. (ed.), *Hegel after Derrida*, 41-63. London, Routledge.

Burns, A. 1948. *Colour Prejudice with Particular Reference to the Relationship between Whites and Negroes*. London, Allen and Unwin.

Cadamosto, L. 1944. *Navegações de Luís de Cadamosto, Texto Italiano, e Tradução Portuguesa do Dr. Giuseppe Carlo Rossi*. Lisbon, Instituto para a Alta Cultura.

Cardozo, M. 1962. A Tradição Náutica na mais Antiga História da Península Ibérica. *Actas do Congresso Internacional de História dos Descobrimentos* 3, 15-42.

Costa, P. F. 2004. Between Fact and Fiction: Narratives of Monsters in Eighteenth-Century Portugal. *Portuguese Studies* 20, 63-72.

Cresques, A. 1375. *El Atlas Catalan, Espagnol 30* (Bibliothèque Nationale de France, Département des Manuscrits Division Occidentale, Paris).

Crone, G. R. 1954. *Memoir Accompanying Reproductions of Early Maps III: The World Map by Richard of Haldingham in Hereford Cathedral circa A. D. 1285*. London, Royal Geographical Society.

Devisse, J. 1979. *The Image of the Black in Western Art 2: From the Early Christian Era to the 'Age of Discovery'*. Cambridge, Mass. and London, Harvard University Press.

Diffie, B. W. and Winius, G. D. 1977. *Foundations of the Portuguese Empire, 1415-1580, Volume 1*. Minneapolis, University of Minnesota Press.

Donelhas, A. 1625. *Outra Relação em 14 Capítolos que fez Andre Donellas, ao Governador e Capitão Geral Fr. de Vaz Concellos da Cunha; Sobre a Serra Leoa, Reys e Senhores que a Habitão, e Secunvezinhos, Ritos, Costumes e Todas Variedades de Rios, Portos, Arvores, Animais Aves Pexes com os Proveitos que Dela se Tirão*. Ms. 51-IX-25, Palácio de Ajuda.

Friedman, J. B. 1981. *The Monstrous Races in Medieval Art and Thought*. Cambridge, Mass., Harvard University Press.

Gomes, D. 1900. Relações do Descobrimento da Guiné e das Ilhas dos Açores, Madeira e Cabo Verde, Versão do latim por Gabriel Pereira. *Separata do Boletim da Sociedade de Geografia de Lisboa*, 17a. Série, No. 5. Lisbon.

Hair, P. E. and Mota, A. T. (eds.) 1977. *Descrição da Serra Leoa e dos Rios de Guiné do Cabo Verde (1625)*. Lisbon, Junta de Investigações Científicas do Ultramar.

Hall, S. (ed.) 1997. *Representation: Cultural Representations and Signifying Practices, Culture, Media and Identities*. London, SAGE.

Harvey, P. D. A. 2002. *Mappa Mundi: The Hereford World Map*. London, Hereford Cathedral and The British Library.

Hawthorne, W. 1998. *Title Interior Past of an Acephalous Society: Institutional Change among the Balanta of Guinea-Bissau, c.1400–c.1950*. Unpublished PhD thesis, Stanford University.

Hopkins, J. E. P. and Levtzion, N. (eds.) 1981. *Corpus of Early Arabic Sources for West African History*. Cambridge, Cambridge University Press.

Jana, P. 2001. African Renaissance and the Millennium Action Plan. *Quest* 15, 38-41.

Lagerlund, H. 2004. Mental Representation in Medieval Philosophy. In E. N. Zalta (ed.), *The Stanford Encyclopedia of Philosophy* (Summer 2004 Edition), 14-16.

Leo Africanus, J. 1632. *The History and Description of Africa*. Vol. I. London, The Hakluyt Society.

Liddell, H. G. and Scott, R. (eds.) 1901. *A Greek-English Lexicon*. Oxford, Clarendon Press.

Livermore, H. 1976 (Second Edition). *A New History of Portugal*. Cambridge, Cambridge University Press.

Lorimer, D. A. 1978. *Colour, Class and the Victorians: English Attitudes to the Negro in the Mid-Nineteenth Century*. Leicester, Leicester University Press.

Lydon, G. 2009. *On Trans-Saharan Trails: Islamic Law, Trade Networks, and Cross-Cultural Exchange in Nineteenth-Century Western Africa*. Cambridge, Cambridge University Press.

Mbeke, T. 1998. *The African Renaissance, South Africa and the World*. http://www.unu.edu/unupress/mbeki.html

Mudimbe, V. Y. 1988. *The Invention of Africa: Gnosis, Philosophy, and the Order of Knowledge*. Bloomington, Indiana University Press.

Münzer. J. 1958. Itinerarium, De Inventione Africae Maritimae et Occidentalis Videclicet Genee Per Infantem Heinrichum Portugallie, fols. 280-88 (1494). In P. A. Brásio (ed.), *Monumenta Missionaria Africana, Africa Ocidental 1342-1499, Segunda Série, I*. Lisbon, Academia Portuguesa da História.

Njeza, M. 1997. Fallacies of the New Afrocentrism. *Journal of Theology for Southern Africa* 99 (November), 47-57.

Pacheco Pereira, D. 1954 (Third Edition). *Esmeraldo de Situ Orbis: Introducção e Anotacões Históricas pelo académico de número Damião Peres. – por Duarte Pacheco Pereire*. Lisbon.

Palmberg, M. (ed.) 2001. *Encounter Images in the Meetings between Africa and Europe*. Uppsala, Nordiska Afrikainstitutet.

Payne, S. G. 1973. *A History of Spain and Portugal*. Madison, University of Wisconsin Press.

Petersen, A. 1996. *Dictionary of Islamic Architecture*. London, Routledge.

Pieterse, J. N. 1992. *White on Black: Images of Africa and Blacks in Western Popular Culture*. London, Yale University Press.

Ramsay, N. 2004. Holdingham, Richard of (*d.* 1278?). *Oxford Dictionary of National Biography*, Oxford, Oxford University Press, 2004. http://www.oxforddnb.com/index/101037891/Richard-of-Holdingham.

Russell, P. E. 1995. *Portugal, Spain and the African Atlantic 1343-1490: Chivalry and Crusade from John of Gaunt to Henry the Navigator*. Aldershot, Variorum,

—2000. *Prince Henry 'the Navigator': A Life*. New Haven. Yale University Press.

Snowden, F. M. 1983. *Before Color Prejudice: The Ancient View of Blacks*. Cambridge, Mass., Harvard University Press.

Shoha, E. and Stam, R. 1994. *Unthinking Eurocentrism: Multiculturalism and the Media*. London, Routledge.

Souto, J. C. 1973. *Dicionàirio de Literatura: Literatura Portuguesa, Literatura Brasileira, Literatura Galega, Estiliìstica Literaìria*. Porto, Figueirinhas.

Strickland, D. H. 2003. *Saracens, Demons, and Jews: Making Monsters in Medieval Art*. Princeton, N. J., Princeton University Press.

Terra, B. 1964. *Guiné do Século XV, Cidades de 200.000 Habitantes: Análise e Resposta a um 'Professor Barbadinho'*. Luanda, Grafica.

Thomas, H. and Cortesão, A. (eds.) 1938. *The Discovery of Abyssinia by the Portuguese in 1520: A Facsimile of the Relation entitled Carta das Novas que Vieram a El Rey nosso Senhor do Descobrimento do Preste Joham (Lisbon 1521)*. London, The British Museum.

Westrem, S. D. 2001. *The Hereford Map: A Transcription and Translation of the Legends with Commentary*. Turnhout, Brepols.

Whitfield, P. 1994. *The Image of the World: 20 Centuries of World Maps*. London, The British Library.

Petrie's Revolutions: The Case of the Qurneh Queen

Bill Manley
National Museums Scotland

Figure 1. The Qurneh burial as photographed by Petrie's team on the day of its discovery, 29 December 1908 (with the lid of the child's coffin removed).

Abstract
Flinders Petrie is the man whose name, more than any other, is associated with the archaeological discovery of Ancient Egypt. However, he came to conclude that indigenous Egyptians have contributed nothing of consequence to civilisation, and that their own civilisation had been the product of a sequence of definitive 'Northern' interventions. The synthesis of his historical and political convictions was a law of the revolutions of civilisation, whereby each nation is subject to cycles of excellence, decline and then conquest. Using the case of the magnificent Qurneh burial-group, which he discovered in 1908, Petrie's law can be understood as an emphatic assertion of the inferiority of indigenous Egyptian, and more generally African, culture at all stages of history. However, his radical beliefs are an original teleology, and cannot be dismissed simply by reference to the endemic racism of European scholarship.

Keywords: archaeology, civilisation, Egypt, Egyptology, eugenics, Nubia, Petrie, social policy, teleology, underclass.

'From the very beginning, intellectuals claimed to possess insights unavailable to ordinary mortals.'
(Feyerabend 1987, 115)

Introduction
In 1939, at the age of 85, Sir Flinders Petrie, the most important figure in British Egyptology, set down *The Making of Egypt* to summarise all he had learned about Ancient Egypt during his seventy celebrated years in archaeology:

'The uniform result is that Egypt never originated any new civilisation, but was a fertile ground for implanting the products of other lands. Each new movement entered Egypt at its best, and deteriorated gradually under the easy conditions of life in Egypt.' (Petrie 1939, 161)

This is the paradox of Petrie: the man whose name, more than any other, is associated with the modern discovery of the splendour that was Ancient Egypt, ultimately maintained that indigenous Egyptians have contributed nothing of consequence to civilisation because the land herself is a succubus. Hence his famously Spartan living regime when working there, which was partly intended to protect his impressionable protégés from the drain of their moral and intellectual stamina (Petrie 1886; Drower 1995, 217, 393). So how do we make sense of Petrie's startling conclusion? Here I would like to consider this paradox in relation to a specific problem: Petrie's ambivalence towards the splendid Qurneh burial-group, now housed at National Museums Scotland (NMS A.1909.527.1-42).

The Qurneh Burial
In the winter of 1908-9 Petrie was at Luxor, working among the northern slopes on the west bank of the Nile, a broad area with the generic name Qurneh. He knew that there were ancient royal cemeteries in the area (Petrie 1909, 2), and no doubt specifically that the burials (or reburials) of King Kamose and Queen Ahhotpe II of the 17th Dynasty (1650-1550 BC) had been discovered nearby in 1857 and 1859 respectively (Miniaci and Quirke 2008, 9-10; Thomas 1966, 34-49). On 29 December 1908, at the foot of a promontory known locally as el-Khōr, his team uncovered a shallow pit containing the intact burial of a woman and child, which at that time formed 'the richest and most detailed undisturbed burial that has been completely recorded and published' (Petrie 1909, 10; Figure 1).

The centrepiece of the burial was an exceptionally tall (2.06m) coffin decorated in the *rīshi*-style, whereby the deceased woman is shown swathed in the feathery embrace of a kite, which lies across her heart. Her face is framed by a striped linen head-cloth and a collar with falcon terminals. The decoration is painted in blue on a yellow ground, with details added in black or highlighted by gilding. The form and decoration of this coffin are datable to the 16th century BC, and, in terms of quality and stature, compare favourably with the kings' coffins known from this time. Inside lay the mummy of a short, slender woman, aged about 18-25, who wore a magnificent four-banded collar made up of 90%-pure gold rings, as well as a pair of 95%-pure gold earrings, two pairs of gold bracelets, and finally a girdle of fine electrum rings that had been worn in life (Troalen et al. 2010). Other items in the coffin included an acacia headrest inlaid with ivory and ebony, and a basket containing the head of a flail-shaped sceptre. Around the coffin were three stools, various ceramic vessels, and a rod strung with ten nets holding more vessels, including six exquisite Kerma-ware pots. There were also offerings of grapes, dates, palm fruits, a pomegranate, and assorted loaves and cakes, while a second basket included a decorated stone bowl, and an oil-horn inlaid with ivory and ebony. Finally, at the foot of the woman's coffin lay the simple, white-painted coffin of a child. The child's remains indicate an age at death of 24 to 30 months, too young for its gender to be discernible, although the mummy's ivory jewellery favours a girl. The presence of two coffins in a single grave suggests that the deceased were related, but it has not been possible to confirm this scientifically. The pit had been deliberately covered with boulders, so there was no intention to re-enter it in ancient times: therefore, the woman and child probably had died at about the same time and been buried together.

The identities of the deceased are not known. The only inscription anywhere among the entire grave-group is a standard funerary prayer, pressed or stamped into plaster on the lid of the woman's coffin. The column measures 1085mm, but the gilded text is now broken away two-thirds of the way down:

An offering which the king gives to Osiris, lord of Djedu, a voice offering of bread and beer, fowl and ox, for the spirit of

What should follow is the statement of the woman's titles and her name but the whole area of plaster has been lost. Nevertheless, the location of the burial and the exceptional assemblage of grave-goods indicate that she held a position at the very top of society, and probably was a member of the royal family. Although a simple pit, the grave indicates 'a level of wealth that would be notable in any period' (Roehrig 2005, 16), and yielded 'the largest group of goldwork that had left Egypt' (Petrie 1932, 212). Indeed, Petrie offered the group to the Royal Scottish Museum (a precursor of National Museums Scotland) partly because 'it must go where there are night watchmen, as the gold is worth £30 intrinsically', according to his letter to the Director, dated 5 August 1909.

The provision of Kerma-ware is unexpected in an Egyptian burial, and indicates that one or both of the deceased had an association with Nubian funerary culture. Petrie himself suggested that the woman's skull was not typically Egyptian (Petrie 1909, 10), although more recent examination of her skeleton to determine her ethnicity has been inconclusive (on this basis she is as likely to be European as Nubian). However, analyses of carbon and nitrogen isotopes in her skeleton have produced striking results: by comparison with published data for ancient remains, her diet falls between that typical of Egyptians and that of Nubians (Eremin et al. 2000). Apparently she was either an Egyptian with a taste for Nubian foods, perhaps through family considerations, or a Nubian who had moved to Egypt while young. In order to explain such a connection, it seems straightforward, if speculative, to invoke two well known cultural phenomena. One is that some of the grave-goods were respectful gifts from a ruler of Kush for a royal burial at Thebes. The other is dynastic marriage, whereby the woman would be a Nubian married into the Theban royal family, or the offspring of such a marriage.

'Taken as a whole, this exceptional group of objects belies the conventional wisdom about Thebes [at this time as] a relatively isolated provincial center cut off from the trade and resources needed to acquire or manufacture luxury items of the type that this burial reveals.' (Roehrig 2005, 16)

How strange, then, that Petrie should comment:

'There was no very valuable article in it, but the whole was an unusual and valuable group.' (Letter dated 18 January 1909 from Petrie to an unnamed correspondent, now among Petrie's papers in University College, London)

In order to explain his ambivalence, we need to understand why Petrie was interested in Egypt at all, and, therefore, what was 'valuable' to him.

Before Qurneh

Born in Kent in 1853, Petrie was a sickly child, effectively unable to attend school. His situation was further complicated by the straitened financial circumstances of his family, which were not in keeping with its social standing, and did not allow for a private tutor (Drower 1995, 15-20). As a result he received little of the formal education he might otherwise have expected, and, instead, mostly taught himself from whichever books took his fancy. The effect of this on his character he summarised much later, aged 44, in a letter courting his future wife:

'I knew that circumstances were against me in my start in life, owing to causes I could not help; and I resolutely avoided any possible entanglement for it would, I always knew, be almost life and death to me to really care about anyone. I drowned my mind in work, and have kept my balance by filling every thought with fresh interests and endeavours, at a cost and strain which I could hardly live under. Success has come to me far more than I expected; the world has been very kind to me, and I have never failed in any serious work that I have undertaken.' (quoted in Drower 1995, 235)

Of course, it would be churlish not to recognise that in this letter Petrie is making love to Hilda Urlin, but the sentiments are consistent with those of a man for whom life was pre-eminently about social and academic achievement, over all but the closest personal relationships (with the presumption that this would recommend him to a prospective wife).

In the event, Petrie grew up to be a precociously talented engineer and surveyor, as well as an austere Christian. As with many scientifically-minded men in the latter half of the 19th century, he was obliged to reconcile post-Darwinian theories of human evolution with his own literal understanding of the Bible. Petrie's own solution was to develop an evolutionary teleology that would underpin all of his later writings on history and sociology. At first his teleological tendencies attracted Petrie to the theories of Piazzi Smyth, Astronomer Royal for Scotland: the proportions of the Great Pyramid at Giza, he claimed, reveal that it was built by a tribe of Israelites, who were in turn the progenitors of the British; and its internal layout maps the progress of civilisation. It was a desire to scrutinise these claims that first took Petrie to Egypt in 1880. As it happens, he was a man of sufficient ability and integrity to demonstrate that there was no empirical basis to the claims of Piazzi Smyth – a family friend – but Petrie was now fascinated by Egypt and what it may reveal about the truth of The Bible.

During the next two decades, Petrie established himself as a phenomenon in Egyptology. Advocating methods of archaeology more rigorous than those usually employed in Egypt, he was concerned with the details of discoveries and the plans of sites, and recognised that the minor aspects of an excavation may reveal the most interesting information. During the 1880s he was able to construct schematic charts of pottery development, which gave a structure to the study of prehistoric Egypt and transformed our understanding of how Egypt emerged as the first great nation-state. In the 1890s, as a sign of growing confidence in his own skills, he excavated a whole city, el-Til el-Amarna. There his most sensational discovery was foreign material imported to Egypt: Mycenaean pottery from the 14th century BC, which demonstrated an unforeseen antiquity for Greek civilisation. However, his own essay on the pottery was intended, not only to demonstrate the antiquity of Greece, but to argue for something much more controversial:

'These are parts of that product of that great Graeco-Libyan conquest, which swept almost over Egypt time after time.' (Petrie 1890, 274)

We may see in this remark only a naïve view of history, but he continued:

'Why may not a similar Mediterranean invasion have poured into Egypt in 2000 BC as it did in 1200, 1100 and 1000? The Libyo-Greek league may have already been strong enough to pour in a horde on the country already beaten down by the Hyksos invasion.' (Petrie 1890, 277)

Emboldened by his speculation, he proposed his final conclusion about the Greeks in Egypt:

'...we have tangible remains of the Greek or Libyo-Akhaian invasions of Egypt as far as [1400 BC]. And ... we have pushed back the hazy and speculative region to before 2000 BC, and shown some reasons for looking to a rise of European civilisation before 2500 BC.' (Petrie 1890, 277)

In other words, in this essay Petrie set out two provocative propositions: that European civilisation was more than two thousand years older than had previously been supposed; and that Egyptian civilisation was the product of a sequence of definitive European interventions. One of his greatest critics at that moment was Cecil Torr, with whom Petrie engaged in a 'long and tedious exchange of letters', according to the latter's biographer (Drower 1995, 185). In fact, in the pages of *The Academy* Torr was able to expose the enormous *non sequitur* at the core of this account, and in the highly personalised debate that ensued, Petrie could not substantiate his conclusions (Manley 2001).

Nevertheless, throughout these years Petrie had been shrewd about popularising himself and his career through books and articles distributed in schools and published by religious societies (Montserrat 2000, 7). Amelia Edwards, founder of the Egypt Exploration Fund, was the principal champion of his work: in 1892 she died, leaving a will that endowed a Chair at University College London, carefully worded to ensure that it would be Petrie who became the first ever Professor of Egyptian Archaeology in the United Kingdom. He was now a man in very different circumstances to those into which he had been born, and apparently through his efforts alone, without recourse to privilege or education. So it was, in the first decade of the new century, that he carried out perhaps his most important archaeological work, at Abydos. The cemeteries there were already known to include the burials of kings, but Petrie was able to demonstrate their full extent and their true importance as our earliest record of pharaonic culture. Central to his own account of the discoveries at Abydos and related sites was the contentious proposal of a 'dynastic race' from Elam, which had led the indigenous people out of dark prehistory into the light of civilisation through 'the conquest and union of the whole land of Egypt' (Petrie 1939, 77). On the eve of discovering the Qurneh burial, Petrie had come to believe that he could identify the very genesis of pharaonic culture in an invasion from the north. His sketch of pharaonic civilisation complete, he was now set to change course as a writer and advocate, and give full vent to his teleological convictions.

The Qurneh Years
In 1907, Petrie published his first overtly political book,

Janus in Modern Life, subtitled *Sociology Essays*. His starting assumption was that he who knows most about the history of mankind knows most about its future:

'And in our day it is only the view of the past and the future which can warn us of evils to come, and save us from violence and confusion.' (Petrie 1907, vii)

Evidently his historical and political views were mutually dependent:

'It is useless to protest that human nature should not act as it always does, or expect it to act differently from what it has done.' (Petrie 1910, 1)

Who knows the past better than the historian? Therefore, who better to dictate social policy than the historian? A reviewer in *The Academy* begged to differ:

'This book, by the best-known of Egyptologists, reminds us of the articles in a certain magazine which were said to be always written by men who were experts on any subjects but those they were asked to write about.' (Anonymous Reviewer 1907, 185)

Nevertheless, Petrie regarded himself 'first and foremost as a historian', for whom archaeology was merely the means to an end and for whom politics was of the utmost importance (Drower 1995, 428-9). For example, in 1914 the Professor of Egyptian Archaeology became President of a political pressure-group, The British Constitution Association, whose letter-head reads:

'To resist socialism: to uphold the fundamental principles of the British Constitution – personal liberty and personal responsibility; and limit the functions of governing bodies accordingly.'

This epitomises Petrie's own view of socialism, not as a specific political development, but as a primitive, historical tendency whereby individuals are subsumed within the masses:

'Broadly speaking, Socialism was far more general in the ruder and earlier stages of society, than it is in the later and more civilised times. The Tribal system has preceded the Individual system. It can still be studied in its present working in most savage tribes, and in the earlier stages recorded in history.' (Petrie 1910, 2)

His most strident political text was a pamphlet written in 1910 for the Anti-Socialist Union, *Socialism in Working Order*, in which he harnessed his knowledge of the ancient world to his political beliefs, and all without reference to Egypt.

The synthesis of Petrie's historical and political convictions became his immutable law of civilisation, whereby each nation is subject to cycles of excellence in art, then science, then wealth, followed by the decline into decadence, ending inevitably in foreign conquest:

'[Civilisations] all begin by a conquest of a decadent race by less civilised and more robust conquerors ... It takes the union of two races to start a new civilisation, as it takes the union of two stocks to start a new variety of plant.' (Petrie (1922, 239)

In 1912, *The Revolutions of Civilisation* offered an empirical demonstration of the reality of these cycles, specifically in art; and likewise how the long-term trend is for Europe to reach greater heights of achievement and for Egypt to decline (Figure 2). Of course, this thesis cannot be separated from his earlier conclusion that the highest achievements in Ancient Egyptian civilisation were driven by decisive European interventions. Essentially, therefore, his account of the 'revolutions' in history indicates *where* the evidence for each advance in human civilisation is to be found; but the *dynamic* driving this process is that, throughout history, Egypt has furnished the 'decadent race' and the North has provided the 'more robust conquerors'.

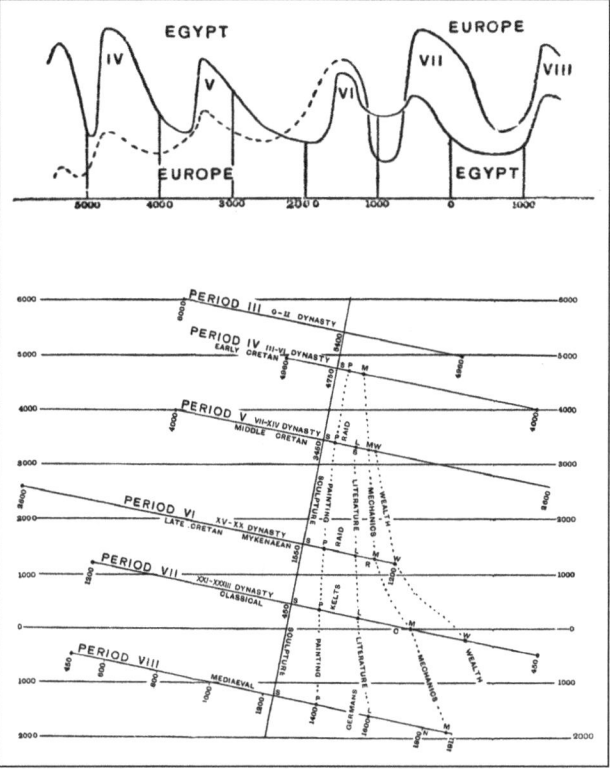

Figure 2. The revolutions of 'Mediterranean civilisation' from 6000 BC to AD 1911, as charted by Petrie (Petrie 1912, 85 plus end-page). Amidst the cycles of improvement and decline, the upper chart indicates a trend through history to overall decline in cultural success for Egypt compared to overall improvement for Europe. In addition, Petrie correlates the improvements in Egyptian civilisation with 'Northern' invasions, peaking eight centuries afterwards (Petrie 1912, 129). The lower chart indicates a trend through history to overall improvement in the arts, mechanics and wealth.

Having demonstrated to his own satisfaction the existence of these cycles – each with a period of 1115 years (Petrie 1938) – Petrie advocated eugenics as a means to forestall the decadence that would otherwise overwhelm western civilisation (Petrie 1911, 131). In giving the Huxley Memorial Lecture to the Anthropological Institute in 1906, he asserted that:

'... the only way to save a country from immigration is to increase the capabilities of its inhabitants by thorough weeding, so that other races cannot get a footing by competition or by force.' (Petrie 1906, 170)

Another solution was to pay working-class people not to breed. Petrie's biographer regards his political views as 'shockingly élitist' but only for a modern audience, and they were certainly viewed with approval by important friends and admirers, such as Francis Galton and George Bernard Shaw. Moreover, they 'attracted little notice in the Press' and were, anyway, peripheral to his work as an archaeologist (Drower 1995, 303). On the other hand, we may rather suppose that his political views were integral to his writing, and were specifically argued out on the basis of his archaeological discoveries. That they 'attracted scant attention in academic circles', as his biographer admits (Drower 1995, 304), and reviewers were 'in general doubtful' was because he openly aligned himself with pressure-groups on the political fringes, while his qualifications to pontificate on such matters were less than obvious to many.

If, as for many, Petrie's confidence in the certainties of European civilisation were shaken by World War I, he rebounded with a series of articles and lectures in which the argumentation employed in *The Revolutions of Civilisation* was harnessed instead to the case for colonial rule, because 'we cannot expect all races to be equally capable of political success in managing themselves or others' (Petrie 1918, 336). Colonialism, he insisted, had helped to resist the otherwise inevitable decline of Africa and the Orient. In the aftermath of a world war, it was even more urgent that the gene-pool within the British Isles should be restricted, in order that the British would best be able to serve as a civilising element for the rest of the world.

The Case of the Qurneh Queen

As Petrie was ignored in politics in his own time, nowadays – except for site publications – he is rarely read in Egyptology, although his published bibliography runs to more than one thousand items (Uphill 1972, and even then crucial articles on colonialism in *The Yale Review* do not appear in Uphill's otherwise admirable synopsis). His law of the revolutions of civilisation is most familiar to modern Egyptologists (and then often hazily and anecdotally) through his theory of the 'dynastic race' initiating pharaonic civilisation. Generally forgotten is his principal thesis that European interventions always underlay, and still ought to underlie, every advance in Egyptian civilisation. Throughout his career he supported his theories by measuring skulls and studying facial types to reveal what he saw as carefully defined racial groups whose teleological interaction was the basis for understanding human history. Indeed, this is effectively the only form of argumentation he employs in *The Making of Egypt*, and the basis for the quote at the beginning of the present article.

Are Petrie's political views relevant to his Egyptology? Of course. For example, he insisted that his archaeological work revealed the existence of a permanent, evolutionary underclass, which was one consequence of the revolutions of civilisation. In Britain this underclass was defined by its moral and intellectual degeneracy compared with Petrie and his peers, and was only to be maintained insofar as it contributed to the overall good of the nation. In Egypt, however, the very nature of the land condemned the entire population to the status of an underclass, which could only survive as a civilised nation through the interventions of a foreign ruling elite. All of this Petrie advocated because history has ever been so, as he himself had demonstrated (to his own satisfaction). To marginalise this aspect of his work would be to deny the heart of his intellectual achievement. It is not sufficient to say, with his biographer, that his views (racist, elitist, historicist, and however else they may be classified) simply embody the standard values and beliefs of his time because this does not credit his originality of thought, his breadth of writing, nor, indeed, the criticism he received from many of his peers.

As for the case of the Qurneh queen? She belonged to the 17th Dynasty – in Petrie's terms a decadent remnant of Middle Kingdom civilisation – and her own cultural ties were with the south of Egypt and probably also Nubia. Petrie believed that the whole dynasty had its roots in Ethiopia (Petrie 1924, 17). However, the culture to which the Qurneh queen belonged was already under siege from 'a sturdy race of horsemen' from the Caucasus, the Hyksos, and the resultant 'Semitising of Egypt ... bore full effect when the fashions, ideas, and manners of Syria were implanted' (Petrie 1924, 24; Petrie 1932, 211; Petrie 1939, 142). As noted above, he also contended that a putative 'Libyo-Greek league may have already been strong enough to pour in a horde on the country already beaten down by the Hyksos invasion', thereby creating a decisive 'union of two stocks' required for the next step forward in the evolution of Egypt. By comparison, all the gold and splendour of the Qurneh queen – an indigenous African – cannot disguise an evolutionary cul-de-sac. Hence, whatever its archaeological significance, the burial held 'no valuable article' for Prof. Petrie, historian and sociologist, for whom Egypt, and indeed Nubia, 'never originated any new civilisation'.

References

Anonymous Reviewer. 1907. Dr Flinders Petrie as Sociologist. *The Academy* (30th November), 185.

Drower, M. S. 1995. *Flinders Petrie. A Life in Archaeology*. Madison and London, University of Wisconsin Press.

Eremin, K., Goring, E., Manley, W. P. and Cartwright, C. 2000. A Seventeenth-Dynasty Egyptian Queen in

Edinburgh. *KMT. A Modern Journal of Ancient Egypt* 11/3, 32-40.

Feyerabend, P. 1987. *Farewell to Reason*. London and New York, Verso.

Manley, W. P. 2001. Cecil Torr, Flinders Petrie and the Ancient World Chronology Question, in J. M. Córdoba Zoilo, R. Jiménez Zamudio and C. Sevilla Cueva (eds.), *El Redescubrimiento del Oriente Próximo y Egipto. Viajes, hallazgos e investigaciones*, 227-32. Madrid, Universidad Autónoma.

Miniaci, G. and Quirke, S. J. 2008. Some Remarks on the Development of *rishi* Coffins, in S. Grallert and W. Grajetzki (eds.), *Life and Afterlife in Ancient Egypt During the Middle Kingdom and Second Intermediate Period*, 94-9. London, Golden House Publications.

Montserrat, D. 2000. *Ancient Egypt. Digging for Dreams*. Glasgow, Glasgow City Council.

Petrie, W. M. F. 1886. A Digger's Life. *The English Illustrated Magazine* 3, 440-8.

—1890. The Egyptian Bases of Greek History. *Journal of Hellenic Studies* 11, 271-7.

—1891. *Illahun, Kahun and Gurob*. London, Egypt Exploration Fund.

—1894. *Tell el Amarna*. London, Egypt Exploration Fund.

—1906. Migrations: Being an Abstract of the Seventh Annual Huxley Memorial Lecture of the Anthropological Institute, delivered on Nov. 1st, 1906. *Man* 6/104, 170ff.

—1907. *Janus in Modern Life. Sociology Essays*. London, A. Constable.

—1909. *Qurneh*. London, British School of Archaeology in Egypt and Egyptian Research Account.

—1910. *Socialism in Working Order*. London, Anti-Socialist Union.

—1912. *The Revolutions of Civilisation*. London and New York, Harper and Bros.

—1918. The Tutelage of the East. *The Yale Review*, 335-49.

—1922. The Outlook for Civilisation. *The Yale Review*, 225-41.

—1923. The Antiquity of Egyptian Civilisation. *Journal of Egyptian Archaeology* 9, 153-6.

—1924. *A History of Egypt, During the XVIIth and XVIIIth Dynasties*. London, Methuen and Co.

—1932. *Seventy Years in Archaeology*. London, Low, Marston and Co.

—1938. Letter. *Nature* 1/10/1938, 620.

—1939. *The Making of Egypt*. London, Sheldon Press.

Rattray, R. F. 1945. A Neglected Prophet. *The Quarterly Review* (October), 443ff.

Roehrig, C. H. with Dreyfus, R. and Keller, C. A. 2005. *Hatshepsut. From Queen to Pharaoh*. New York, New Haven and London, Metropolitan Museum of Art with Yale University Press.

Thomas, E. 1966. *The Royal Necropoleis of Thebes*. Princeton, private publication.

Torr, C. 1896. *Memphis and Mycenae. An Examination of Egyptian Chronology and its Application to the Early History of Greece*. Cambridge, Cambridge University Press.

Troalen, L., Guerra, M.-F., Manley, W. P. and Tate, J. 2010. Technological Study of Gold Jewellery from the 17th and 18th Dynasties in Egypt. *ArcheoSciences: revue d'archéométrie* 33 (forthcoming).

Uphill, E. P. 1972. A Bibliography of Sir William Matthew Flinders Petrie (1853-1942). *Journal of Near Eastern Studies* 31, 356-79.

Public Understandings of Ancient Egypt in the Formation of Dalit and Afro-American Identities and History Curriculum

Clyde Ahmad Winters
Governors State University, Illinois

Abstract
In this paper I will discuss the role Ancient Egypt has played in the identity formation of Dalits and Afro-Americans, why both groups see a direct link between themselves and the Ancient Egyptians, and why they made this a major part of their history curriculum within the context of their civil rights movements.

Keywords: curriculum, Dalit, haplogroup, indentured servant, segregation, lascars.

Introduction
Two principal minorities in the United States and India are Afro-Americans and the Dalits, formerly known as the Untouchables of India. W. E. B. DuBois in *Africa and the World* (1965), V. T. Rajshekar in *Dalits: The Black Untouchables of India* (1995), and the Dalit Bishop Rev. Azariah in *A Pastor's Search for Dalit Theology* (2002) have linked Afro-Americans and East Indians to an African origin. Although these minorities are separated by thousands of miles, both ethnic groups locate their origins in Africa and see Egyptian civilisation as part of their ethnic heritage. This idea of Egyptian heritage is part of the liberation history curriculum taught in their schools. Recently in the United States the history curriculum has been changing in relation to how Afro-Americans are represented in United States text books. The changing demographics in many American schools have led to educators seeking to be more multicultural in their outlook towards education. In the Chicago Public Schools in the Chicago, Illinois, region students come from homes where over twenty non-English languages are spoken. In CPS we find that there has been an increase in the number of Spanish speaking children as well as a significant number of students in Chicago's western suburbs from Arabic speaking backgrounds.

This movement toward multiculturalism is welcome to many Afro-Americans, but this shift to multiculturalism as a curriculum idea is not new. In many parts of the United States, up until the desegregation of American schools in 1954, Afro-Americans attended schools which were segregated. In the 19th century Afro-Americans began to write textbooks which were used in segregated Afro-American schools and which included material about the history of Blacks in Africa and the ancient world, especially Egypt. In the segregated schools Afro-American school administrators used a history curriculum that included Afro-American and African history, including Egypt.

Slavery in the United States
Afro-Americans are deeply interested in the study of ancient world history and the role of Blacks in this history. Many Afro-Americans believe that writing ancient history is a political act. Carter G. Woodson, in *The Mis-Education of the Negro* (1933) observed that '[The oppressor p]lays up before the negro, then, his crimes and shortcomings. Let him learn to admire the Hebrew, the Greeks, the Latin, and the Teuton. Lead the Negro to detest the man of African blood—to hate himself' (p. 192). These scholars see the writing of ancient Black history as an anecdote to White supremacy. Woodson, again in *The Mis-Education of the Negro* wrote: 'The oppressor, however, raises his voice to the contrary. He teaches the Negro that he has no worthwhile past, and that his race has done nothing significant since the beginning of time, and that there is no evidence that he will ever achieve anything great. The education of the Negro then must be carefully directed lest the race may waste time trying to do the impossible… If you teach the Negro that he has accomplished as much good as any other race he will aspire to equality and justice without regard to race. Such an effort would upset the program of the oppressor in Africa and America' (p. 192).

The Atlantic slave trade (*c.* AD 1631-1865) played an important role in how Afro-Americans viewed the development of their history curriculum. This historical experience led to the African holocaust in which W. E. B. DuBois claimed 100 million Blacks died crossing the Atlantic Ocean during the Middle Passage or on slave plantations throughout the Americas (DuBois [1915] 2001, 93).[1] The African origin of Afro-Americans led to the desire among many members of this population for an understanding about their African homeland. They also wanted to know about the history of their people in the United States.

It was during the period of the slave trade and slavery that Afro-Americans and Dalits (East Indians) generally met, as a result of the fact that many East Indians came to the United States as slaves from Madras, Bombay, Surat, Cochin and Calcutta (Chatterjee and Easton 2006). Some of these East Indian slaves were *lascars* (Indian sailors) of the Dutch East India Company, carried to the USA by Dutch, French and English captains, while other slaves were captured in slave raids in India and sold into chattel slavery in America (Asissi 2009; Kaiwar and Muzamdar 2003). The first East Indian slaves were situated in Jamestown, Virginia. In 1622, there is a report of an East Indian slave or servant of Captain George Menefie (Assisi 2009). As early as 1667 East Indian slaves were

---

[1] 'The American slave trade, therefore, meant the elimination of at least 60,000,000 Negroes from their fatherland. The Mohammedan slave trade meant the expatriation or forcible migration in Africa of nearly as many more. It would be conservative, then, to say that the slave trade cost Negro Africa 100,000,000 souls. And yet people ask today the cause of the stagnation of culture in that land since 1600!' DuBois, 1915, 93. Retrieved 5/21/2010 at: http://www.sacred-texts.com/afr/dbn/dbn11.htm

being sold in the New World (Kaiwar and Muzamdar 2003). For centuries some East Indians were traded as slaves by American slave traders who were always on the lookout for the cheapest slaves they could find from India and East Africa. In the Virginia Gazette, 4th August 1768, there is a report that acknowledges a young 'East Indian' who had 'a thin visage, a sly look'. Another East Indian was identified as 'an East Indian negro man' who spoke French and English (Assisi 2009). And on 13 July 1776, the Virginia Gazette reported an escaped East Indian servant as follows: 'Servant Man named John Newton, about 20 Years of Age, 5 feet 6 inches high, slender made, is an Asiatic Indian by Birth, has been about twelve months in Virginia, but lived ten Years (as he says) in England, in the Service of Sir Charles Whitworth' (Assisi 2009). Court documents provide us with details about East Indian slaves in New England and Virginia. In these records East Indian slaves were identified as 'East India Indians', 'Asiatic Indians' and 'East Indians': 'This East Indian was named Tony, and was used as a headright' (Assisi 2009).

Court documents and newspaper advertisements provide historians with indisputable evidence for the earliest historical link between people from the Indian subcontinent and America. Since many of these East Indians were held in bondage as chattel slaves over the years these East Indians were absorbed into the Afro-American slave population (Chatterjee and Easton 2006). This allows Asian Americans and African Americans, particularly those with South Asian ancestry, to re-vision their history and claim their full heritage.

Slavery and Beyond
During and after slavery in the United States, state and national history curriculums portrayed Afro-Americans as backwards and ignorant. The curriculum maintained that African people had always been slaves and contributed nothing to ancient history. After slavery Afro-Americans began to write history and establish their own history curriculum. This curriculum was based on the 'Ancient Model' of history. This 'Ancient Model' of history was based on references to Africans and Black people in the Classical literature and The Bible.

There are four philosophical schools associated with the Afro-American history curriculum: perennialist, essentialist, existentialist and progressivist. The taxonomic system we use to classify the various Afro-American history philosophical positions and related values affecting the Afro-American history curriculum are modelled on philosophical developments associated with education. We can use taxonomies of educational philosophies to discuss the Afro-American history curriculum because both education and philosophy are 'cultural experiences'. Moreover, because the Afro-American history curriculum seeks to explain and delineate the story of African people, it clearly is a field of study which encompasses all aspects of the culture of Black and African people (Asante 1990, 1991; Winters 1994).

The Afro-American perennial scholars study the great works such as The Bible and the writings of the classical scholars. The adherents of this school include Cornish and Russwurm (1827), Edward Blyden (1869, 1887, 1890, 1905), Frederick Douglas (1966) and Martin Delaney (1978). These Afrocentrists see knowledge as truth, which is eternal.[2] Essentialist Afro-American history researchers emphasise in their writing data that is well established through scientific research. Afrocentrists of this philosophical school include W. E. B. DuBois (1924, 1965, 1970), John Jackson (1974), Leo Hansberry (1981) and C. A. Winters (1985a, 1985b, 1989a, 1990, 1994). They believe that, as new research is published, it should be analysed to discover how it relates to the ancient history of Africaan and Black people to enrich our understanding of the past. The existentialist Afrocentrists believe that africalogical studies should strive to teach African people to know more about themselves so we can have a better world. The Afrocentric existentialist social scientists include G. M. James (1954), Marcus Garvey (1966), J. A. Rogers (1967), Cheikh Anta Diop (1974, 1991) and A. A. Schomburg (1979). The final philosophical school is progressivist. The progressivist believes that we should have knowledge of the process and futuristic focus on Afrocentric studies. The major exponent of this frame of reference is Molefi K. Asante (1991).

With regard to the Afrocentric view that the Egyptians were Black Africans we must look to the perennialists. The perennialist school, associated with Frederick Douglas (1966) and Martin Delaney (1978), founded the Afro-American history curriculum. These Afrocentrists, writing in the 19th century, placed the great works of the past centre-stage in the formulation of their Afrocentric ancient history knowledge base. The perennialists postulated that you should use The Bible and the writings of the classical scholars who recognised the 'Ancient Model' of history (i.e. that Blacks played a major role in ancient history) in deciding what to teach people in relation to the ancient history of African Americans. The Old Testament provides annals of the ancient empires of Africa and Mesopotamia. In the Old Testament the Blacks are recognised as the sons of Ham. According to the Old Testament narrative found in the Book of Genesis (10:6), the children of Ham are alleged to be the founders of **all** the ancient civilisations including Kush (the Ta Seti, and C-Group cultures of Nubia and the Sudan; the Sumerians of Mesopotamia and the Elamites of Iran), Mizraim (the founder of the Egyptians), Phut (the civilisations of ancient Ethiopia/South Arabia), and Canaan (the early Canaanites and Hattians of ancient Palestine). The Old Testament narrative and the classical literature were important to the perennialists because it already recognised the division of Black people of Africa into two groups: the Semitic (Canaan and Phut) speakers and Black African (Egypt, Sumer and Elam) speakers (Winters 1985a, 1989a, 1990).

---

[2] An Afrocentrist can be defined as a social science researcher who uses traditional social science research methods to explain and discuss the history of African people from an African-centred perspective.

Africalogical Paradigms of Ancient History

As a result of the 'Ancient Model' of history the scientific efforts of africalogical ancient history researchers of the diverse philosophical schools discussed above were organised around two theoretical or empirical generalisations, or paradigms. An empirical generalisation is 'an isolated proposition summarizing observed uniformities of relationships between two or more variables' (Merton 1957, 95); a 'scientific law' is 'a statement of invariance derivable from a theory' (Merton 1957, 96). The two paradigms associated with the africalogical study of African history (ASAH) developed by the perennialist Afrocentric scholars are:

1. Black/African people are the children of Ham;
2. Blacks founded the first civilisations in Asia (Sumer, Babylon and Elam), Africa (Egypt, Ethiopia, and Libya/North Africa) and Europe (Greece and Crete).

The normal scientific research in africalogical ancient historical studies is directed toward the articulation of those phenomena and theories supplied by the ASAH to deduce new paradigms. Due to the foundation of africalogical ancient research by the Afrocentric perennialists, ASAH research is paradigm-based. The perennialists made Egypt the centrepiece of the Afro-American history curriculum.

As a result, fact-gathering is done by employing historical, linguistic and anthropological research methods. Using these research methods Afro-American scholars taught that Egypt was a Black African civilisation. This history curriculum was reinforced by the Black Church which, every Sunday, taught Afro-Americans about the Hamites, central to which group were the Ancient Egyptians. By the late 19th century Afro-American researchers began to write text books on Afro-American history. In these textbooks Afro-American educators not only discussed the history of Africans in the USA. and Africa, they also discussed the ancient civilisations founded by Blacks in Egypt and Mesopotamia. The scholarship of these researchers was based on contemporary archaeological and historical research indicating the African/Black origin of civilisation throughout the world. These Afro-American scholars, mostly trained at Harvard University (one of the few universities that admitted Blacks in the 19th century) provide the scientific basis for Afrocentrism and the global role played by African people in civilising the world. These researchers practiced Afrocentrism; Afrocentrism and the africalogical study of ancient Black civilisations were initiated by Afro-Americans.

The foundation of any mature science is its articulation in an authoritative text (Kuhn 1996). The africalogical textbooks published by Williams (1883), Perry (1893) and Hopkins (1905) provided the vocabulary and themes for further Afrocentric social science research and curriculum development. The pedagogy for ancient africalogical research was well established by the end of the 19th century by Afro-American researchers well-versed in the classical languages and knowledge of Greek and Latin. Cornish and Russwurm (1827), in the *Freedom Journal*, were the first Afro-Americans to discuss and explain the 'Ancient Model' of history. These Afrocentric social scientists used the Classics to prove that the Blacks founded civilisation in Egypt, Ethiopia, Babylon and Nineveh. Cornish and Russwurm made it clear that archaeological research supported the classical, or 'Ancient Model' of history. Edward Blyden (1869) also used classical sources to discuss the ancient history of African people. In his work he not only discussed the evidence for Blacks in West Asia and Egypt, but also the role of Blacks in early America (Blyden 1869, 78). In 1883, G. W. Williams published the first textbook on African American history, *History of the Negro Race in America*, which provided the schema for all future africalogical history texts. Dr. Williams, who trained at Howard, confirmed the classical traditions for Blacks founding civilisations in both Africa (Egypt, Ethiopia) and West Asia. In addition to confirming the 'Ancient Model' of history, Dr. Williams also discussed the presence of Blacks in Indo-China and the Malay Peninsula. A decade later R. L. Perry (1893) also presented evidence to confirm the classical tradition of Blacks founding Egypt, Greece and the Mesopotamian civilisation. He provided empirical evidence for the role of Blacks in Phoenicia, thus increasing the scope of the ASAH paradigms. Pauline E. Hopkins (1905) added further articulation in understanding the role of Blacks in Egypt as well as providing further confirmation of the role of Blacks in Southeast Asia, and expanding the scope of africalogical research to China.

This review of the 19th century africalogical social science research which is the foundation of the Afro-American history curriculum theories serves to confirm the 'Ancient Model' for the early history of Blacks. We also see a movement away from self-published africalogical research, to more formal publication of research, research articles on Afrocentric themes, and the publication of textbooks. It was in these books that the paradigms associated with the 'Ancient Model' and Afro-American study of ancient history were confirmed, and given reliability by empirical research. It was these texts which provided the pedagogic vehicles for the perpetuation of the africalogical normal social science. The Afrocentric textbooks of Williams (1883), Perry (1893) and Hopkins (1905) proved the reliability and validity of the ASAH paradigms. The discussion within these texts of contemporary scientific research findings proving the existence of ancient civilisations in Egypt, Nubia-Sudan (Kush), Mesopotamia, Palestine and North Africa lent congruence to the classical literature which pointed to the existence of these civilisations and their African origins (i.e. founded by the children of Ham= Khem=Kush?).

The authors of the africalogical textbooks reported the latest archaeological and anthropological findings in their textbooks, adding precision to their analysis of the Classical and Old Testament literature. This, along with the discovery of artefacts on many ancient sites depicting Black/African people, proved that the Classical and Old

Testament literature, as opposed to the 'Aryan Model', objectively identified the Black/African role in ancient history. The 'Aryan Model', created during the Slave Trade era, claimed that African peoples had no history. Finally, these textbooks confirmed that any examination of references in the classical literature to Blacks in Egypt, Kush, Mesopotamia and Greece/Crete was consistent with the evidence recovered from archaeological excavations in the Middle East and the Aegean. These researchers disconfirmed the 'Aryan Model', which, according to their research, proved to be a falsification of the authentic history of Blacks in early times.

The creation of africalogical textbooks provided us with a number of facts revealing the nature of the Afrocentric ancient history paradigms. They include a discussion of:

1. the artefacts depicting Blacks found at ancient sites recovered through archaeological excavation;
2. the confirmation of the validity of the Classical and Old Testament references to Blacks as founders of civilisation in Africa and Asia;
3. the presence of isolated pockets of Blacks existing outside Africa;
4. the fact that the contemporary Arab people in modern Egypt are not the descendants of the ancient Egyptians.

The early africalogical textbooks also outlined the africalogical themes research should endeavour to study and serves as content for the Afro-American history curriculum. The data collected by the africalogical ancient history research pioneers by the end of the 19th century led to the development of four questions which needed to be solved by the Afrocentric paradigms:

1. What is the exact relationship of Ancient Egypt to Blacks in other parts of Africa?
2. How and when did Blacks settle America, Asia and Europe?
3. What is the contribution of the Blacks to the rise and cultural expression of ancient Black/African civilisations?
4. Did Africans settle parts of America in ancient times?

In the early 20th century new researchers began to investigate the history of Egypt. These researchers include Leo Hansberry and W. E. B. DuBois. They argued, as their predecessors had, that the original Egyptians were Black Africans. There is no one who can deny the fact that Leo Hansberry, who was a professor of Howard University, founded African Studies in the USA. Hansberry was primarily interested in the Classical references to Blacks in Egypt and elsewhere. It is the Classical literature which linked Africans and East Indians; the Classical writers maintained that there were two Ethiopias of Kush: one in Asia and the other in Africa. Herodotus wrote: 'The Eastern Ethiopians differed in nothing from the other Ethiopians, save in their language, and the character of their hair. For the Eastern Ethiopians have straight hair, while they of Libya are more woolly-haired than any other people in the world' (from *The History of the Persian Wars*, VII.70).

DuBois is also considered a content specialist when writing the Afro-American history curriculum. His major contributions to this area are *The World and Africa* (1965) and *The Negro* (1970). In these books Egypt's African heritage is explained and discussed in detail. Up until the 1950s the most popular Afro-American history text used in Afro-American public schools was *The Negro in Our History* (1922) by Carter G. Woodson and C. H. Welsley. Carter G. Woodson founded the *Journal of Negro History* in 1916, and his textbook was extremely popular, going into a number of editions. Many Afro-American teachers graduated from southern Negro Colleges and they encouraged the use of *The Negro in Our History* in schools in the large cities of the United States. By the 1960s the leading Afro-American history text was *From Slavery to Freedom: A History of Afro-Americans* (1947) by John Hope Franklin. This book is one of the most comprehensive Afro-American history texts ever written, giving a fine history of Africa and Afro-American history, and it continues to be used not only at many colleges in the United States, but also in high school history programs.

Dalit History Curriculum
The Dalit civil rights struggle was initiated in 1928 by Dr B. R. Ambedkar (1891-1956), a leading Indian scholar and political leader, who articulated the dreams and aspirations of the Dalits. Dr Ambedkar was the major spokesman in India for Dalits to be given their human rights and not be treated unjustly by their fellow Hindus. He was awarded India's highest Civil Award posthumously in 1990. There are 160 million Dalits in India, sharing with Afro-Americans a history of segregation and slavery (Rajshakar 1995). In the past Dalits were called outcastes or 'Untouchables'. Mohandas Ghandhi called them Harijans, 'children of God'. The term Dalit means 'crushed and broken'. The Dalits believe that their ancestors originated in the Sudan, from where they migrated to the Indus Valley (Winters 1985b), and they regard their relationship to Egypt and the Sudan as a link to Afro-Americans and Africans. According to the Dalits, this link allows them to have allies outside of India where they are harassed and discriminated against. V. T. Rajshekar is a major Dalit leader, and one who accepts the African origin of the Dalits, based on the Classical literature, and genetic and linguistic research that links Dravidians and Africans. After a long period of silence, the Dalits have begun a civil rights movement in India, with V. T. Rajshekar as one of their most articulate leaders. The Dalits identify with their African ancestry and are enamoured of Afro-Americans (Paswan and Jaidevd 2003). The Dalits idolised the Black Panther Party, and, in 1972, the Dalit Black Panther Party was founded in Bombay, India (Kapoor 2004).

The Dalit history curriculum is founded on research linking Dravidian speakers to Africa. It is already recognised that there are known Indian populations of African ancestry (Indian Genome Variation Consortium

(IGVC) 2008). The archaeological and genetic evidence suggest that the Dravidians may have originated in Africa (Sergent 1992), and it appears from the linguistic evidence as well that some Dravidian speakers originated in Africa (Winters 2007). Aravanan (1976) and Upadhyaya and Upadhyaya (1983) provide considerable evidence that Dravidian originated in Africa, not Eurasia. Using osteological data researchers have established that the Dravidian speakers of South India and the Indus Valley were primarily related to the ancient Capsian population (c. 21,000-12,000 BP; Gates 1961; Guha 1935), which originated in Africa. Lahovary (1963) and Sastri (1955) maintain that this population was unified over an extensive zone from Africa to South India. B. B. Lal (1963) argued convincingly that the Dravidians were related to the C-group people of Nubia based on the fact that both groups used, 1) a common black-and-red ware pottery (BRW); 2) a common burial complex incorporating megaliths and circular rock enclosures; and, 3) a common type of rock cut sepulchre. Rao (1972) pointed out that the BRW industry diffused from Nubia across West Asia into Rajastan, and thence to East, Central and South India. In addition, Singh (1982) made it clear that he believes that the BRW radiated from Nubia through Mesopotamia and Iran southward into India.

Many researchers, especially Dravidian speaking linguists, maintain that the Dravidian languages are genetically related to the Niger-Congo family of languages (Aravanan 1976, 1979; Upadhyaya and Upadhyaya 1976, 1979, 1983; Winters 1989a, 1989b, 1990, 1994, 2007b, 2008a). The Niger-Congo speakers originated in Nubia, the same location as the archaeological evidence linking the Dravidian speakers to the C-Group culture of Nubia who lived in Africa around 3000 BC (Lal 1963; Winters 2008a). Millet was probably introduced to India from Africa by Dravidian speakers (Winters 2008b). Winters (1999a, 1999b, 2000, 2008a) has reconstructed the Paleo-African-Dravidian terms for the hoe, millet, cattle, sheep and goats. Balakrishnan (2005) claims that onomastics indicate an African 'root' for the language of the Dravidian-speaking tribes. He presents data indicating that the names for rivers and hills in Koraput, for example are identical to the names for rivers and hills in Africa. Today many Niger-Congo speakers are spread across Africa and carry the M1 haplogroup which is also found in India (Gonzalez *et al.* 2006; Kivisild *et al.* 1999). Cordaux *et al.* (2003) and Winters (2010) noted that Africans and Dravidians share a number of haplogroups. The archaeological evidence makes it clear that the Dravidians and C-Group people of Nubia shared the same culture. The congruity that exists between the date for the C-Group culture, and the genome evidence of Reich *et al.* (2009) which suggests that the earliest Dravidian speakers lived around 3000 BC, supports the view that the Dravidian people originated in Africa, and are not autochthonous in India.

Conclusion

The Dalits and Afro-Americans do not look at Egypt solely as a major civilisation but rather they see Egypt as a symbol of the greatness of their ancestral civilisation. Egypt, to the Dalits and Afro-Americans, gives them pride in their heritage, and recognition that they have not always been poor. Recognition of Egypt as their ancient homeland gives Afro-Americans and Dalits hope that one day they will experience true citizenship without the status of being recognised as different by the dominant cultural groups in India and the United States. The key element in Afro-American understandings of Egypt comes from the Black Church. The Black Church has been a constant source of healing and comfort for many Afro-Americans. It was here, through Sunday School, that Black children were taught that the Egyptians were Black Africans and descendants of Ham. Since Afro-Americans learned in church that Ham was the father of the Negro/African people, including Egyptians, this has kept alive for the last 200 years the popular idea that the Egyptians were Black.

References

Aravanan, K. P. 1976. Physical and Cultural Similarities between Dravidians and Africans. *Journal of Tamil Studies* 10, 23-7.

—1979. *Dravidians and Africans*. Madras, Paari Nilayam.

Asante, M. K. 1990. *Kemet, Afrocentricity and Knowledge*. Trenton, N.J., Africa World Press.

—1991. The Afrocentric Idea in Education. *Journal of Negro Education* 60(2), 170-80.

—1992. Afrocentric Curriculum. *Educational Leadership* 49(2), 28-31.

Assisi, F. C. 2009. Indian Slaves in Colonial America. *Indian Currents*, May 2007. http://www.indiacurrents.com/news/view_article.html?article_id=e26c1cc3bcc0503da89fc4511af72bd5

Blyden, E. W. 1869 (January). The Negro in Ancient History. *Methodist Quarterly Review*, 71-93.

—1887. *Christianity, Islam and the Negro Race*. Edinburgh, Edinburgh University Press.

—1890. *The African Problem and the Method for its Solution*. Washington, D.C., Gibson Brothers.

—1905. *West Africa before Europe*. London, C. M. Phillips.

Balakrishnan R. 2005. African Roots of the Dravidian-speaking Tribes: A Case Study in Onomastics. *International Journal of Dravidian Linguistics* 34, 153-202.

Chatterjee, I. and Easton, R. M. (eds.) 2006. *Slavery and South Asian History*. Bloomington, Indiana University Press.

Cordaux, R., Saha, N., Bentley, G. R., Aunger, R., Sirajuddin, S. M. and Stoneking, M. 2003. Mitochodrial DNA Analysis Reveals Diverse Tribal Histories of Tribal

Populations from India. *European Journal of Human Genetics* 11(3), 253-64.

Cornish, S. and Russwurm, J. B. 1827. European Colonies in America, *Freedom Journal* 1.

Delany, M. R. 1978. *The Origin of Races and Color.* Baltimore, MD., Black Classic Press.

Diop, C. A. 1974. *The African Origin of Civilization.* Edited and translated by M. Cook. Westport, Lawrence Hill and Company.

—1991. *Civilization or Barbarism: An Authentic Anthropology.* Translated by Y-L. M. Ngemi, edited by H. J. Salemson and M. de Jager. Westport, Lawrence Hill and Company.

Douglas, F. 1966. The Claims of the Negro Ethnologically Considered. In H. Brotz (ed.), *Negro Social and Political Thought*, 226-44. New York, Basic Books.

DuBois, W. E. B. 1896. *The Suppression of the African Slave Trade.* Harvard University Historical Series 1. Harvard, Harvard University Press.

—1924. *The Gift of Black Folks.* Boston, The Stratford Co.

—1965. *The World and Africa.* New York, International Publishers.

—1970 [1915]. *The Negro.* New York, Oxford University Press.

Garvey, M. 1966. Who and What is a Negro? In H. Brotz (ed.), *Negro Social and Political Thought*, 560-2. New York, Basic Books.

Gates, R. R. 1961. Early Mediterranean Traits in the Leptorhine Elements in the Kurumbas and Other Tribes of S. India. *Mankind* 1(4), 20-3.

Gonder, M. K., Mortensen, H. M., Reed, F. A., de Sousa, A. and Tishkoff, S. A. 2006. Whole mtDNA Genome Sequence Analysis of Ancient African Lineages. *Molecular Biology and Evolution* 4(3), 757-68.

González, A. M., Cabrera, V. M., Larruga, J. M., Tounkara, A., Noumsi, G., Thomas, B. N. and Moulds, J. M. 2006. Mitochondrial DNA Variation in Mauritania and Mali and their Genetic Relationship to Other Western Africa Populations. *Annals of Human Genetics* 70(5), 631-57.

González, A. M, Larruga, J. M., Abu-Amero, K. K., Shi, Y., Pestano, J. and Cabrera, V. M. 2007. Mitochondrial Lineage M1 Traces an Early Human Backflow to Africa. *BMC Genomics* 8, 223-35.

Guha, B. S. 1935. The Racial Affinities of the People of India. *Census of India 1931, Vol. I, India, Pt. 3A*, 2-22. Delhi, Government of India Press.

Hansberry, L. H. 1981. *Africa and Africans: As Seen by Classical Writers.* Vol. 2. Washington, D.C., Howard University Press.

Herodotus. 1862. *The Histories.* Trans. G. Rawlinson. New York, Dutton and Co.

Hopkins, P. E. 1905. *A Primer of Facts Pertaining to the Early Greatness of the African Race and the Possibility of Restoration by its Descendants - with Epilogue.* Cambridge, Mass., P. E. Hopkins and Company.

Indian Genome Variation Consortium (IGVC). 2008. Genetic Landscape of the People of India: A Canvas for Disease Gene Exploration. *Journal of Genetics* 87(1), 3-20.

Jackson, J. 1974. *Introduction to African Civilization.* Secaucus, N.J., Citadel Press.

Kaiwar, V. and Muzumdar, S. (eds.) 2003. *Antinomies of Modernity: Essays on Race, Orient, Nation.* Durham (USA), Duke University Press.

Kapoor, S. D. 2004. *Dalits and African Americans: A Study in Comparison.* Delhi, Kalpaz Publication.

Kivisild, T., Kaldma, K., Metspalu, M., Parik, J. and Papiha, S. 1999. The Place of the Indian mtDNA Variants in the Global Network of Maternal Lineages and the Peopling of the Old World. In R. P. Deka (ed.), *Genomic Diversity*, 135-52. London, S.S. Kluwer Academic/Plenum Publishers.

Kuhn, T. S. 1996. *The Structure of Scientific Revolution.* Chicago, University of Chicago Press.

Lahovary, N. 1963. *Dravidian Origins and the West.* Madras, Longman.

Lal, B. B. 1963 (20 April). The Only Asian Expedition in Threatened Nubia: Work by an India Mission at Afyeh and Tumas. *The Illustrated Times.* London.

Merton, R. K. 1957 [1949]. *Social Theory and Social Structure.* Glencoe, IL., Free Press.

Paswan, S. and Jaidevd, P. (eds.) 2003. *Encyclopaedia of Dalits in India.* Vol. 10 (Education). Delhi, Gyan.

Perry, R. L. 1893. *The Cushite.* Brooklyn, The Literary Union.

Rajshekar, V. T. 1995. *Dalit: The Black Untouchables of India.* Atlanta, Clarity Press.

Rao, B. K. G. 1972. *The Megalithic Culture in South India.* Prasaranga, Mysore.

Sastri, K. A. N. 1955. *History of South India from Prehistoric Times to the Fall of Vijayanagar.* Madras and New York, Oxford University Press (Indian Branch).

Schomburg, A. A. 1979. *Racial Integrity.* Baltimore, MD., Black Classic Press.

Sergent, B. 1992. *Genèse de l'Inde.* Paris, Payot.

Shaffer, R. 1954. *Ethnography of Ancient India.* Wiesbaden, Harrassowitz.

Singh, H. N. 1982. *History and Archaeology of Black and Red Ware.* Delhi, Sundeep Prakashan.

Upadhyaya, P. and Upadhyaya, S. P. 1976. Affinités ethno-linguistiques entre les Dravidiens et les Négro-Africains. *Bulletin de l'Institut Français d'Afrique Noire* 38(1), 127-57.

—1979. Les liens entre Kerala et l'Afrique tels qu'ils resosortent des survivances culturelles et linguistiques. *Bulletin de l'Institut Français d'Afrique Noire* 1, 100-32.

—1983. *Dravidian and Negro-African: Ethno-Linguistic Study on their Origin, Diffusion, Prehistoric Contacts and Common Cultural and Linguistic Heritage.* Udupi, Samshodhana Prakashana on behalf of Rastrakavi Govind Pai Research Institute.

Williams, G. W. 1869. *History of the Negro Race in America.* New York, G. P. Putnam.

Winters, C. A. 1985a. The Proto-Culture of the Dravidians, Manding and Sumerians. *Tamil Civilization* 3(1), 1-9.

—1985b (September 16th). African Origin of the Glorious Dalits. *Dalit Voice,* 1-4.

—1989a. Tamil, Sumerian, Manding and the Genetic Model. *International Journal of Dravidian Linguistics* 18(1), 98-127.

—1989b. Review of Dr. Asko Parpola's 'The Coming of the Aryans'. *International Journal of Dravidian Linguistics* 18(2), 98-127.

—1990. The Proto-Sahara. In V. I. Subramoniam (ed.), *Dravidian Encyclopaedia.* Vol. 1, 553-6. Thiruvananthapuram, International School of Dravidian Linguistics.

—1994. The Dravidian and African Languages. *International Journal of Dravidian Linguistics* 23(1), 34-52.

—1999a. Proto-Dravidian Terms for Cattle. *International Journal of Dravidian Linguistics* 28, 91-8.

—1999b. Proto-Dravidian Terms for Sheep and Goats. *Pondicherry Institute of Linguistics and Culture (PILC) Journal of Dravidian Studies* 9(2), 183-7.

—2000. Proto-Dravidian Agricultural Terms. *International Journal of Dravidian Linguistics* 30(1), 23-8.

—2007. Did the Dravidians Speakers Originate in Africa? *Bio Essays* 27(5), 497-8.

—2008a. Origin and Spread of the Dravidian Speakers. *International Journal of Human Genetics* 8(4), 325-9.

—2008b. *African Millets Carried to India by Dravidian Speakers?* Annals of Botany (Electronic Letters) http://aob.oxfordjournals.org/cgi/eletters/100/5/903

—2010. Y-Chromosome Evidence of an African Origin of Dravidian Agriculture. *International Journal of Genetics and Molecular Biology* 2(3), 30-3.

Woodson, C. G. and Wesley, C. H. 1972. *The Negro in Our History.* Washington, D.C., The Associated Publishers.

Curating Kemet, Fear of a Black Land?

Sally-Ann Ashton
Fitzwilliam Museum, University of Cambridge

Abstract
This paper documents a number of initiatives in which the Fitzwilliam Museum's Egyptian collections have been used in order to present Egypt in its African context. Drawing upon the results of qualitative research, community engagement and individual research, the paper will also consider how re-situating Ancient Egypt as Kemet impacts on museum-users and audiences. The themes of racialised identities, perceived expertise and Egyptology as an academic discipline will also be explored in order to contextualise key issues within the Eurocentric versus Afrocentric debate.

Key words: Afro-centrism, Ancient Egypt, Kemet, museums.

Introduction
In July 2003 I was asked, as part of my role as curator of the Egyptian collections at the Fitzwilliam Museum in Cambridge, to present a lecture at a maximum security prison in England. At the time, my research interests were concentrated on the Ptolemaic period of Egyptian history and I was involved with archaeological fieldwork in Alexandria. When the regular tutor collected me at the station she made a comment that has resonated since. She asked me about the subject of my talk, and then explained that her students were mostly Black and that they resented the ancient Greeks, because they had appropriated African culture and ideas. I trained as a Classicist and was aware of the so-called *Black Athena* debate (Bernal 1991, 2001), which argued that Egypt influenced Western philosophy and science. This concept is still controversial amongst mainstream academics in the UK and US (Lefkowitz and MacLean Rogers 1996). However, I personally have always seen the Ancient Egyptians as African. Greek and Roman historians confused the Ancient Egyptians with Ethiopians, and when they depicted an Ancient Egyptian it was with dark brown or black skin, 'afro' hair and a wholly different appearance from the Greeks.

The following year I returned to the same prison to present another lecture to a much larger group on an exhibition that I had curated entitled *Roman Egyptomania* (Ashton 2004). Another important theme emerged when a member of the audience stood up and declared, with a degree of force, that 'the Ancient Egyptians were Black'. I had never assumed otherwise and replied as such. In response, the person who had raised the issue repeated his statement, perhaps initially believing that I had misheard him the first time. I recount this incident for two reasons. Firstly, it shows that some Black community members assume that all White academics view Ancient Egypt from a wholly different perspective. Although this may be true of some Egyptologists, it is certainly not the case for all. Curators of university collections in particular are making efforts to review their collections with the aid of community groups and to adapt their presentation of material culture accordingly. Secondly, the episode was also important because, after I had left the class, I started to think about how Egypt was presented in the academic literature and by popular media such as films and documentaries, and how post-war politics have racialised history in relation to cultural heritage. This paper will explore these key issues through qualitative studies, anecdotes, consultations with community groups, exhibitions and academic study.

Egypt is geographically part of the continent of Africa. It should therefore follow that Egypt is part of African history and cultural heritage; however, this is rarely the case in the literature (Davidson 1991). Even in the standard *Atlas of Ancient Egypt* the country of Egypt is situated within a map of the Middle East rather than Africa (Baines and Malek 2000, 12-13). African-centred Egyptology promotes Ancient Egypt as a legitimate part of Black cultural heritage, a view widely held amongst Black British people. Unlike the teaching of Egyptian history in the United States, where it is promoted in schools as part of African-American culture, Britain has chosen to promote slavery as the dominant component of Black history in schools. The fact that Ancient Egypt is forced to justify its African identity through its geographical location has not gone unnoticed (Karenga 1993). Egyptology as a subject traditionally covers the period from around 5000 BC until the arrival of Alexander the Great in 332 BC. More recently the discipline has been expanded to include the Ptolemaic and Roman periods, Christianity and the Islamic settlement in AD 642, though it is fair to say that the later periods are often excluded from mainstream university degree courses in Egyptology in the UK. However, critics of the mainstream Eurocentric view of Ancient Egypt claim that not only is the connection between Egypt and Africa neglected, it is consciously denied (Clarke 1994). This is partly the legacy of the 'rediscovery' of Egypt by Europe at the end of the 18th century. In addition to this historical context, Egyptology as a discipline is dominated by scholars who are White Europeans or North Americans. This paper will address ways in which a Eurocentric view of Ancient Egypt can be challenged, and will consider how presenting Ancient Egypt within the cultural as well as geographical context of Africa impacts on museums, academics and community groups.

History, His Story, Our Story
That fact that placing Ancient Egypt within an African context, geographically or otherwise, is labelled African-centred or Afrocentric suggests that Ancient Egyptian culture has, in many respects, been de-contextualised as a discipline, as well as in the way it is currently presented by museums, in the media and in schools. This paper is primarily focused on museum interpretations and

museum-based learning and it is important to remember that material culture is de-contextualised as soon as it is brought into a museum environment. It is the interpretation that needs to be truthful in relation to the evidence, located with historic specificity, and honest in its declaration of any speculation.

Kemet was, of course, one of the names used by indigenous people in the country the Greeks named Egypt. However, in a modern context it is used to situate Ancient Egypt as an African culture and will be used throughout this paper to refer to an African-centred approach. The problem with the interpretation of Egypt as Kemet is not simply a case of Eurocentric versus Afrocentric points of view. The issue is more complex and is embedded in perceived expert and non-expert opinions, and more specifically between some 'White' or European/Western Egyptologists and some 'Black' community members. The former group distance themselves from the latter, with the result that the motives behind any 'White' Egyptologist who chooses to view Egypt as Kemet are questioned by 'Afrocentrists' and 'Eurocentrists' alike. There is also the fact that this academic sub-category has been dominated by, but not exclusively involved, scholars of African descent, whose credentials have been unjustifiably questioned by some mainstream specialists in Ancient Egypt (Cannon-Brown 2006, 342). As a result of this, there sometimes remains a degree of suspicion surrounding White Egyptologists who adopt an African-centred approach to their subject. An example of this can be cited from the questions following the oral presentation of this paper at the Egypt in its African Context conference. A delegate recounted a conversation that she had heard on the train from London to Manchester, involving two 'Black men' who were discussing why it was only White female Egyptologists who taught African-centred Egyptology. Her question to me was why this approach to Ancient Egypt was dominated by White women rather than men? The men involved in this remarkable conversation on the train were misinformed. There were two White male curators present at the conference who have been involved in the presentation of their collections as part of African cultural heritage.

I mention this episode here because I cannot help but wonder if there is an underlying supposition that there is another motive for White women being involved in Black history/culture with Fanonian undertones (Fanon 1952). I have also been asked if I have a personal reason for wanting to promote Ancient Egypt as African, for example, whether members of my family are African or of African descent. In contrast I was once asked by a White student why I was 'letting the side down' by promoting Egypt as part of Black History when I myself am White. My motives are very simple and are linked with my own academic background and experiences, as noted above. It is also notable that in all of the time that I have studied and been seen as a professional Egyptologist, my identity with regard to, and motives for, writing papers on the Ptolemaic dynasty, for example, have never been questioned in the same way that my work on presenting Ancient Egypt in its African context have been probed. It is perhaps significant that when you ask people if the Ancient Egyptians were African, the majority will say yes on account of the country's geographical location. However, if you ask 'Were the Ancient Egyptians Black?' you will get a different response. In this paper I will use the racialised concept of 'Black' in its current sense, as we define it today in the UK. For the second half of the 20th century 'Black' was used to identify a universal political association of all those who experienced racism and were non-White. It was a word that reflected solidarity and assertion in the face of brutal inequality and subjugation. However, more recently, some people of African descent make reference to the negative connotations of the word 'Black' both in terms of the semantics but also contemporary 'Black' culture. That is not to say that skin colour and tone were not relevant in the ancient world. The very fact that on wall paintings in tombs from all periods we see people with different shades of brown skin indicates that people were conscious of this. A modern parallel can be found in the Caribbean where people will quite often, when describing a person, say 'brown-skinned' or 'dark'.

It is clear that some people of African descent feel disconnected from mainstream British history and the interpretation of history in schools, colleges and museums. During 2008 I was invited to attend a Black History discussion group that had been established and held by men serving prison sentences with whom I had previously worked. I was the only White person attending and found the experience to be extremely helpful in terms of looking at history through a different lens. During these meetings and a subsequent course that I ran with one of the members, there were several references to his/story as a means of recognising that history is rarely inclusive and typically exclusive with respect to people from the African diaspora. The idea is not a new one. In 1990 Public Enemy made a similar reference in one of their songs on the album 'Fear of a Black Planet':

To the brothers in the Streetschools and the prisons
History shouldn't be a mystery
Our stories real history
Not his story.
(Brothers Gonna Work It Out, www.publicenemy.com)

Released in April 1990, Public Enemy's third studio album, 'Fear of a Black Planet', questioned social injustice and advocated empowerment for African-Americans, commenting on many of the problems that were faced collectively by this group in the United States in the late 20th century, and in fact continue to impede people of African descent. Several tracks on the album make reference to Black history, either directly through the use of the voice leading Black historical figures, or more generally, as above. Hip Hop is not the only Black music genre to make reference to history. Reggae music often makes reference to the history of the African diaspora and its impact on people today, and free jazz references the African-American experience with regard to Kemet, including such artists as Sun Ra. Some parts of

Black music still express a creative language about the past and deal with inequality. Mainstream White/European culture also does this through its absorption of Black music.

There is often an assumption that personal knowledge or experiences are somehow less valid than the specialist knowledge that comes from formal education. However, in an ideal world the academic/curator and the community member should be able to work together and to learn from each other. During classes that I have taught with community groups it has been common for students with connections to West Africa to find parallels between traditional objects in their country of origin and some of the ancient Egyptian artefacts, such as headrests. And of course objects such as hair combs (Figure 1) are a good example of objects that people of African origin can connect with. Cultural anthropology as a discipline is embedded in this process, and yet Egyptologists rarely utilise it. One student commented that the wooden head of Queen Tiye now housed in the Egyptian Museum, Berlin reminded him of his mother, most especially the look that she gave him when he had done something wrong. His mother was from North-East Africa.

Figure 1. Predynastic hair comb (The Fitzwilliam Museum, Cambridge, E.GA.3204.1943).

However, some Black community members are cautious about sharing their thoughts and ideas with White academics, most probably because of a general feeling of mistrust. Some members of Black communities in the USA and UK believe that there exists an academic, and therefore White, conspiracy to divorce Ancient Egypt from Africa. In her 1995 essay to the American Research Center in Egypt newsletter, and 1996 on-line publication, 'Building Bridges to Afrocentrism', Ann Macy Roth lists this idea amongst the four most common 'misconceptions'.[1]

Roth explains the reaction of the majority of mainstream Egyptologists to the concept of Kemet by observing that Egyptology as a discipline is often ostracised from related fields of archaeology, anthropology and African history. As a consequence of their traditional training, many Egyptologists de-contextualise Egypt without a second thought. In other words, if Egyptologists are not privy to other views of their subject it may never occur to them to think differently. Roth also suggests that specialists are loathe to communicate with community members because they fear their subject is already popularised by members of the aforementioned disciplines (1996).

Community group concerns are not unfounded. Some early Egyptologists viewed the Africans pejoratively, and some Egyptologists have denied that the Ancient Egyptians were Africans (Manley, this volume). Morton suggests that although Negroes [sic.] populated Egypt they were part of an enslaved class rather than the elite (1844, 33-61). My work with Black community groups has fundamentally changed the way in which I approach Ancient Egypt, both as an academic discipline and in the interpretation of the collections that I curate. Our views were not dissimilar, but one approach was passive, the other active. For the remainder of this paper I will summarise different ways in which I have tried to bridge the gaps between 'Egyptology' as academic discipline and between people of different cultural, educational and racialised backgrounds.

Egyptology in Prisons
Inspired by my initial teaching experiences in prisons, in the autumn of 2007 I began a Knowledge Transfer fellowship and two-year leave of absence from my post as curator to develop resources and classes that present Ancient Egypt as part of African cultural heritage. During this time I worked full-time in prisons using the Fitzwilliam Museum's collections to teach Ancient Egypt from an African perspective and researching people's attitudes towards this idea, looking carefully at variables such as ethnic background, age and level of education. I have been extremely fortunate that those attending my classes have shared their own ideas and interpretations of the culture that I claim to have specialist knowledge of. The relevance of the environment where this project took place, with respect to this paper, is negligible.[2] More significant is the fact that by teaching in prison education departments I was able to work with community members from a wide variety of backgrounds and nationalities, and so obtained a more rounded understanding of key issues when teaching Egyptology from an African-centred perspective.

---

[1] I use the term misconception because this is how the four grievances are portrayed in Roth's essay. The other three are that the Ancient Egyptians were Black; that Ancient Egypt was the greatest civilisation; and that Ancient Egypt had an extensive influence on Europe and Africa.

[2] However, the associated study on the impact of teaching relevant cultural heritage courses on the self-concept of Black male prisoners explores whether there is a difference in the way in which Black community members who are at liberty and engaged with public life everyday interpret Ancient Egypt, as opposed to those people who have had their liberty constrained. It also explores whether exclusion from society affects our interpretation of racial past and inequality (Ashton forthcoming).

During this period I also studied criminology and this move into the social sciences has impacted significantly on how I interpret and look at my core subject area. This is because for two years I have been able to take my criminological research back to the people I have been working with to ensure that I have not misrepresented them. I have also noticed that disclosing identity, background and experiences, and how they might impact on our interpretation of cultures, both past and present, is not standard practice within the field of Egyptology, and yet in the social sciences it is crucial that you include this information and acknowledge how it will impact on your research.

The prison population in Britain has almost doubled in the past ten years with Black and Minority Ethnic groups over-represented at all levels within the criminal justice system (Edgar 2007, 268-92). I observed a high level of interest in exploring Kemet in some parts of the prison estate, particularly amongst Black British students, and to a lesser extent people of Jamaican or West African origin. There were naturally substantial differences for each of those groups depending on where they were brought up, which school system they went through and also with regard to their religion. Nevertheless what three individual studies demonstrated was the importance of Kemet within the study of Black history and also the positive impact it could have on potential and in some cases offending behaviour (Ashton forthcoming).

With regard to attitudes towards history, there was a difference in the responses of participants who had explored Egyptian history on their own, or who had attended lectures on the subject, and those who had not been exposed to Egyptian history. Those people who had been involved in classes or personal study all believed that Ancient Egypt was part of African history. The importance of exposure to books, lectures or information on African history was indicated by a 39 year old participant in the study, who said, 'I feel that Egypt is part of Black history, but only because of what I've been reading recently'. This is why museums wishing to act as agents of social change should perhaps consider adopting a more active role in exploring Ancient Egypt as part of Africa with all community groups.

During the conference discussion following the presentation of this paper, a number of members of the audience asked if it was 'right' to use African-centred Egyptology as a 'therapy'. As one of the other key speakers pointed out in a response to that question (Shomarka Keita), it is noteworthy that when members of the African diaspora access their history it is often labelled as 'therapeutic' and yet when other groups learn about their cultural heritage or history no such connection is made. I pointed out then and I reiterate here, that I do not see the Egyptology project in prisons as a form of therapy. The project aims and objectives remain as they have always been, to give people who are currently unable to visit our museum in person access to the collections and an alternative way of viewing this important African culture. The research tried to understand why Kemet was important to people, and to share with non-African communities the personal connections that people of African descent have made. The aim was that in doing so the concept of 'Kemet' would be treated with more regard and engaged with openly and critically.

African history is not simply a history for people of African descent. However, I have found that if a lecture is advertised as Black history I will get almost exclusively Black students attending; if a talk is advertised as 'Ancient Egypt' then a more mixed audience attends. I have also noticed the impact of presenting Egypt as an African culture and, more to the point, Ancient Egyptians as 'Black' people, on non-Black community members – as I noted above, people respond differently to the use of the terms 'African' and 'Black', being more likely to agree with the former, whereas the latter will provoke more of a reaction, often negative. In most cases, however, it is easy to get people to change their perceptions by simply giving them access to the evidence. Many of my students who are White British have been fascinated by the concept that Egypt is an African culture. One expressed outrage at the fact that the media and education system had suggested otherwise; he felt that he had 'been duped'.

Virtual Kemet
In an article in the *Museums Journal* in December 2007 Felicity Haywood wrote that 'Egypt is de-Africanised' at the Fitzwilliam Museum's re-display of the collection, which took place in 2005/6, and asked, 'Is it more important to protect the sensibilities of the white academics and visitors to a museum in Cambridge, than to tell the truth?' (p. 21)

I feel that Ms Hayward's assumptions with regard to protecting the sensibilities of White academics and visitors were a knee-jerk reaction of a type that is fortunately uncommon but not isolated. Had she not attended a panel at the Museum's Association Conference in Glasgow in October 2007, where the Museum's African-centred Egyptology programme had been discussed, her conclusions might have been justified. In addition, the programme of African-centred Egyptology described in this paper was in its early stages and had she contacted the Museum prior to her visit I would have gladly gone through our plans for considering Egypt in a more African-focused manner.

Ms Hayward's comments also illustrate the passive versus active approach to presenting Kemet. Perhaps the biggest challenge for many curators is the limited amount of space for information and interpretation of the collections on galleries. This is where web space and special exhibitions can play a key role in inviting people to look at the evidence. Community engagement is crucial to this process.

When I consulted the community groups that I work closely with, they struggled to explain how you might successfully present Kemet in a gallery. I wish to stress that the material speaks for itself, but as I have said I wanted people who have perhaps not viewed Egypt in this way before to look at it again, and to take a more active approach. In the physical gallery we have an information panel explaining about the concept of Kemet and explain how Egypt and its population have changed over time, citing examples like the well-known Herodotus description of the people of Kemet. However, it was really in the virtual version that we were able to more successfully 'brand' or, rather, 're-brand' Egypt as 'Kemet' (Figure 2).

Figure 2. Banner from the top of the Virtual Kemet web-page, designed by Weston Digital Imaging.

The idea of creating a virtual version of our Egyptian galleries came from the initial group of long term prisoners who I presented a lecture to in July 2003. I returned the following year with an example of pages that included text and an image. However, the response of two groups was that this was not an appealing way to access the collections. It soon became apparent that allocated funding was necessary if the project was to be developed in a suitable and appealing way. Because the initial idea and subsequent development had focused on allowing access from a closed environment where people do not have access to the internet, there were these additional barriers to overcome. In 2007 the Fitzwilliam Museum was awarded a Your Heritage, Heritage Lottery grant in order to develop the project further. A specialist company was engaged to work closely with me and the community groups who had thought of the idea have been consulted throughout the process. Comparisons between the initial versions of the gallery with the final product show that a conscious attempt has been made to embed the collections within an African context. Strong images remain at the top of each page. Egypt has been replaced with Kemet in all labels and information panels prior to the Ptolemaic conquest of the country, and a series of tours stressing links with Africa and African culture have also been integrated into the main galleries. In this way we have attempted to avoid tokenism and hope to present the material from a non-Eurocentric viewpoint. To accompany the gallery two booklets have been produced, one entitled *Kemet, Remnants of an African Past* (Figure 3) and the other *Kush, Remnants of an African Past* (Figure 4). Writing with a non-specialist but well informed Black community member has once again reminded me that although I might be considered by many as an Afrocentric, there are still fundamental differences in the way in which people of different backgrounds view and interpret material. Many community members write as they see and with great passion, whereas as academics we tend to place an emphasis on minutiae and referencing, and this is where museums can perhaps play a greater role in encouraging a range of views and approaches to be shared.

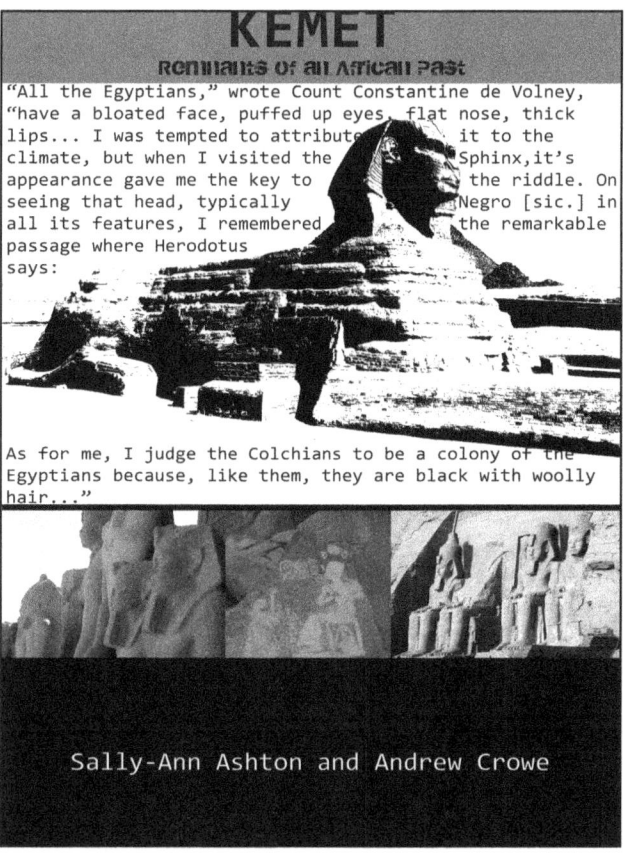

Figure 3. Front page of the educational booklet on Egypt and Nubia.

Figure 4. Front page of the educational booklet on the archaeology of Sudan.

Conscious of the fact that Egyptology is dominated by White European or North American scholars, as part of the Heritage Lottery-funded Virtual Kemet project, the Fitzwilliam Museum with the support of the Petrie Museum of Egyptian Archaeology at University College London organised three workshops in which community groups were invited to raise key issues with regard to the presentation of Ancient Egypt with key African intellectuals. The first session was with Dr Ossama Abdel Meguid, Director of the Nubia Museum in Aswan, who is a Nubian; the second was with Dr Shomarka Keita, a biological anthropologist and medical doctor who is a Senior Research Associate at the National Human Genome Centre at Howard University and Research Associate in the Department of Anthropology at the Smithsonian Institute; and finally the third session was presented by Dr Mpay Kemboly who, after completing his PhD in Egyptology at the University of Oxford, returned to the Democratic Republic of Congo in Africa, where he is a Roman Catholic priest and member of the religious Order of the Jesuits. This workshop focused on spirituality and the Ancient Egyptians and modern interpretations or uses of Ancient Egyptian religion and culture.[3]

Special Exhibitions

The first thing that curators and museums can do is to acknowledge that how we view the world can be influenced by our experiences, our identity and our background. When teaching classes on Ancient Egypt from an African-centred perspective many students who are not of African descent have voiced the fact that they had never really thought about the Ancient Egyptians as Africans, partly because of media portrayals. However, once made aware of this approach to the subject they accept the new way of viewing Ancient Egypt and on occasion people have asked why they have not been made aware of this approach before, for example, at school. This also demonstrates how we can transcend our subjective outlook.

In April 2009 the Centre for African Studies in Cambridge hosted an exhibition of an experiment with two photographers – one Black British (Andrew Crowe) and the other White British (Michael Jones). I visited sites in southern Egypt with both photographers during our time away from working on a survey, and I asked them to take and select photographs that they felt captured their impressions of Ancient Egypt. Andrew Crowe had visited Egypt on one occasion before, but not this region, and this was the first time that Michael Jones had been to Egypt. The results were interesting in that one photographer chose to concentrate mainly on statues, revealing the identity of Ancient Egyptians as Africans, and the other concentrated on the architecture as well as on how tourists interacted with the antiquities (Figures 5 and 6). Neither selection was misleading, they were simply different. However, someone unfamiliar with the sites would be forgiven for thinking that the photographs had come from different places. If we consider this observation within a museum context it is possible to see how easily Egypt can be de-contextualised, without thought.

Figure 5. Photograph by Andrew Crowe: statue of Ramesses II at the Ramesseum.

Figure 6. Photograph by Michael Jones: tourists at Karnak.

---

[3] The workshops can be viewed on the Fitzwilliam Museum's web pages: http://www.fitzmuseum.cam.ac.uk/dept/ant/egypt/outreach/kemet/resources/index.html

It could be argued that Ancient Egypt is African and if people choose not to see it as African, then so what? However, I take the view that the role of museums should be to act as agents of social change, challenging people's perspectives and often stereotypes of cultures with which they have no personal connection. In short, it should not only be people who have a direct connection to Africa or an African heritage who view Ancient Egypt as Kemet. It is important for all of us to consider Ancient Egyptian culture and language within its African framework, because in removing it we fail to consider it as a whole. I also feel that it is important to acknowledge that Kemet has an important place within contemporary 'Black' culture and identity, which is recognised less here than in the United States.

In an attempt to present the concept of Kemet the Fitzwilliam Museum held an exhibition of photographs and film footage taken by the aforementioned Black British photographer Andrew Crowe entitled 'Black to Kemet' in October 2009 (Figures 7 and 8). The exhibition was shown on six television screens in the courtyard of the Fitzwilliam Museum and was also available on-line. A series of lectures on African-centred Egyptology was also presented throughout the three-week run to support the main theme. The concept of the exhibition was to show images that strongly support the idea that the people of Ancient Kemet were what we would consider today Black Africans.

A computer survey was also undertaken, with 70 respondents, in order to assess the impact on the Museum's regular visitors. When asked to describe the exhibition 38 out of the 41 comments that were written were positive:

'Excellent images. Some were convincing as black Africans; for example Ramose; others such as the priests were not so secure. An interesting project; well worth doing.'

'A different perspective and a new way to look at history and the way it is been taught. This is done in the context of Egypt and its links with African race.'

'It is good to see a truthful representation of ancient Egyptian history in an educational institution.'

Only two people made negative comments, describing the exhibition as 'very vague', 'biased' and 'pointless'. The dataset from the survey was too small to run any significant statistical analysis. However, visitors' comments and the discussions involving the public following the associated talks and presentations at the Museum, showed that by presenting Egypt as part of African cultural heritage a dialogue can be initiated between people of different backgrounds and an exchange of knowledge and experiences can be achieved.

Figure 7. Photograph by Andrew Crowe: Sohail inscription, from the exhibition, 'Black to Kemet'.

Figure 8. Poster advertising the exhibition, 'Black to Kemet'.

Cleopatra, an Impromptu Social Experiment

Perhaps the most contentious issue within the field of African-centred Egyptology is the question which, as Roth (1996) noted, strikes fear into the hearts of most American Egyptologists, namely, 'What colour were the Ancient Egyptians?'

Figure 9. Display case in the Kerma Museum (image: author's own).

I say contentious because many academics and biological anthropologists in particular do not wish to categorise historical groups according to modern racialised identities (Roth 1996). This makes life difficult when dealing with a non-academic audience or indeed an audience that is academic but not trained in biological anthropology. The public know what they mean by 'Black', albeit that this is a concept that many people of African descent do not now wish to be associated with because of negative modern cultural or semantic connotations. It is therefore frustrating for people to be told that their question is irrelevant because the Ancient Egyptians did not view themselves in this way. One way around this issue is to ensure that any reconstructions have dark skin, brown eyes and hair that would be appropriate for people from this region. In the Sudan National Museum, Khartoum a reconstruction of a human face shows the subject with dark brown skin, and the image of a person wearing adornments in the museum at Kerma (Figure 9). This is in contrast to the recent reconstructions of Tutankhamun in 2005 for the special exhibition 'Tutankhamun and the Golden Age of the Pharaohs', where the ruler was shown with a skin tone that would be more typical of people from Northern Europe. In the US in particular many African-American groups were horrified and openly protested against the depiction of Tutankhamun as a non-African. However, showing historical figures with dark brown skin often provokes a backlash from some people of non-African descent, some of whom go as far as questioning the knowledge or qualifications of the Egyptologist involved. It is a great pity that such exercises provoke outrage rather than discussion.

In the summer of 2008 I was asked to work on a computer-generated image of Cleopatra VII for a television documentary. I agreed to do this only if the London-based company Atlantic Productions would show the queen as part African rather than European. The rationale behind this request was not based on my own supposition, and I am not the first to suggest that Cleopatra VII was Egyptian and so African. It has been suggested that Cleopatra was part African through her mother and paternal grandmother, who, it has been argued, were likely to have been Egyptian rather than Greek (Ashton 2008, 1).

The process took several weeks of consultation, producing a computer-generated image from a statue that has been identified from a sanctuary of Isis in Rome (Ashton 2008, 118, fig. 5.1). The process was significant from the start because the team working on the computer image initially replaced the features of the statue with a longer, narrower nose, an elongated face and pointed chin. When asked why they had done this they said that they had also used a profile of Cleopatra on a coin, minted late in her reign in Syria. When it came to skin colour and hair type I made it clear to the reconstruction team that the hair should be braided (which is how the hair appears on the aforementioned coin), and that the skin colour should be acceptable for a person who was of mixed parentage but erring on the side of darker rather than lighter, assuming that both the mother and maternal grandmother had been Egyptians and so Africans.

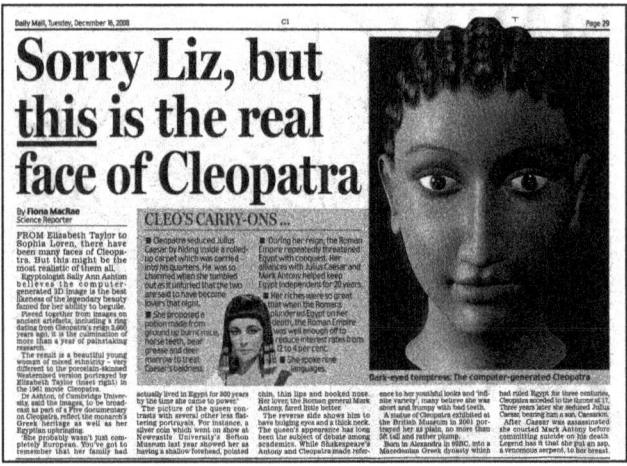

Figure 10. The Daily Mail article on the facial reconstruction of Cleopatra (16th December 2008).

As is often the case, two filming sessions were cut down to around one minute of the final documentary and the viewer was left with the impression that the reconstruction had been based on a ring rather than a statue. However, the pre-showing of the film caught the attention of the Daily Mail newspaper, which ran an article on the 16th December 2008 entitled 'Sorry Liz but THIS is the real face of Cleopatra' (http//www.dailymail.co.uk/sciencetech/article-1095043/Sorry-Liz-THIS-real-face-Cleopatra.html; Figure 10).

The Daily Mail's article provoked 229 comments on the newspaper's blog and has provided an interesting social commentary on attitudes towards race and ownership of history. The majority of comments ranged from indignant disagreement to outrage, and it is noteworthy that the response to people who wrote in support of the idea that Cleopatra was of mixed parentage received a negative rating from the viewers. In addition to the wider issue of attitudes to race and racialised identities, a number of sub-themes emerged from the blogs: orientalist or colonial attitudes, an assumed personal or expert knowledge of the physical appearance of the queen, a pre-occupation with how physically attractive the reconstruction was deemed to be, and a lack of understanding of the importance of recognising African historical figures as African. The question is often neglected and even deliberately ignored by some Afrocentrists:

'As far as McWhorter (2000) is concerned, one has to understand that whether Cleopatra was Black or White is not an Afrocentric issue. Most scholars know that she was a descendant of Ptolemy, the Greek, left in charge by Alexander. However, it is argued that some of her ancestors were Egyptians, Black. But the reason that is not a major issue with Black Studies scholars is that she is relevant only because of Shakespeare's account of her chasing Mark Anthony. Cleopatra is not a great ruler. She is not a Hatshepsut, the first woman to rule Egypt in her own right. One must dismiss this as a serious discussion about an African queen.' (Cannon-Brown 2006, 343)

As someone who has spent the past 10 years looking at Cleopatra, I would disagree with the statement that she is relevant only because of Shakespeare's account of her chasing Mark Anthony. Cleopatra ruled in her own right and during her rule proved herself to be an astute political figure in a Eurocentric and male dominated world (Ashton 2008). Cleopatra's political credentials aside, there are two important points that are missed if we dismiss Cleopatra's potential as an African queen. Firstly, is it right to pick and choose which historical figures are accepted into an African-centred approach to Ancient Egypt? And secondly, as a Black British student once pointed out to me in answer to the question, does it matter if Cleopatra was Black? What matters is, if she was Black and people are trying to hide this fact.

This latter point featured within the comments on the Daily Mail blog. Some examples are quoted below, the others are still available at the time of going to press on the Daily Mail website:

'The ancient Egyptians were (as any historian who has studied accounts of the time will tell you) white caucasian Europeans. Cleopatra was white with possibly sun kissed features, she wouldn't have been a black African as the picture tries to suggest.'

'I thought the Greek Macedonians that ran Egypt did not marry outside the ruling elite; so how is it possible that Cleopatra was of 'mixed ethnicity'? It's more likely her Greek blood was undiluted, and last time I looked Greeks are Europeans. This attempt to Africanise Cleopatra is just more anti-Western, multicultural rubbish. The Greek [sic.] that ruled Egypt looked down on Egyptian culture and were keen to preserve their distinct Greek culture and protect their separateness. The Greeks rarely adopted Egyptian customs and when they did it was for political reasons, to make their rule more palatable.'

'Why are people so caught up with colour[?] History is the issue here not the colour of those [who] were reported in history. Achievements, mistakes, knowledge – these are the things we should be asking, not what people may have looked like. What a waste of time, effort and money. It's about time people stopped classifying themselves in terms of colour.'
(All at:
http://www.dailymail.co.uk/sciencetech/article-1095043/Sorry-Liz-THIS-real-face-Cleopatra.html)

The high number of responses was most likely provoked by the physical reconstruction of a historical figure. The moment that a piece of visual evidence is placed in front of an audience it becomes somehow more real. If the documentary had expressed the belief verbally that Cleopatra was African then it is unlikely that as many people would have responded. If the documentary had stated that Cleopatra was 'Black' then a similar response may have ensued. This is because many people in Britain distinguish between the racialised terms 'Black' and 'African'.

I cite this as an example of just how powerful visual representations of past peoples and cultures can be, and this is why and where museums can play a role in changing public perceptions of Ancient Egypt or in representing Kemet in its modern sense of the word. I also refer to this case study as a reminder of how some people respond to the idea that a prominent figure or, in the case of Egypt, a prominent civilisation, is part of African rather than European or Middle Eastern history.

Does it Matter?
The simple answer to this question is, yes it does. Not simply for the reason that including Ancient Egypt as part of African history offers a positive addition to the study of the history of early Africa, or that Kemet is cited as a significant factor in a number of publications of studies on Black (mainly African-American) self-concept (Allen 2001, 22-3). This issue is not concerned with direct

cultural ownership and the inclusion/exclusion of certain racialised groups, or about who owns knowledge of that culture. As previously stated, it should not only be people with a direct connection to Africa who explore the concept of Kemet, and this is not what the so-called Afrocentrics are advocating. On the contrary, the 'Afro-centric movement has tried for decades to get mainstream Eurocentric Egyptologists to engage with the subject from their viewpoint' (Cannon-Brown 2006, 341-2). Exploring and promoting an ancient culture within its original context, and acknowledging and transcending modern political and ethnicised boundaries by adopting an African-centred approach to this material, awards academics, museums and community groups the potential to be more inclusive rather than exclusive.

Acknowledgements

I am especially grateful to Saira Law, who worked as the project co-ordinator for the Virtual Egypt in Prisons project, for her comments and input. I would also like to thank David Evans and Andrew Crowe for their comments and discussion of various aspects of this paper.

References

Allen, R. L. 2001. *The Concept of Self. A Study of Black Identity and Self-esteem*. Detroit, Wayne State University Press.

Ashton, S.-A. 2004. *Roman Egyptomania*. London, Golden House Press.

—2008. *Cleopatra of Egypt*. Oxford, Wiley-Blackwell.

—(forthcoming). *Imprisoned Black Voices. Teaching African History in Prisons*.

Baines, J. and Malek, J. 2000. *Atlas of Ancient Egypt*. Oxford, Andromeda.

Bernal, M. 1991. *Black Athena: The Afroasiatic Roots of Classical Civilization. Volume I. The Fabrication of Ancient Greece, 1785-1985*. London, Vintage.

—2001. *Black Athena Writes Back*. London and Durham, Duke University Press.

Cannon-Brown, W. 2006. Decapitated and Lynched Forms: Suggested Ways of Examining Contemporary Texts, in M. K. Asante and M. Karenga (eds.), *Handbook of Black Studies*, 333-51. California, Sage Publications.

Clarke, J. H. 1994. *Who Betrayed the African World Revolution? And Other Speeches*. Chicago, Third World Press.

Davidson, B. 1991. The Ancient World and Africa, Whose Roots? In Van Sertima, I. (ed.), *Egypt Revisited: Journal of African Civilizations* 10, 39-52. New Brunswick, Transaction Publishers.

Edgar, K. 2007. Black and Minority Ethnic Prisoners. In Y. Jewkes (ed.), *Handbook on Prisons*, 268-92. USA and Canada, Willan Publishing.

Fanon, F. 1952. *Peau noire, masques blancs*. Paris, Éditions de Seuil.

—2008. English edition, *Black Skin, White Masks*. London, Pluto Press.

Karenga, M. 1993. *Introduction to Black Studies*. Los Angeles, University of Sankore Press.

Lefkowitz, M. R. and MacLean Rogers, G. (eds.) 1996. *Black Athena Revisited*. North Carolina, The University of North Carolina Press.

Morton, S. G. 1844. *Crania Aegyptiaca, or, Observations on Egyptian Ethnography, Derived from Anatomy, History and the Monuments*. Philadelphia, J. Pennington.

McWhorter, J. H. 2000. *Losing the Race. Self-Sabotage in Black America*. New York, Free Press.

Roth, A. M. 1995. Building Bridges to Afrocentrism, a Letter to my Egyptological Colleagues. In *American Research Center in Egypt Newsletter* 168 (December 1995), 15-21.

—1996. Building Bridges to Afrocentrism, a Letter to my Egyptological Colleagues. http://www.hartford-hwp.com/archives/30/134.html

www.ingramcontent.com/pod-product-compliance
Lightning Source LLC
Chambersburg PA
CBHW041706290426
44108CB00027B/2868